In this book Pamela Thurschwell examines the intersection of literary culture, the occult and new technology in the *fin de siècle*. She argues that technologies such as the telegraph and the telephone annihilated distances that separated bodies and minds from each other. As these new technologies began suffusing the public imagination from the mid-nineteenth century on, they seemed to support the claims of spiritualist mediums. Talking to the dead and talking on the phone both held out the promise of previously unimaginable contact between people: both seemed to involve 'magical thinking'. Thurschwell looks at the ways in which psychical research, the scientific study of the occult, is reflected in the writings of such authors as Henry James, George Du Maurier and Oscar Wilde, and in the foundations of psychoanalysis. This study offers new and provocative interpretations of *fin-de-siècle* literary and scientific culture in relation to psychoanalysis, queer theory and cultural history.

PAMELA THURSCHWELL is a lecturer in twentieth-century literature at University College London. She is the author of *Sigmund Freud* (Routledge Press, 2000). Her recent articles on Henry James and psychoanalysis have appeared in *Textual Practice* and *differences*. She has also published on popular music and culture.

CAMBRIDGE STUDIES IN NINETEENTH-CENTURY
LITERATURE AND CULTURE 32

LITERATURE, TECHNOLOGY AND MAGICAL THINKING, 1880–1920

Nineteenth-century British literature and culture have been rich fields for interdisciplinary studies. Since the turn of the twentieth century, scholars and critics have tracked the intersections and tensions between Victorian literature and the visual arts, politics, social organization, economic life, technical innovations, scientific thought – in short, culture in its broadest sense. In recent years, theoretical challenges and historiographical shifts have unsettled the assumptions of previous scholarly synthesis and called into question the terms of older debates. Whereas the tendency in much past literary critical interpretation was to use the metaphor of culture as 'background', feminist, Foucauldian, and other analyses have employed more dynamic models that raise questions of power and of circulation. Such developments have reanimated the field.

This series aims to accommodate and promote the most interesting work being undertaken on the frontiers of the field of nineteenth-century literary studies: work which intersects fruitfully with other fields of study such as history, or literary theory, or the history of science. Comparative as well as interdisciplinary approaches are welcomed.

A complete list of titles published will be found at the end of the book.

LITERATURE, TECHNOLOGY AND MAGICAL THINKING, 1880–1920

PAMELA THURSCHWELL

CAMBRIDGE
UNIVERSITY PRESS

PUBLISHED BY THE PRESS SYNDICATE OF THE UNVERSITY OF CAMBRIDGE
The Pitt Building, Trumpington Street, Cambridge, United Kingdom

CAMBRIDGE UNIVERSITY PRESS
The Edinburgh Building, Cambridge CB2 2RU UK
40 West 20th Street, New York NY 10011–4211, USA
10 Stamford Road, Oakleigh, VIC 3166, Australia
Ruiz de Alarcón 13, 28014 Madrid, Spain
Dock House, The Waterfront, Cape Town 8001, South Africa

http://www.cambridge.org

First published 2001

Printed in the United Kingdom at the University Press, Cambridge

Typeface 11/12.5pt Baskerville   *System* 3B2   [CE]

A catalogue record for this book is available from the British Library

Library of Congress Cataloging in Publication data
Thurschwell, Pamela, 1966–
Literature, technology and magical thinking, 1880–1920 / Pamela Thurschwell.
p.   cm.
Includes bibliographical references (p. 180) and index.
ISBN 0 521 80168 0
1. English literature – 19th century – History and criticism. 2. Magic in literature.
3. Literature and technology – Great Britain – History – 19th century.
4. Literature and technology – Great Britain – History – 20th century.
5. English literature – 20th century – History and criticism.
6. Psychoanalysis and literature. 7. Homosexuality and literature.
8. Spiritualism in literature. 9. Occultism in literature. 10. Telepathy in literature.
I. Title.
PR468.M34T48 2001
820.9′37–dc21   00-065987

ISBN 0 521 80168 0 hardback

Contents

Acknowledgements

I would like to thank the institution and fellows of Queens' College, Cambridge for the generous research fellowship that allowed me to complete this monograph with a minimum amount of stress and a maximum amount of pleasure. Several libraries were helpful in providing me with access to their resources and permission to quote from archival material: the Society for Psychical Research; the University Library, Cambridge; the Wren Library, Trinity College and the Houghton Library, Harvard.

An early version of chapter three appeared in *Modernist Sexualities*, edited by Hugh Stevens and Caroline Howlett (Manchester University Press, 2000). Part of chapter four appeared in *Textual Practice* 13: 1 (1999), and material from chapter five appeared in *differences* 11: 1 (1999).

I have been fortunate in having many good friends and advisors over the years who have made this book intellectually and emotionally possible. For sharp readings, good suggestions, tea and sympathy over the long haul, I want to thank: Tim Armstrong, Gillian Beer, Bonnie Blackwell, Nicola Bown, Suzanne Canally, Cynthia Chase, Pete Coviello, Jason Edwards, Maud Ellmann, Geoffrey Gilbert, Sarah Goldfine, Liz Guzynski, Richard Hardack, Sally Jacob, Dana Luciano, Roger Luckhurst, Scott MacKenzie, Anne Mallory, Jodie Medd, Dorothy Mermin, Yasmin Mohsenzadeh, Cordelia Molloy, Tim Murray, Chris Nealon, Anna Neill, Leah Price, Adam Roberts, Talia Schaffer, Adam Schnitzer, Mark Seltzer, Hugh Stevens, Shannon Summers and Trudi Tate. Linda Bree, Rachel DeWachter, and others from Cambridge University Press have been enormously helpful throughout.

To my endlessly wonderful family, Charlotte and Hubert, Eric, Adam, Cathy, Walter and Sophie, I can only offer many thanks for a lifetime of support. Jim Endersby has made finishing this book, and being in the world, something to celebrate – I'm lucky to even know him.

If I believed in book dedications this book would be for Geoff for thinking magically, and for sharing his thoughts; the dangerous influences of which saturate my own.

Introduction

> Intimacy between people, like occult phenomena, is fundamentally bewildering.[1]

In 1921 Sigmund Freud was invited to co-edit three periodicals dedicated to the study of occultism. He refused all three invitations. However, according to Hereward Carrington who issued one of them, he did so reluctantly, saying to Carrington: 'If I had my life to live over again I should devote myself to psychical research rather than psychoanalysis.' Later an irritated Freud denied ever having expressed such sentiments, and the task of imagining a Freud who traced his patients' mental illnesses to unruly ghosts rather than to unruly sexuality has been left to the occasional novelist.[2] Freud, the full-fledged psychical researcher, was never born. But as any viewer of *The X-Files* knows, today's popular parapsychology owes him a great deal.

Psychical research, the scientific study of the occult which emerged as a discipline in the late nineteenth century, has usually been dismissed as a pseudo-science, an embarrassing sideline to the otherwise serious careers of figures such as William James, Henri Bergson and Henry Sidgwick. In this book I argue that, on the contrary, interest in nineteenth-century parapsychology and psychical research suffuses late Victorian literary and scientific culture, and helps spawn psychoanalysis. Through examining the works of the Society for Psychical Research, the society formed in Cambridge in 1882 in order to investigate scientifically the claims of spiritualism and other paranormal phenomena, it becomes clear that the concerns of psychical research are centrally related to a late nineteenth-century fascination with the modus operandi of cultural transmission and communication. Psychical researchers' debates about the possibility of telepathy, hypnosis and survival after death contribute to wider reconceptualizations of the borders of individual consciousness and emerge together with new communication technologies such as the telephone and the telegraph, and new psychological theories such as crowd theory, the hypnosis debates of the 1880s and 1890s, and psychoanalysis. These occult reformulations of community and communication also appear in the literary work of the time. Authors such as Oscar Wilde, Henry James, George Du Maurier and Sigmund Freud often explain cultural and communicative transmission by implicitly or explicitly invoking occult concepts such as ghosts and telepathy. Through readings of late nineteenth-century writings including Du Maurier's *Trilby*, Wilde's *The Picture of Dorian Gray*, and James's *In the Cage*, *The Sense of the Past*, letters, and autobiographical material, I relate literary extensions of individual consciousness to questions that are raised by psychical researchers about what separates one mind from another and what separates the living from the dead. Occult ways of imagining cultural transmission and communication, which organizations such as the Society for Psychical Research are attempting to make scientifically plausible, are used by a wide variety of writers of the period to create phantasmatic spaces in which they redefine intimate, sexual, familial and national ties between people against the usual patriarchal models of inheritance and community via marriage and the nuclear family. In the works I examine, occult transmission can be doubly transgressive, disrupting both sense boundaries and traditional codes of behaviour and alliance.

During the 1880s and 1890s various discourses – occult, literary, scientific, psychological, and technological – converge to inaugurate shifting models of the permeability and suggestibility of the individual's mind and body. It is by now standard to note that the 1890s is also the decade in which anxieties about the permeability and suggestibility of bodies and minds erupt in crises around sexuality. Sexual and gender panic manifests itself in representative figures such as the New Woman and the dandy, in public scandals such as Oscar Wilde's trials, and in the reification of medicalizing, pathologizing, and criminalizing discourses around homosexuality.[3] Deep and far-reaching anxieties about the stability of the traditional grounds of gender and sexuality pervade *fin-de-siècle* culture.

Literature, Technology and Magical Thinking, 1880–1920 seeks to relate these anxieties to a series of real and fantasized connections which are being made at the *fin de siècle* between the occult world, innovative technologies of communication and intimate bonds between people. Teletechnologies such as the telegraph and the telephone suggested that science could help annihilate distances that separate bodies and minds from each other. When these new technologies begin suffusing the public imagination from the mid-nineteenth century on they appear to support the claims of the spiritualist mediums; talking to the dead and talking on the phone both hold out the promise of previously unimaginable contact between people. Intimacy begins to take on new, distinctively modern forms.

Excellent recent work has shown the ways in which much modernist writing responds to, and emerges from, technological innovation, whether that writing is in agreement with, or in protest against, the forces of modernity.[4] Theodor Adorno's influential argument that literary and artistic Modernism was largely a reassertion of the aura of the work of art in reaction to the commodification and bureaucratization of the individual in modern mass culture, has been modified by recent critics to encompass a wider variety of reactions to modernity. Furthermore, critics have argued that many of the defining formal aspects of Modernism emerged in dialogue with developments in the mass market and technologies of communication.[5] This book supports these compelling claims while tactically shifting their scale and emphasis to encompass the uncanny nature of technological transmission as it was imagined at the *fin de siècle*. Modernism's technological roots affect and are affected by a supernatural erotics of bodily and cultural transmission that emerges sharply in the anxious cultural context of Wilde's trials, in turn of the century high and popular literature, and in psychoanalytic writing, as well as in the writings of the Society for Psychical Research. These fantasies of supernaturally enhanced intimacy alternatively embrace, and are threatened by, modernity's technological and cultural disjunctions. Yet it would be misleading to label these imaginings straightforwardly Modernist. The mutually constitutive sexual, technological and occult beliefs and desires that I focus on become particularly acute in the 1890s, reverberating between the poles of psychical research and psychoanalysis. If anything, this work is a contribution to what might (rather sheepishly) be labelled studies in the long *fin de siècle*. Even with that caveat, the rough periodization, 1880–1920, is in fact somewhat misleading, since some of the Freud and Ferenczi material, and Theodora Bosanquet's automatic writing correspondence with James, extends the book well into the 1920s and 1930s. This is the price one pays for working with the dead. James's reincursion into Bosanquet's life in the 1930s may be taken as emblematic of the dangers of too-assured periodizing: a reminder that even an author's death date may be insufficient evidence for fixing an endpoint to a literary career or historical phenomenon. Howsoever dead the authorial body may appear, technological resuscitation is always possible from the end of the nineteenth century onwards: phonographs and automatic writing assure that spectral authors can always re-emerge.

In the works I examine cultural imaginings of technologically uncanny contact are intertwined with an expanding sense of sex and gender flexibility. Ideas about sexuality inevitably engage fears of transmission – what types of contact are people having and imagining having? What is exchanged during these contacts? This book concerns itself with these, at times, basic questions, performing a reduction of sex to proximity and distance (or materialized and dematerialized contact) in order to explore the relationship between the emerging science of sexuality – psychoanalysis, and the emerging (soon to be submerging) science of the occult – psychical research. At the turn of the century, theories of occult and technological transmission subtend the psychic and social construction of transgressive sexual desires and encounters. As the history behind psychoanalysis's fraught relationship to occultism reveals, fantasies of occult transmission cannot be reduced to the repressed secrets of sex. Rather psychoanalysis emerges from the same questions which mobilize psychical researchers.

Psychoanalysis still provides one of the few compelling critical languages for talking about affective ties and intimate attachments. Yet, over the past twenty years, psychoanalysis as a discipline and a philosophy, has suffered a barrage of attacks. One important root of this dissension can be found in Freud's early attempts to elaborate the origins of sexuality in children and the paths of psychical transmission that sexuality takes. A major and continuing source of tension for psychoanalysis has been the vexed relationship between psychoanalysis's emphasis on fantasy, and the actual contingent events that happen to a person during the course of his or her life. Critics have accused psychoanalysis of ignoring the effects of history or the 'real event' that impinges upon a person from the outside, in favour of psychical reality – the inner desires, fantasies and repressions which are equivalent to reality for the subject.[6] A sustained attack on psychoanalysis of this sort began with Jeffrey Masson's 1984 book, *The Assault on Truth: Freud's Suppression of the Seduction Theory*.[7] In *The Assault on Truth*, Masson claims that Freud was correct in his initial postulation of the seduction theory as the source of his patients' hysterical illnesses: Freud's patients were, in fact, sexually assaulted by their fathers. According to Masson, when Freud renounced the seduction theory in favour of fantasy to found what we now think of as psychoanalysis, he betrayed not only his women patients but history as well, moving from the real world of events to the staged and therefore inauthentic world of the psyche and fantasy.

Psychoanalysis responds to this charge by emphasizing the importance of psychical reality, the ways in which fantasy takes on the force of reality for the patient. The world of the psyche may be staged for a variety of unconscious motivations, but that in no way makes it inauthentic to the person who experiences it. Yet the question of what constitutes psychic or historical authenticity has remained a vexed one for psychoanalysis, prompting other more recent attacks. Returning once again to Freud's earliest theories, Mikkel Borch-Jacobsen has claimed that psychoanalysis's building blocks – Freud's women patients' fantasized seductions by or of their fathers – have shaky foundations. If, according to Freud, psychoanalysis discovered the inner truth of desiring fantasy; and if, according to Masson, Freud disavowed the outer truth of the histories of sexual abuse that his patients told him; then according to Borch-Jacobsen there never were any histories, either real or fantasized, until Freud created them. The real truth of psychoanalysis is that of the suggesting therapist and the suggestible patient. Through suggestion, Freud installed his own theoretical (Oedipal) framework in his patients, and now we all live with the consequences, the culturally seductive, egoistic dream of Sigmund Freud.[8]

It is not the place of this study to adjudicate amongst these positions. That an event that did happen to a person probably will have different effects on her than an event that did not, seems like a relatively uncontroversial statement.[9] However, the potentially wayward workings of unconscious fantasy make it impossible to state categorically that we can predict how any event, either real or fantasized, will be experienced. Similarly, people are undoubtedly suggestible, but some more so than others; some suggestions work while others do not. One reason Freud gave up hypnosis was not that it worked too well, but rather that he couldn't get it to work well enough, and that he risked losing his credibility and authority by his failure.[10] If certain suggestions (for instance, the Oedipus complex) have successfully accrued to the collective and individual psyches of our culture, then simply pointing out that these suggestions were based on the mistaken impositions of one turn-of-the-century Viennese nerve specialist who hated his father and loved his mother, will not necessarily undo their effects. Nor will it explain why this particular suggestive fantasy 'took' – had the far-reaching consequences it did, while another (Fliess's belief in male cyclicality, for instance) did not.

What I offer in this book is not so much a settlement of the Freud wars as a new way of understanding why psychoanalysis 'took' by examining it through the lens of late nineteenth-century/early twentieth-century literary and scientific interest in occult forms of intimacy and transmission. Psychoanalysis's volatile relations to questions of history, memory and suggestion can be seen as part and parcel of its inviting and disavowing magical thinking, or 'the omnipotence of thought' that Freud found in children, obsessive compulsives, psychotics and primitive societies.[11] Magical thinking is the belief that thoughts and desires can directly transfer themselves to, and transform, the material world, other people, the future. As Freud explains in *Totem and Taboo*, quoting J. G. Frazer: 'Men mistook the order of their ideas for the order of nature, and hence imagined that the control which they have, or seem to have, over their thoughts, permitted them to exercise a corresponding control over things.'[12] Like telepathy and contact with the dead, magical thinking collapses distances: 'since distance is of no importance in thinking – since what lies furthest apart both in time and space can without difficulty be comprehended in a single act to consciousness – so, too, the world of magic has a telepathic disregard for spatial distance and treats past situations as though they were present.'[13] Psychoanalysis claims mastery over these beliefs by analysing them and identifying their sources in the infant's rapidly disappearing but endlessly desired sense of its own omnipotence. Yet, Freud's description of magical thinking also works as a description of the unconscious which knows no time or distance. When magical thinking is mobilized, the unconscious's reality, psychical reality, becomes impossible to distinguish from outer reality. As Freud and Breuer discover in *Studies on Hysteria*, through the hysterical symptom, hysterics' bodies seem magically to translate the psychic into the somatic, registering the effects of psychic troubles directly on the body. Psychoanalysis's original task was to trace the paths of transmission of those effects.

A desire for the effectivity of magical thinking unites the literary and cultural discourses I discuss. Psychoanalysis cannot finally endorse magical thinking, but at crucial moments it relies on it as a bridge between unconscious desire and worldly effects. In their work, James, Wilde, Du Maurier and other turn-of-the-century writers employ magical thinking as a powerful tool to expand the potential effects of consciousness and the possibilities for intimate ties and identifications. Psychical researchers search for the mechanism of these magical transmissions to explain apparently inexplicable trafficking between minds and bodies, while the emergence of new technologies creates new imaginative correspondences for delineating these psychic and physical transmissions.

Psychoanalytic ways of reading inform this study to the extent that I find the category of fantasy helpful for interpreting these manifestations of magical thinking, and to the extent that I believe psychoanalysis can provide compelling, if sometimes limiting, narratives of the forms and formations of psychic and social fantasy. But the impetus of my work is to show that the cultural fantasies I discuss are as formative for psychoanalysis as they are able to be analysed by it. To employ psychoanalytic interpretative techniques without uncovering their historical roots would be mistaken. Friedrich Kittler's Foucauldian analyses of the medical, technological, scientific and literary discursive networks which run throughout turn-of-the-century European cultural production have proved helpful to my own project. In Kittler's work the Derridean deconstruction of the western metaphysical tradition sometimes serves as the uncertainly historicized grounds from which he builds his apparently historically determined arguments. Although my work is similarly implicated in this critical see-saw of historical and theoretical arguments for the development of cultural and literary forms, my emphasis on the affective investments and fantasies these forms provoke and/or satisfy means that the assignment of specific historical moments for the emergence of these forms is not my primary object. Rather I situate my work at the conjunction of psychoanalysis, deconstruction and a Foucauldian historicism, in order to analyse both the affective and historical consequences of certain late nineteenth-century cultural fantasies of transmission, and the less securely historicizable logics of affect these fantasies mobilize. This study is also centrally indebted to recent work in queer theory in that these logics of affect are often perverse and fantastic – aligning subjects and their desires in unexpected and culturally unacceptable ways (affiliations between the living and the dead being one limit-case example). Magical thinking is, in Freud's terminology from *The Three Essays on Sexuality*, another factor to consider in the dramatically unstable relation between sexual aim and sexual object. Ideally, I hope that this work, like Freud at his best, has something to contribute towards un-covering the unfixed nature of those physical and mental connec-tions that we group under the umbrella of sex; to ask why and how those connections were being constructed in the period from around 1880 to around 1920.

My first chapter, 'The Society for Psychical Research's experiments in intimacy', argues that the Society for Psychical Research's writings on telepathy indicate that the existence of telepathy was taken for granted and became a basis for 'scientifically' explaining the spiritu-alist claims of contact with the dead. Through readings of the journals and letters of the Society, I show how this presumed existence of direct contact between minds was an object of intense erotic invest-ment for some of the Society's members. Even as the Society attempted to maintain a code of scientific objectivity, the séance became a place for transgressive cross-class/cross-gender contact, as well as a site for communication with a desired other world. Similarly, the possibility of telepathy, legitimated by comparisons to the tele-graph and telephone, focused erotic fantasies of minds and bodies merging, as well as utopian hopes for better communication. Through readings of Rudyard Kipling's story 'Wireless', Bram Sto-ker's *Dracula*, and the anonymously written *Teleny*, I elucidate some of these hopes and fears for telepathic and séance transmission at the turn of the century. Although the Society for Psychical Research set itself up against the mystical claims of the spiritualists, its 'scientifi-cally' validated championship of telepathy endorses an occulted erotics of communicative contact, which can later be traced through Freud and other turn-of-the-century theorizations of transmission.

Chapter Two, 'Wilde, hypnotic aesthetes and the 1890s' argues that as the hypnotizing villain became a staple of *fin-de-siècle* fantasy and horror literature, anxieties about the limits of suggestibility diffused throughout *fin-de-siècle* culture. 1890s Britain found itself fascinated by a courtroom scene that raised the question of dangerous influence – Oscar Wilde's 1895 trials for gross indecency. During the trials Wilde's writings, such as *The Picture of Dorian Gray* (1891) and his homosexuality were portrayed as substitutable for one another, and as dangerously influential and contaminating. In the eyes of the prosecuting attorneys and the press, Wilde was a monster of influence. In this chapter I examine Wilde's trials, and *Dorian Gray*, along with two other 1890s portrayals of suggestibility run amok – George Du Maurier's best-selling *Trilby* (1894) (with its evil hypnotizing musician Svengali) and J. MacLaren Cobban's *Master of his Fate* (1890) (with its Charcot-trained, hypnotizing, aesthetic villain who resembles Wilde) to argue that the aesthete encapsulated a constellation of fears and desires in the 1890s about hypnotic effects, both of the market and of new transgressive sexual possibilities. I argue that the paradigm shift around homosexuality, which Foucault and others have located in the late nineteenth century, intersects significantly with popular and scientific debate about hypnosis. In *Master of his Fate* after the villain Julius Courtney has hypnotically (and homoerotically) drained the life from a young soldier on a train from Brighton, *The Daily Telegraph* appeals to the police 'to find the man who has alarmed the civilised world by a new form of outrage'. This chapter explores the ways in which hypnotic influence contributes to the spectacular public imagination of new forms of outrage in the 1890s.

Chapter Three, 'Henry James's lives during wartime', explores how Henry James's very late work constructs the possibility for intimate knowledge of others through his expansive use of identification, specifically in relation to his reaction to World War I. I read James's participation in the war effort – his patriotic fervour, his adoption of British citizenship – along with his final unfinished ghost novel, *The Sense of the Past*, to argue that the structures of imaginative ghostly identification with the past which are at work in the novel are also employed by James in his taking on of a new national identity at the end of his life, and that the anxieties about identificative failure which palpably haunt the novel also appear in James's uncertain relationship to the war as evidenced by his war writings, especially his book of propaganda, *Within the Rim*. In order to overcome his sense of exclusion from a wartime community, because of his age, his nationality and, crucially, because of anxieties about his previously inactive status during the American Civil War, James overcompensates with jubilant, homoerotically charged identifications both with fighting and wounded soldiers, and with the nation as a whole. James's identificatory strategies performatively, even wilfully, enact his version of community through repeated rehearsings of a nationalistic, patriotic 'we'. His wartime identifications allow him to play out transgressive homoerotic desires within a sanctioned patriotic arena, while simultaneously, it is the very erotics of those identifications which make for hegemonic cultural transmission and community formation.

Chapter Four, 'On the typewriter, *In the Cage*, at the Ouija board', suggests that Henry James's ghost stories, such as *The Turn of the Screw*, may not be the only or the best places to look for the ways in which James creates the consciousnesses of his characters as shared, occult places. In her book *Thinking in Henry James*, Sharon Cameron claims that thought is portrayed in late James as shared, and that consciousness is impossible to pin down securely to any one mind. In this chapter I trace this telepathic effect back through James's middle period to his engagement with new forms of communication technology. In his novella about a telegraph office, *In the Cage*, James externalizes the possibility of intimate knowledge of another person through the commercially and materially mediated transactions of the telegram. The erotics of the story, in which a young, working class telegraphist constructs a relationship with an upper class customer through her picture-perfect knowledge of his telegraphing habits, depend on a melding of commercial and sexual transactions which coalesce around the new forms of access to knowledge of others provided by new communication technologies and the workers who run them. These erotics of the technological storehouse are also detectable in James's relationships to his secretaries to whom he dictated his work at the end of his life. I compare the mediated intimacy of *In the Cage* to the extensive automatic writings of James's final secretary Theodora Bosanquet, a dedicated psychical researcher, who, after James's death, spent a good deal of time channelling him as well as other literary figures. Specifically new forms of commercialization of intimacy, with precursors that encompass both prostitution and paying mediums for séances, begin to gather force with the revolution in communication technology at the end of the nineteenth century, creating a new figure, the (primarily female) information worker, whose access to others' minds results in anxieties about the permeable boundaries of individual knowledge.

James's writings on and through new communication technologies
extend the definition of consciousness as a shared category as I have
defined it in my third chapter in relation to James's jubilantly
desiring wartime 'we'. The two chapters together situate some of
James's less well known writings in relation to his more famous late
novels' refining and troubling of the notion of individual consciousness, in the process historically locating James's expansive definitions
of consciousness in a context of late nineteenth-century scientific
interest in telepathy, the onset of telecommunication, and versions of
shared consciousness necessitated by war.

My final chapter, 'Freud, Ferenczi and psychoanalysis's telepathic
transferences', argues that turn-of-the-century anxieties about and
desires for intimacy are endemic to the structure of psychoanalysis.
Linking several constitutive outsides of psychoanalysis, themes which
Freud discarded or resisted approaching – his reluctance to treat
psychotics, his desire to distinguish psychoanalysis from telepathy,
and his founding privileging of fantasy over the real event – I argue
that when the mind is imagined as being filled up with actual
transferable material (as both psychosis and thought transference
suggest in different ways) it endangers both the theoretical structure
of psychoanalytic transference and the imagined boundaries of the
subjects who established psychoanalysis as a practice. The accusations of plagiarism engaged in by Freud and other early analysts
suggest that psychoanalysis desires a single traceable origin for ideas,
while its theoretical consequences make the trafficking of ideas
between minds unpoliceable. Freud's correspondence with Sandor
Ferenczi, and the *Clinical Diary* Ferenczi kept in the final years of his
life, indicate that Ferenczi's interest in telepathy and mediums, his
overt transferential desire for Freud, and his turn back to the
seduction theory are all aspects of a fascination (both his and
psychoanalysis's) with dangerous intimacy – bodies and minds which
overlap in ways which are too close, too inextricable.

Recent critical discussion both within and outside of psychoanalysis
over the competing claims of fantasy and history in psychoanalytic,
literary-critical and media debates about trauma and repressed
memory, replay the stakes of these nineteenth-century psychotic and
psychoanalytic fantasies of intimate access to the psyche. *Literature,
Technology and Magical Thinking* uncovers some of the sources of these
debates in the compelling literary, technological and psychological
fantasies and realities of our previous turn of the century.

CHAPTER I

The Society for Psychical Research's experiments in intimacy

IMAGINING INTIMACY AT THE TURN OF THE CENTURY

How do we conceive of intimacy with another human being? What do we mean when we say we know someone 'inside and out'? In the 1880s and 1890s one way to answer these questions is to take them literally, to imagine bodies and minds spatially. In Bram Stoker's *Dracula* (1897) or the psychotic judge Daniel Paul Schreber's *Memoirs of my Nervous Illness* (1903), minds and bodies are invaded by hostile outsiders, filled up with foreign contents, sucked dry of their own. Buildings, bodies and minds can be seen to house ghosts, invaders from the past. Economic models of invasion are often correlated with linguistic models of communication. The dead want to communicate with the living, delivering messages through mediums; the rays which invade Schreber's body are made out of language; Dracula finds himself telepathically connected to the victims whose blood he ingests. At the turn of the century fantasies about language, communication and suggestion are being worked out through economic models, just as formulations, in literary and scientific texts, of the 'actual' contents of the body and mind invoke fantasies about how language works to enable and disable communication. What barriers do these fantasies cross? What barriers do they establish?

Consider the following series of scenarios: imagine that you can communicate with the dead; imagine that you can communicate with someone miles away through a telegraph or on the telephone; imagine that God is sending rays made of language into your body and that his lackeys are recording every one of your thoughts and utterances; imagine that two people in the enclosed space of an office, one of whom spews out uncensored language while the other listens, can come to some sort of understanding of, or cure for, the pathologies of the speaker; imagine that there is telepathy, that thought can be transmitted directly from mind to mind. Each of these fantasies is, of course, differently situated culturally and suggests a different social status. Yet I would maintain that all of these scenarios, from what eventually becomes the most widespread and technologically banal (the telephone) to the most obscure and specific (Schreber's delusions), are related to a nexus of late nine-teenth-century concerns about the shape and configuration of the mind, and the volition of the subject whose mind just may be under attack.

The invasion of the self by a potentially hostile outsider is not an idea that originates in the nineteenth century. The Gothic tradition depends on the notion of being haunted or possessed by forces outside oneself. Terry Castle has noted how Ann Radcliffe's novels register this phenomenon of invasion by rationally explaining the supernatural, while simultaneously supernaturalizing everyday life.[1] From the end of the eighteenth century onwards, Castle claims, the mind is a potentially occupied site. Radcliffe's heroes and heroines carry with them the ghosts of their dead, or presumed dead, loved ones: 'to be haunted . . . is to display one's powers of sympathetic imagination . . . Those who love, by definition, are open to the spirit of the other.'[2] This permeable, occulted psyche of the Gothic novel, one aspect of the Romantic subjectivizing of experience, in which the mind, as its own place, is capable of both inhabiting its surroundings and being inhabited by them, precedes the turn of the century narratives of occupation I explore in this book. Following Friedrich Kittler's lead in *Discourse Networks*, I will argue that ways of imagining the supernaturally occupied mind change with historical shifts in technologies of transmission of information, which affect the available store of mediums and material through which subjectivity is manufactured. For Kittler, as for Foucault, language is a domain resistant to any humanizing internalization. Its effects can only be understood by tracing the material conditions under which it operates: 'A notation system or . . . a discourse network has the exterior character – the outsideness – of a technology . . . such technologies are not mere instruments with which "man" produces his meanings . . . Rather they set the framework within which something like "meaning," indeed, something like "man", becomes possible at all.'[3] Kittler shows how the Romantic discourse network, which privileges the maternal voice as the origin and guarantor of meaning in the written word, precedes and differs from the modern discourse network, in which writing is understood as detached from subjectivity, aligned with the fragmentary and repetitive and incapable of anchoring any sort of coherent self. I argue that the narratives which contribute to creating Kittler's networks are also affectively and erotically charged allegories of invasion and intimacy, distance and spatial collapse. The Gothic novel's tales of desiring, sympathetic and haunted invasion of and by the other are revisited in turn-of-the-century literary, technological, and scientific writings, and also in the naturalized supernatural narratives of psychical societies. The apparatuses of data storage and retrieval which set the terms for Kittler's discourse networks work also to manufacture erotic longing and occult knowledge in the subjects who operate within the space of these networks.

At the end of the nineteenth century new ideas about communication technologies, new ideas about the mind and new ways of thinking about the supernatural help shape changing notions of intimacy and communication. Interest in telepathy can be seen as a focal point for these concerns. As a newly coined word (by F. W. H. Myers in 1882) telepathy is connected to other forms of tele-technology, and often imagined as functioning in the same way that these other technologies do, with the same popular 'scientific' explanations or lack of them. Genealogically linked to the older concept of sympathy and the newer word empathy, telepathy is also related to love – the desire for complete sympathetic union with the mind of another. In this chapter I look at how telepathy was imagined during the 1880s and 1890s, when the Society for Psychical Research was conducting a series of thought transference experiments. What did it mean at that historical moment to have an interest in telepathy? I argue that championing of telepathy was not confined to a group of too-gullible Cambridge scientists, but rather that the popularity of the word, almost from its inception, indicates that as a cultural phenomenon, telepathy, whether disputed as myth or endorsed as reality, was effective beyond the confines of the Journal and Proceedings of the Society for Psychical Research. By contrasting the place of thought transference experiments within the workings of the Society to its other main experimental activity – séances with mediums – the significance of proximity (touch) and distance in what I am calling the erotics of psychical research becomes clear. I conclude by examining two novels which explore the threats as well as the promises of telepathy at the turn of the century.

THE SOCIETY FOR PSYCHICAL RESEARCH

In Cambridge in 1874, Henry Sidgwick, F. W. H. Myers, Edmund Gurney, A. J. Balfour and Eleanor Balfour (soon to marry Sidgwick) began a systematic investigation of occult phenomena such as spiritualism and thought transference. These investigations eventually led to the founding of the Society for Psychical Research in 1882.[4] The stated aim of the Society was simply to study objectively claims for the existence of supernatural phenomena, such as spiritualism, but, as many have argued, its emotional impetus was towards countering the pessimism of a materialist and scientifically determined world view.[5] For Frederic Myers and others like him, the driving desire was to find scientific proof of survival after death, and thus ally the claims of nineteenth-century positivist science with the older claims of religious faith. The typical late nineteenth-century psychical researcher tended towards this combination of religious hopefulness and materialist scepticism. As Janet Oppenheim puts it:

. . . it would not be an exaggeration to say that the early leaders of the SPR zealously explored the terra incognita of telepathy with the aim, whether purposeful or subconscious, of providing new, unassailable foundations for religious beliefs.[6]

Psychical researchers' investigations fell somewhere between the new scientific and the old religious orthodoxies. Neither science nor the clergy was pleased with the claims of spiritualism and related phenomena:

By and large the clergy discarded spiritualism on the grounds that it was either fraud or a work of the devil. With a few notable exceptions, including William Crookes, William Barrett, and Alfred Russel Wallace, men of science and naturalistic writers also dismissed hypnotism, mesmerism, telepathy, and spiritualism. Like the clergy, most scientists considered the psychical occurrences fraudulent. A few actually did investigate séances. The scientific reductionism of others made them ill-disposed to consider the possibility that mind might exist separately from its physical organism.[7]

If one impetus of the Society for Psychical Research was to set the mind free of its materialist moorings, then another was to chart out a new map for understanding its intricacies. New phenomena in psychology such as hypnotism, hysteria, aphasias and multiple personalities, which suggested that the mind had unexplored regions, were of intense interest to psychical researchers. If the mind were structured like a haunted house, the hope was that science, stretched far enough, would be capable of exploring its hidden rooms.[8] Today psychical research is usually dismissed as a pseudo-science or looked on as a best-forgotten sideline to the careers of such nineteenth century men of letters as Sidgwick and William James. Its inheritors are television shows such as *The X-Files* and the recent spate of alien abduction stories. I want to take a different, less dismissive approach to psychical research and read its concerns as coextensive with a late nineteenth-century fascination with the modus operandi of cultural transmission and communication. From its inception the Society for Psychical Research's primary concern was for communication that transgressed obvious boundaries. Spiritualism creates contact across inaccessible time, with the dead; telepathy creates contact across inaccessible space, with others who are out of the range of the usual forms of sensory communication.

The SPR set up the first of its six working committees to pursue thought transference: 'An examination of the nature and extent of any influence which may be exerted by one mind upon another, apart from any generally recognised mode of perception.'[9] Its other committees were devoted to studying mesmerism, apparitions and haunted houses, the theories of Reichenbach (a German investigator who invented the theory of an odic force, a unifying fluid similar to Mesmer's magnetic fluid), the physical phenomena of mediums, and to collecting and collating information on the history of psychical occurrences.

The initial aim of the Society was to apply scientific methods to phenomena that the standard prejudices of scientists prevented them from investigating. As Henry Sidgwick put it in his presidential address to the Society in 1888, speaking of the Society's beginnings six years earlier:

We believed unreservedly in the methods of modern science, and were prepared to accept submissively her reasoned conclusions, when sustained by the agreement of experts; but we were not prepared to bow with equal docility to the mere prejudices of scientific men. And it appeared to us that there was an important body of evidence – tending *prima facie* to establish the independence of soul or spirit – which modern science had simply left on one side with ignorant contempt; and that in so leaving it she had been untrue to her professed method, and had arrived prematurely at her negative conclusions.[10]

As a professor of moral philosophy at Cambridge, Henry Sidgwick's investment in psychical research was in large part an ethical one. He wanted to find a basis for an ethical relation to others in a world shorn of religious certainty. As he said in the same presidential address, '. . . when we took up seriously the obscure and perplexing investigation which we call *Psychical Research*, we were mainly moved to do so by the profound and painful division and conflict as regards the nature and destiny of the human soul, which we found in the thought of our age'.[11] While men of science such as Herbert Spencer looked to evolutionary models to ground their theories of human behaviour, Sidgwick and other psychical researchers turned towards new expansive theories of the mind and consciousness to reconstruct an ordered, ethical universe.

In different ways, spiritualism and thought transference, the Society's main objects of interest, can both be seen to hold out the promise of new grounds for ethical relations. Alex Owen has indicated the connections between nineteenth-century spiritualism and various political reform movements. The desire to attain individual and social perfection on earth was seen as preparation for a progressive evolutionary drive towards the next world: '. . . although there were certainly class tensions within the spiritualist movement, adherents across the spectrum of social class . . . were committed to the amelioration of social abuses and working-class ills'.[12] Organizations such as the British National Association of Spiritualists (BNAS), established in 1874, linked radical social politics with the promise of a spiritualist utopia after death. The BNAS's prospectus 'stated that the Association sought to "reunite those who are now too often divided by seemingly material conflicting interests"', and that it was dedicated to remedying the '"excessive irregularity in the distribution of wealth" with its resulting "crying social evils."'[13] Spiritualism, with its quest to form communities between the living and the dead, was an interest often shared by those who were committed to other radical reforms that aimed to stretch the boundaries, and assert the rights of other under-represented communities such as women, the working class, and, through vegetarianism and anti-vivisectionism, animals.[14]

The Society for Psychical Research's relationship to spiritualism shifted over the years. Some of the Society's original members were committed spiritualists, but by 1886 a rift had developed between the spiritualists and Sidgwick's more sceptical contingent. Most of the serious spiritualists left the Society in that year after taking offence at some of Eleanor Sidgwick's critical writings on the slate-writing of

W. Eglinton.[15] Later in the chapter I will return to the ways in which class and gender divisions between the Society's members and the spiritualists contributed to stretching and delimiting the acceptable boundaries of interaction between living minds, living bodies and ghostly materializations. The methods of spiritualism and psychical research responded both to radical and conservative impulses, and to less easily discernible desires.

One person who embodied many of the conflicting impulses of the Society in its early years was F. W. H. Myers (1843–1901). Myers was obsessed with the possibility of life after death. His *magnum opus*, the enormous two volume *Human Personality and its Survival of Bodily Death*, is a tribute to his faith in survival, but it is also a testimony to his engagement with new materialist and anti-materialist psychological theories. In order to explain phenomena such as hypnotism and multiple personalities, Myers postulated the existence of a subliminal consciousness, similar in part to Freud's unconscious.[16] Myers conceived of human personality along the model of an iceberg, only a small percentage of which, the supraliminal 'everyday' self, extended above the waterline. Like his friend and fellow psychical researcher William James, Myers believed that the greater portion of consciousness, the subliminal self, was submerged, elusive, and shifting:

. . . the stream of consciousness in which we habitually live is not the only consciousness which exists in connection with our organism. Our habitual or empirical consciousness may consist of a mere selection from a multitude of thoughts and sensations . . . I accord no primacy to my ordinary waking self, except that among my potential selves this one has shown itself the fittest to meet the needs of common life.[17]

For Myers, the subliminal consciousness extended further than the supraliminal, opening up the possibility of engaging in 'a far wider range both of physiological and of psychical activity'.[18] The supraliminal self could, under certain conditions, share the wealth of knowledge and insight that the subliminal self contained. The evidence of this communication between selves was what interested psychical researchers. According to Myers's theories, automatic writing, table-rapping, hallucinations, clairvoyance and dreams are all attempts by the subliminal self to deliver information to the supraliminal self.[19] In Myers's theories, as in Freud's, the human subject, in its combination of psychic and bodily automatisms and symptoms, is a relay station for information. For Freud, this information tends to be inward-looking, reflecting the subject's past history. For Myers, the information is more compelling when it is outward-looking, foreseeing the future, the possibility of surviving death, the potential for extra-sensory connections between minds. Myers's hope is for a human body and mind that would intimate immortality; Freud is looking for different things (the Oedipus complex, infantile sexuality, etc.), but both participate in versions of a late nineteenth-century hermeneutic project in which the subject is understood both as a text to be read and a space through which information flows.[20]

Myers was responsible for introducing Freud's work to England, delivering a paper on 'Hysteria and Genius' to the Society in 1897, in which he gave an account of Freud and Breuer's *Studies on Hysteria*.[21] Myers's work raises questions about the relationship between the dissolution of subjectivity and its conservation in the discourses of psychical research. *Human Personality and its Survival of Bodily Death* encapsulates two contradictory strands of thought. On the one hand, human personality seemed infinitely more pliable, doubled, and easily broken down than had been previously suspected. Hypnotism, multiple personalities and hysteria all indicated a subject which was potentially not one and not always present to itself. On the other hand, spiritualism (and Myers) pinned its hopes on the possibility that human personality actually survived death. As Myers puts it in an introductory syllabus in his book: 'The new evidence adduced in this book, while supporting the conception of the composite structure of the Ego, does also bring the strongest proof of its abiding *unity*, by showing that it withstands the shock of death.'[22] This breakdown of the subject, together with its simultaneous reassertion, anticipates a dynamic that recent critics have seen at work in psychoanalysis. Mikkel Borch-Jacobsen, for instance, suggests in *The Freudian Subject* that Freud finally preserves the unified subject at each moment when it seems most threatened, shifting its location from the conscious to the unconscious, or the individual to the crowd, but maintaining its basic unity. In Borch-Jacobsen's view, Freud needs to anchor the psychoanalytic subject firmly in his or her own egoistic identity in order to defend psychoanalysis from charges that it is indistinguishable from hypnotism, charges that while claiming to uncover psychic dynamics, it really installs its own predetermined structures and stories in a pliable, suggestible subject.

Although this dynamic of dispersed and reassembled subjectivity can be seen as endemic to the western philosophical tradition since

Descartes,[23] as Kittler suggests, at the turn of the century the mind is imagined as inhabited, unified, dispersed and communicating in specific ways which are influenced by a nexus of scientific, literary and popular discussions. This account needs to be supplemented with what we might call a historical and affective understanding of fantasy. When we ask what factors contribute to late nineteenth-century ideas about the shape and configuration of the mind, subjectivity and communication, we need to think about what might compel people to want their minds to look certain ways. Whether we care about permanent metaphysical structures, the latest technologies or haunted houses, our explanatory models are bound to reflect these investments. Fantasies, especially site-specific academic fantasies of causal explanation, are often totalizing (i.e. the idea that this or that phenomenon is entirely the product of historical determinants, or entirely the product of a western metaphysics of presence); the appeal of the totalizing fantasy is as visible in the Society for Psychical Research's discussions of telepathy as in late twentieth-century literary theory. The point of the following discussion is not to endorse or critique these fantasies of totalization, but rather to try and understand how various imagined effects of collapse, communication and intimate contact with others' bodies and minds contributed to creating a permeable, boundary-crossing, potentially telepathic subject at the turn of the century.

TELEPATHY

In October 1884 Samuel Clemens wrote to the editor of the *Journal of the Society for Psychical Research* to express his appreciation of the experiments the Society had been conducting on thought transference:

Dear Sir, I should be very glad indeed to be made a Member of the Society for Psychical Research; for Thought-transference, as you call it, or mental telegraphy as I have been in the habit of calling it, has been a very strong interest with me for the past nine or ten years. I have grown so accustomed to considering that all my powerful impulses come to me from somebody else, that I often feel like a mere amanuensis when I sit down to write a letter under the coercion of a strong impulse: I consider that the other person is supplying the thoughts to me, and that I am merely writing from dictation . . . I have been saved the writing of many and many a letter by refusing to obey these strong impulses. I always knew the other fellow was sitting down to write when I got the impulse – so what could be the sense in both of us writing the same thing? People are always marveling because their letters 'cross' each other. If they would but squelch the impulse to write, there would not be any crossing, because only the other fellow would write.[24]

Clemens's engagement with the Society's work is recognized as at least partially ironic by the editors of the *Journal* who reproduce the letter with an introduction, 'the following characteristic letter from Mr. S. L. Clemens (Mark Twain) will, doubtless, entertain many of our readers.-Ed.'[25] Yet to dismiss Twain's interest in the Society as entirely facetious would be mistaken. He not only became a member of the Society but also corresponded with Frederic Myers, to whom he writes about subjects such as the functioning of consciousness and unconsciousness during an experience of blacking out.[26] In an 1891 article in *Harper's Magazine* 'Mental Telegraphy', Twain reiterates his early belief in telepathy and his support of the Society for Psychical Research: 'Within the last two or three years they [the SPR] have penetrated toward the heart of the matter . . . and have found out that mind can act upon mind in a quite detailed and elaborate way over vast stretches of land and water. And they have succeeded in doing, by their great credit and influence, what I could never have done – they have convinced the world that mental telegraphy is not a jest, but a fact, and that it is a thing not rare, but exceedingly common.'[27] Twain's fascination with telepathy clearly dovetailed with his interest in new communication technologies such as the telephone line he early had installed, and the type-setting machine he invested in heavily.[28]

It appears from the letter to the Society that Twain's enthusiasm for thought transference is primarily for its money and time saving potential, as he makes clear when he describes a mental transaction which saves him the cost of a 50 cent telegram. He is not particularly interested in telepathy's metaphysical, spiritual or scientific consequences. Rather, for Twain it would be an economic advantage if mediation could be dispensed with and thought could be instantaneously shared:

In my own case it has often been demonstrated that people can have crystal-clear mental communication with each other over vast distances. Doubtless to be able to do this the two minds have to be in a peculiarly favourable condition for the moment. Very well, then, why shouldn't some scientist find it possible to invent a way to *create* this condition of *rapport* between two minds, at will? Then we should drop the slow and cumbersome telephone and say 'Connect me with the brain of the chief of police at Peking.' We shouldn't need to know the man's language; we should communicate by thought only, and say in a couple of minutes what couldn't be inflated into words in an hour and a-half. Telephones, telegraphs and words are too slow for this age; we must get something that is faster.[29]

This is the American can-do version of thought transference. Telepathy promises to displace mediation and do away with the necessity for transmission, translation, even for language itself, in the service of efficiency. When Twain points out that words themselves, not just telephones and telegraphs, are too slow for this age, he takes telepathy towards its logical conclusion: a collapsing of communication upon itself. No communication would be necessary in Twain's utopia, no transference of anything from one place to another, because there would be no distancing to begin with. To employ poststructuralist terminology, there would be no differentiation from the other, no loss, and no language needed to try to make good that loss. For Twain in this letter, lack of differentiation becomes entirely a matter of economics. No loss means nothing to pay in order to send one's message through.

In Twain's logics of media extension (reaching over farther and farther distances) and contraction (collapsing distance onto itself), telepathy is just a form of communication-enhancing technology that will make things faster, easier, better for market relations and productivity – a sort of Taylorization of the soul. At the turn of the century, telepathy, as has been pointed out, is only one in a whole series of new 'tele' communications.[30] Recently, in the work of theorists such as Kittler, Nicholas Royle and Avital Ronell, 'tele' or technology studies has formed an uneasy alliance with deconstructive theory.[31] On the one hand, it seems that new communication technologies introduce, in a sort of epistemic break, new ways of conceiving of our relations to our minds and bodies, to other minds and bodies, and to time. But, on the other hand, deconstructive theory suggests that the modes of communication transmission employed by these new technologies are structural constants. Our forms of communication, inter- and intra-subjective, are now, and have always been, structured the same way that the telephone line is structured. Even with the knowledge that all communication is 'tele', at a distance, the unfulfillable desire for the collapse of that distance, for 'full' presence, remains. Hence Twain's ironic desire to do away with words.

The flip side of this collapse of communication on itself is the prosthetic extension of the senses into previously unimaginable realms, the fantasy that new technology could retrieve the absolutely lost. Twain's cheerful fantasies of immediacy resemble those of Thomas Edison, another relentlessly non-melancholic deployer of technological know-how. Edison, in his memoir, *The Diary and Sundry Observations of Thomas Alva Edison*, wants to bring science to the afterworld. The final chapter of Edison's musings is devoted to 'The Realms Beyond' in which the scientist discusses the valve he is building to communicate with the dead, or at least to increase the volume level, so that if the dead are trying to get in touch with the living we'll have a better chance of hearing them: '. . . if personality exists, after what we call death, it is reasonable to conclude that those who leave this earth would like to communicate with those they have left here. Accordingly, the thing to do is to furnish the best conceivable means to make it easy for them to open up communication with us, and then see what happens.'[32]

Twain and Edison assume a continuity between the teletechnology they are involved in inventing and deploying and the crossing over into a paranormal world. If you can talk to people at a distance on the phone, the logic runs, why shouldn't you be able to talk to the dead? Friedrich Kittler points out the connections between the nineteenth century's new forms of communication technology and the spiritual world:

the tapping specters of the spiritualistic séances with their messages from the realm of the dead, appeared quite promptly at the moment of the invention of the Morse alphabet in 1837. Promptly, photographic plates – even and especially with the camera shutter closed – provided images of ghosts or specters which in their black and white fuzziness, only emphasized the moments of resemblance. Finally one of the ten uses Edison predicted . . . for the recently invented phonograph was to preserve the 'last words of the dying'.[33]

In other words there is always already a ghost in the machine, a telepath on the telephone wire. What is the force of this logic of extension? It may be grasped perhaps if we first consider the specific anxieties and hopes about telepathy within the Society for Psychical Research.

Although not such an obviously widespread cultural phenomenon as the mid-century craze for spiritualism, thought transference by the 1880s was a popular subject for debate. Rather like interest in

the seemingly magical but less and less disputed powers of hypnotism
and suggestion, at the end of the century telepathy begins to be taken
for granted by some sections of the population. The Society for
Psychical Research's interest in telepathy extended in several different
directions. Chiefly through the early efforts of Myers and Edmund
Gurney, the Society collected people's stories of their experiences of
visual hallucinations and published them in the enormous *Phantasms
of the Living* in 1886.[34] The book told a repeated story of a dying person
appearing to a loved one far away at the moment of death, which
Gurney and Myers postulated was potentially caused by a telepathic
projection. Whether these crisis apparitions were telepathic transferences sent out by the person at the moment before death or actual
appearances of someone after death was a crucial question for
members of the Society who accepted the evidence of *Phantasms* as
proof of some sort of image transference. Was there survival after
death, or could the evidence that pointed to it be explained away by
that other extra-sensory, but comparatively mundane phenomenon,
telepathy? For Myers and others, therefore, telepathy was double
edged: both a step on the way towards proof of survival after death
and a potentially less outlandish explanation for phenomena generated by mediums which might otherwise point towards proof of
survival. It is in part because of this use of telepathy as the less
radical explanation for spiritualists' evidence that telepathy itself
comes to be assumed truly to take place, or at least to be plausible.

The Society's first and initially most successful thought transference experiments were carried out on the Creery sisters by the
physicist William Barrett.[35] The 1881 successes with the Creery girls
became the basis for a firm belief by Barrett, as well as other
members of the Society, that thought transference was a proven
phenomenon.[36] However, the Creerys were caught using a code
when tested again in 1887. Other thought transference and hypnotic
experiments carried out by Edmund Gurney in the 1880s, which
seemed to point towards startling evidence for telepathy, were also
partially discredited by doubts about the experimentees.[37] But the
fact that many of the major experiments that acted as cornerstones
for the Society's faith in telepathy were later shown to be untrustworthy is not my primary concern. Rather, I am more interested in
the ways in which belief in telepathy was dispersed through the
Society and outside it, despite lack of unimpeachable scientific
evidence for its existence.

Henry Sidgwick thought that telepathy was still the most promising line of inquiry for the Society, even if there was not yet convincing evidence for its existence. In an 1888 journal entry he writes, 'I have not much hope of our getting out positive results in any other department of inquiry, but I am not yet hopeless of establishing telepathy.'[38] A theory of telepathy was what was needed to convince the rest of the scientific world. 'If only I could form the least conception of the *modus transferendi!*'[39] Sidgwick's desire to believe but inability to understand how telepathy actually functioned indicates the role telepathy was fulfilling in the collective psyche of nineteenth-century psychical researchers. It was useful for explaining other phenomena, but seemed to have no explanation itself. Yet its popularity grew. Sidgwick's wife, Eleanor, another intrepid psychical researcher, writes, 'telepathy . . . had now become a catchword of the man in the street, who used it like "electricity" to explain anything mysterious. Meantime telepathy had hardly moved an inch in the favour or respect, of the professional scientist.'[40]

As well as both being handy if mystifying explanations for transmission, telepathy and electricity share other characteristics. They both inspire fantasies of community – instant access to others. If the world becomes a smaller place because of telecommunication, telepathy too is imagined to create connections with even more startling potential effects. In his book *On the Threshold of the Unseen*, William Barrett, one of the staunchest supporters of the truth of telepathy, imagines a telepathic utopia where social justice would follow inevitably from shared thoughts:

If we were involuntarily sharers in one another's pleasures and pains, the brotherhood of the race would not be a pious aspiration or a strenuous effort, but the reality of all others most vividly before us; *the* factor in our lives which would dominate all our conduct. What would be the use of a luxurious mansion at the West End and Parisian cooks if all the time the misery and starvation of our fellow creatures at the East End were telepathically part and parcel of our daily lives? On the other hand what bright visions and joyous emotions would enter into many dreary and loveless lives if this state of human responsiveness were granted to the race![41]

In this scenario, the ethical consequences of telepathy would mean that the rich would have to think about the poor and the poor could telepathically share the privileges of the rich. For Myers as well, the existence of telepathy implied utopian bonding. In his essay 'Science and a future life', he claims: '. . . that same direct influence of mind on mind' which telepathy revealed '*in minimis* would, if supposed operative *in maximis*, be a form of stating the efficacy of prayer, the communion of saints, or even the operation of a Divine Spirit'.[42] Telepathy here becomes a dramatic and scientifically sanctioned method for transporting words such as sympathy or the recently coined 'empathy' from the realm of the way things should be to the way things actually could be, the way things *will* be if thought is effectively shared.

Telepathy was imagined in a variety of ways. Both telepathy itself and the tendency to believe in it were subsumed by contemporary theories that posited what Robert Nye has called the two fallacies of nineteenth-century cultural anthropology: 'the presumption that modern savage societies represented carbon copies of their historical predecessors "frozen" in time, and the notion that primitive institutions could be logically inferred from a study of their "survivals" in contemporary social forms'.[43] Telepathy was sometimes put in the service of Barrett's collective utopia but it was also seen as a throwback to a previous evolutionary state. Frank Podmore thought that telepathy was one of several 'long lost but once serviceable faculties' which man, ages ago, used consciously, but which since had become involuntary residuals.[44] Against telepathy, James Frazer and others argued that it was the *belief* in phenomena such as telepathy and ghosts, not the phenomena themselves, that was a survival of the superstitions of the savage mind which had not yet been ousted from the modern one.[45] Henry Sidgwick mockingly described a *Pall Mall Gazette* article of 21 October 1882 which warned against the dangers of succumbing to belief in ghosts. The article 'urged its readers to abstain from inquiring into ghost stories on account of the dangerous tendency to give them credence which, on the principle of evolution, must be held to exist in our brains. Owing to the many generations of our ancestors who believed in spirits, we retain, it seems in our nervous mechanism, "innumerable connections of fibers", which will be developed into superstitious beliefs if we give them the slightest opportunity . . . "The scientific attitude can only be maintained by careful abstention from dangerous trains of thought."'[46]

The idea of telepathy as evolutionary survival was also used to connect humans to animals, particularly insects, who were pictured as employing forms of telepathic communication. Barrett suggests that, 'the habits of ants and bees seem to indicate the possession of a mode of communication unknown to us. If our domestic animals are in any degree open to thought-transference, may we not get into somewhat closer communication with them?'[47] Although lacking the desire to talk to the animals, Freud, in his article 'Dreams and Occultism', is not far from Barrett when he suggests that telepathy might be an atavistic sense in humans, still at work in insects:

. . . it is a familiar fact that we do not know how the common purpose comes about in the great insect communities; possibly it is done by means of direct psychical transference of this kind. One is led to a suspicion that this is the original, archaic method of communication between individuals and that in the course of phylogenetic evolution it has been replaced by the better method of giving information with the help of signals which are picked up by the sense organs.[48]

Myers and others, however, saw telepathy as a progressive evolutionary step rather than a movement back towards a lost atavistic sense: 'telepathy is surely a step in evolution. To learn the thoughts of other minds, without the mediation of the special senses, manifestly indicates the possibility of a vast extension of psychical powers.'[49] In the emerging theories of crowd behaviour, telepathy held an important if unexamined explanatory place. The crowd mind, often thought of as a primitive one, had to be imagined as telepathically created in order for it to act en masse. Gabriel Tarde postulates in *The Laws of Imitation* that sociality itself, in its most radical form, would be telepathic: 'in its hypothetical form it would consist of such an intense concentration of urban life that as soon as a good idea arose in one mind it would be instantaneously transmitted to all minds throughout the city.'[50] Gustave LeBon, in his enormously popular *La Psychologie des foules* (1895) posits '*the law of the mental unity of crowds*', suggesting that crowds form themselves through contagion of a hypnotic order.[51] Although the unthinking, primitive crowd is for LeBon inferior to the reasoning individual, he also suggests that the crowd can at times rise above itself, somewhat in the manner of Myers's progressive evolutionary hopes for telepathy:

So far as the majority of their acts are considered, crowds display a singularly inferior mentality; yet there are other acts in which they appear to be guided by those mysterious forces which the ancients denominated destiny, nature or providence, which we call the voices of the dead, and whose power it is impossible to overlook, although we ignore their essence. It would seem, at times, as if there were latent forces in the inner being of nations which serve to guide them. What, for instance, can be more complicated, more logical, more marvelous than a language? Yet whence can this admirably organised production have arisen except it be the outcome of the unconscious genius of crowds?[52]

Language, LeBon suggests, is not developed through individual communicative interactions. Rather it arises spontaneously in the group mind, creating, amongst other things, national identity. If for Freud, telepathy is potentially an archaic, pre-linguistic method of communication, then for LeBon, language itself arises telepathically, instantaneously, contagiously in the mind of the crowd. Telepathy is imagined as the origin of language, sociality and nationhood.

Telepathy was clearly a contradictory creature. Sometimes imagined as the path towards spiritual or earthly utopia through shared sensations, it could also be viewed as the mechanism behind a collapsing of all thought in the primitive, riotous, unthinking crowd mind. Physical explanations for its existence were often contradictory too. Telepathy was most often explained by recourse to analogies to electricity and other dematerialized, non-visible forms of transmission. The Society's 'First Report on Thought-Reading' quotes a Dr T. A. McGraw from the *Detroit Review of Medicine* to support their beliefs about the plausibility of thought transference:

'It seems to me there is a hint towards the possibility of the nervous system of one individual being used by the active will of another to accomplish certain simple motions. There would be nothing inherently impossible in this when we recollect the strong similarities that exist between nervous and electrical forces; and as we know, it is possible to generate induced currents of electricity in coils of wire that are near to a primary electric coil; so we can imagine the nervous current to be continued into . . . another body and act there upon the automatic centres of action . . .'[53]

Such explanations borrow from older explanations of mesmerism, harkening back to come up with a new, technologically updated version of the bodily magnetism initially thought responsible for mesmeric effects. The 'First Report on Thought-Reading' attempts to set thought transference in a continuum with other forms of dematerialized transmission once thought impossible but now scientifically accepted:

It is quite open to surmise some sort of analogy to the familiar phenomena of the transmission and reception of vibratory energy . . . One tuning-fork or string in unison with another will communicate its impulses through the medium of the air . . . A permanent magnet brought into a room will throw any surrounding iron into a condition similar to its own; and here the medium of communication is unknown though the fact is undisputed. Similarly, we may conceive . . . that for every thought there is a corresponding motion of the particles of the brain, and that this vibration of molecules of brain-stuff may be communicated to an intervening medium, and so pass under certain circumstances from one brain to another, with a corresponding simultaneity of impressions.[54]

This desire to link mind and brain in a psycho-physical materialist explanation of the transference of thought goes hand in hand with the recognition of transmission's expansion into realms in which proximity or touch are not necessary to its workings. At the end of the nineteenth century science is severing the links between materiality, visibility and transmission, allowing for a sort of telepathic imaginary. In his 1886 novel *Tomorrow's Eve*, Philippe Villiers de l'Isle Adam has a fictional Thomas Edison deploy telepathy as well as a plethora of new technologies in the invention of an android woman. The book's hero, Lord Ewald, cannot understand how his robotic lover can be telepathically controlled and 'electrified' from a distance. He says:

Just a minute . . . I'm sure it's already a remarkable thing that electric current can now transmit energy to great heights and over enormous, almost limitless distances . . . This trick is perfectly comprehensible, given the use of tangible conductors – magic highways – through which the powerful currents flow. But this INSUBSTANTIAL transmission of my living thought, how can I imagine it taking place, at a distance, *without conductors or wires, even the very thinnest* ?[55]

Ewald's doubts suggest that one limit of conceiving of transmission at that particular moment in the historical development of electrical technology was materiality itself. Wires, even wisp thin ones, are still a substantial link between one thing and another. When these wires are snapped and transmission still takes place, then, for Ewald, we have crossed a line which divides science from the occult. Without a visual or substantial guarantee of the materiality of information flow, without some sort of promise about the empirical connection between cause and effect, we come face to face with the unknown. Anything can happen. Bring out your dead, bring on the mind-readers.

Rudyard Kipling's 1902 tale 'Wireless' engages precisely this nexus of concerns about the line that divides science from the occult, but dispenses with Ewald's anxious tone. The story sets up an analogy between early wireless radio technology and spiritualist séances, and pictures both as untrustworthy methods of information transmission. 'Wireless' rests on a simple conceit. In the back room of a chemist's shop an electrician sets up a wireless Morse conductor in order to receive signals from a friend in Poole. While the electrician waits for his signals to come through, in the front of the shop a young chemist's assistant, Mr. Shaynor, falls into a drug-induced stupor and apparently begins channelling the spirit of John Keats by attempting to compose or transcribe 'The Eve of St. Agnes'. The narrator, who has come to witness the wireless communication, goes back and forth between the two scenes noting similarities between the two partially successful transmissions: the chemist gets a few verses almost right; the electrician fails to reach Poole but picks up the signals of two ships off the Isle of Wight which are unable to make contact with each other. The narrator surmises that the chemist's channelling of Keats, whom the chemist has not read, is due to a general resemblance in their situations. Like Keats, Shaynor is a tubercular chemist. He is also in love with Fanny Brand, a woman identified with modern commercial culture who, 'distantly re-sembled the seductive shape on a gold-framed toilet-water advertise-ment' – a mass-produced, brand-named Fanny Brawne.[56]

The narrator of 'Wireless' suggests that the electrician's inability to explain electricity – '"Ah, if you knew *that* you'd know something nobody knows. It's just It – . . ."' – allows it to function both as an analogy to and explanation for the chemist's mediumistic trance. Here electricity is a 'black box', a system in scientific discourse contained in such a way as to enable its utilization without under-standing its components.[57] As Eleanor Sidgwick also pointed out, electricity functions as an explanation for which no explanation is required. The narrator 'explains' to himself in terminology which could be a parody of a Society for Psychical Research explanation for séance phenomena: 'it's the . . . Hertzian wave of tuberculosis, *plus* Fanny Brand and the professional status which, in conjunction with the main-stream of subconscious thought common to all mankind, has thrown up temporarily an induced Keats'.[58] In 'Wireless' this heady combination of a shared store of thought and 'Hertzian waves' – a scientific-sounding phrase which purports to explain all sorts of transmission – makes for another example of the potential pleasures and dangers of severing wires, transgressing sense boundaries, and delivering unexpected messages through unintentional mediums.[59] Analogies between electricity and extrasensory forms of communication such as telepathy and contact with the dead function in this story and in the writings of the Society for Psychical Research as the non-causal, causal ground for a range of desires and fantasies about new ways of knowing, both others and information.

'Wireless' makes no judgements about the potential truth or falsity of unconscious channelling of the dead; it simply observes the similarities between various forms of channelling. If Kipling's story rests on a straightforward analogy between science and séance, it is worth remembering that his sister, Alice Fleming, was a medium, who spent some time being dictated to by the deceased F. W. H. Myers amongst others.[60] In the period in which Kipling was writing 'Wireless' it was not uncommon to have all sorts of media and mediums functioning in one house. Texts such as *Tomorrow's Eve* and 'Wireless' point towards the structural analogies and the black-boxing of explanation which make these narratives of occult/technological transmission so compelling for turn-of-the-century culture. In experimenting with thought transference and searching for the *modus transferendi* of telepathy the Society for Psychical Research explored new relationships between the material and the psychic and between proximity and distance. The ways these turn-of-the-century experiments with and theorizations of telepathy become intertwined with an erotics of knowledge can be traced, in part, through the shift in the Society's experimentation from sittings with physical mediums to thought transference and mental mediums.

The Society's members, in general, quickly lost faith in the so-called 'physical mediums', nearly all of whom were discovered in trickery at some point during their careers.[61] Physical mediums were often paid for their performances and engaged in theatrical displays, moving tables and furniture and conjuring spirits while supposedly securely locked in a cabinet.[62] The later mental mediums the Society turned towards tended to be from a different class background from their predecessors. Studies of their automatic writing fed into psychical researchers' psychological interests in the subconscious or subliminal consciousness. William James in his presidential address to the SPR in 1896 expressed his relief at being able to discard the dubious displays of the physical mediums: 'It is pleasant to turn from phenomena of the dark-sitting and rat-hole type (with their tragi-comic suggestion that the whole order of nature might possibly be overturned in one's own head, by the way in which one imagined oneself, on a certain occasion, to be holding a tricky peasant woman's feet) to the "calm air of delightful studies".'[63]

'Holding a tricky peasant woman's feet' combines the class and sexual politics of the physical séance in one concise image. The Society's early séance experiments involved upper class university-educated men locking themselves in rooms with working-class, sometimes foreign women, for hours on end.[64] In order to detect and prevent fraud, the mediums were often held on to during the sittings and searched thoroughly before and after. When physical mediums locked themselves in closets in order to provoke visible bodily spirit manifestations, they were kept under surveillance through a series of complicated tests.[65] As Alex Owen has described, the body of the medium became a site of intense interest to the scientific investigators, and the séance became a site for transgressive contact between men and women of different classes.[66] When spirits materialized they were touched, embraced, kissed, in the name of testing the limits of their materiality, and they in turn touched, embraced and kissed their investigators. James's desire to turn away from the dubious job of holding a tricky peasant woman's feet should be read in this light.

But what exactly was he turning towards? If the erotics of the physical séance were centred around the physical manifestations of bodies which needed to be touched to ensure their materiality, is there an erotics of telepathy? From the first the goal of the Society's thought-transference experiments was to get away from physical contact: 'The primary aim in all cases must be to get the results *without physical contact* or anything approaching it . . . in no other way can the hypothesis of "muscle-reading" be with certainty eliminated . . .'[67] If any of the potential consequences, scientific, religious, metaphysical, utopian, of telepathy were to be realized, it required that that wire, the physical connection, be severed. But in the popular imagination, this very severing became the source of new and intense imaginings of proximity. These are the erotics of mind melding.

In a letter to George Eliot in 1872 Myers wrote despondently:

Life has come to such a pass – now that there is no longer any God or hereafter or anything in particular to aim at – that it is only coming into contact with some other person that one can be oneself. There is no longer anything to keep a [sic] isolated fire burning within one. All one can do is to feel the sparks fly from one for a moment when one strikes a kindred soul. Such contact in real life can make one feel for the moment immortal, but the necessary circumstances are so unusual.[68]

Here Myers employs a metaphorics of physical contact, the striking of matches or flint to start a fire, to describe the contact of souls. Years later, after Edmund Gurney's death in 1888, Myers spoke of his grief in these terms: 'For fifteen years we had been as intimate and as attached to each other as men can be; – every part of our respective natures found response by comprehension in the other. But I will not say more of that.'[69] Myers's response to his close friend's death is cast in the language of sentiment, friendship, homosocial bonding, but it is also in the language of telepathy as the desire for absolute knowledge and melding with another, inevitable perhaps between two friends who spent much of their time experimenting with thought transference. The type of rhetoric Myers uses to describe his relationship to Gurney moves us towards an explicitly erotic aspect of telepathy. The dematerialization, the lack of physical contact, required for scientific proof of telepathy in the Society seems to make it safe from a distracting erotics, untainted by desire. Minds should meet but not bodies, much to the relief of William James and the other scientists of the Society. But the types of investments in telepathy inside and outside the Society would indicate that the potential nature of the intimacy circumscribed by thought transference is not containable in these terms.

Two 1890s novels suggest how telepathy can signify dangerous proximity in this period. When one thinks of the perils of intimacy in Bram Stoker's *Dracula*, telepathy might not immediately spring to mind. Neither might the phonograph, for that matter, but both telepathy and phonographs threaten to invade and discover the secrets of the insides of minds in the novel, just as vampires threaten to suck dry the insides of bodies. When it becomes necessary for the vampire hunters to collect and process the information about Dracula's whereabouts that is contained in the various journals they all separately have been keeping, Mina Harker, who is trained in shorthand, agrees to listen to and transcribe the journal that Dr Seward had been recording on phonograph. Unfortunately, the phonographic recording contains, amongst other things, the record of his unrequited love for Lucy Westenra. Mina says to Seward:

'That is a wonderful machine, but it is cruelly true. It told me, in its very tones, the anguish of your heart . . . I have copied out the words on my typewriter, and none other need now hear your heart beat as I did.'[70] Hearing someone's heart beat is, of course, a figurative expression for intimacy. But the phonograph, as a re-cording instrument, at least suggests the possibility of taking this literally, while simultaneously being entirely removed in space and time from the person to whom that heart belongs. Similarly, Mina, when under bodily attack from Dracula, becomes the victim of a telepathic or hypnotic attack on her mind. Dracula can gain access to her mind for information about the movements of the men who are pursuing him, because the sexualized, bodily-enervating vam-piric attack also creates a telepathic corollary. The mind is open to invasion, and bodily intimacy becomes impossible to extricate from 'tele' intimacy: the all knowing intimacy created by a machine like the telephone, the distant but penetrating access to another.

A final example of the dangers of the telepathic imagination comes from the anonymous pornographic novel *Teleny*, written by several people one of whom was probably Oscar Wilde. It was first published in a limited edition in 1893. The story of a tortured love affair between the pianist Teleny and the narrator Des Grieux, *Teleny* begins with a series of shared hallucinations between the two at a concert Teleny plays in: 'Do you believe in the transmission of thought, of feelings, of sensations?' Teleny asks Des Grieux when they first meet.[71] Teleny's very name conjures up tele-communi-cation as well as his telepathic connection to Des Grieux. The love between Teleny and Des Grieux is described in terms of electrical currents and shocks (p. 40). When Teleny spends a night with a woman, Des Grieux experiences the encounter simultaneously, as if he were there, explaining to his interlocutor '"There was, as I told you before, a strong transmission of thoughts between us. This is by no means a remarkable coincidence. You smile and look incredulous: well follow the doings of the Psychical Society, and this vision will certainly not astonish you any more"' (p. 79).[72]

In *Teleny* telepathy is radicalized towards narcissistic collapse, an economy of the same. When the Countess who spent the night with Teleny gives birth to a son nine months later he looks like Des Grieux. But then Des Grieux looks like Teleny, so who is to say who is the father, or who is who? In *Teleny* telepathy seems to function as trope and ground for a phantasmatic homosexual male sexuality based on narcissism and non-differentiation.[73] A few years later in his article 'On Narcissism', Freud will reductively diagnose homosexuality as a disease of arrested auto-eroticism. Homosexuals, Freud asserts, are 'plainly seeking *themselves* as a love-object'.[74] At times *Teleny* reads like a textbook enactment of Freud's theories, for example when Des Grieux describes his embrace of Teleny: 'As my hands wandered over his head, his neck, his shoulders, his arms, I could not feel him at all; in fact, it seemed to me as if I were touching my own body' (p. 110). Telepathy, seemingly the most disembodied method of contact, can lead, as it does in *Teleny* to an almost unbearably collapsed physicality.

As I hope I have amply indicated, desires for telepathic communication at the turn of the century were by no means necessarily sexual, nor were they inevitably solipsistic; the ultimate goal of telepathy was not necessarily speaking only to oneself. On the contrary, as a fantasy position, telepathy suggested a whole range of possibilities, from Mark Twain's cost-efficient replacement for the telegraph to William Barrett's dream of talking to the animals in a telepathic world of shared sensation and wealth. In the Society for Psychical Research in general, however, and certainly for someone such as Myers, telepathy seemed to fulfill two apparently contradictory functions. On the one hand, the Society's experiments in thought transference were a turn away from the dubious class and sexual connotations of séances with physical mediums towards scientifically reliable, dematerialized experiments within the confines of laboratory conditions. Crudely put, emphasizing thought transference rather than séances allowed the Society to move from touching (primarily) women to not touching (primarily) men.[75]

On the other hand, the Society's members who pinned their hopes for transcendent meaning on the SPR's findings were heavily affectively invested in thought transference experiments. Myers's desire to feel the sparks fly from his soul to another's is a fantasy which is imaginatively entwined with the image of a scientific laboratory filled with people not touching each other as they read each others' minds. One fantasy grounds itself in the other, and the hopes for what telepathy might mean both for other-worldly transcendence and for this world's intimate relations are bound up in that moment of scientific proof the Society felt was always so near and which always just eluded it.

Poststructuralist theory in the tradition of Derrida informs us that self-presence is the western metaphysical fantasy par excellence. What we want and what we can never have is plenitude and non-differentiation, a version of love that would be beyond language or make it unnecessary. Telepathy at the turn of the century can be read in the light of this overarching schema, but also more specifically in terms of the available cultural material around which these fantasies structure themselves. The ways in which new technologies of communication are severing the wire of visible, materialized transmission in the last decades of the nineteenth century help create a new metaphorics for imagining intimate relations with others. How a piece of information ('I'm thinking of a number from one to ten') gets from one place to another, and what that means in terms of the relationship between the bodies and minds that pass that information along is not as simple a problem as it may first appear. For psychical researchers, as for other commentators at the time, telepathy both promised and threatened that the mind was not necessarily a sealed and protected space. Critical interpretation of telepathy suggests that the mind's potential porousness was made to serve the purposes of the most erotically charged, as well as the most scientifically removed purposes, in a telepathic dialectic of touch and distance.

CHAPTER 2

Wilde, hypnotic aesthetes and the 1890s

The psychical researchers who were stretching the boundaries of the mind through their investigations of telepathy were also intrigued by another phenomenon that indicated the porousness of the mental apparatus: hypnosis. At the *fin de siècle*, hopeful cultural fantasies of the possibilities of telepathic contact were balanced by an anxious sense that someone or something might get inside one's mind and control one's actions. Although hypnosis has a long history, the *fin de siècle* is a peculiarly suggestible time, brimming with anxieties about the complete extinction of will brought about by the stage mesmerist, the medical practitioner, and the Society for Psychical Research experiment.[1] Psychical researchers such as Edmund Gurney and F. W. H. Myers studied hypnosis for what the phenomenon could tell them about the vicissitudes of conscious and subconscious thought, but hypnosis also had an audience outside the medical and scientific arenas. By the 1890s the hypnotically threatening figure was a staple of popular literature; Rider Haggard's *She* (1888), Stoker's *Dracula* (1897) and Richard Marsh's *The Beetle* (1897) take over the minds as well as the bodies of their entranced victims. George Du Maurier's 1894 novel *Trilby*, the sensational story of a Bohemian artist's model who becomes an operatic star and sexual slave through the mesmerizing influence of the demonic Jewish musician Svengali, was one of the most popular novels of the decade in Britain and America.[2] Hypnosis, appropriately enough, com-pelled attention – in scientific and press contexts, but also in the rapidly expanding book market. As the runaway success of *Trilby* shows, hypnosis sold.

What made someone seem 'hypnotic' in the 1890s, in both the technical and popular usages of the word? After first meeting Oscar Wilde, Max Beerbohm made a note in his diary of his impressions of him: 'Effeminate but vitality of twenty men, magnetism – authority.

37

Deeper than repute or wit, Hypnotic.'[3] In Beerbohm's paradoxical description Wilde eludes easy categorization. Effeminate but with superhuman strength and vitality, an authoritative manner and a hypnotic effect on those he meets; is he aggressive or passive, masculine or feminine? Wilde's peculiarly 'magnetic' combination of attractions makes him resemble one version of the late nineteenth-century hypnotizing villain – the sophisticated, ambiguously sexual aesthete – an amoral artist figure who values art over life, and who sometimes, quite literally, sucks the life out of his victims.[4]

The spectre of Wilde's corrupting 'influence' on young men hovered over his criminal trials in 1895; the word 'influence' was invoked repeatedly by the prosecution. Recent critics have read the word as it appears in both the transcripts of the trials and in Wilde's own work, as a coded expression for the rapidly opening secret of homosexuality. Influence clearly is used in this way, as my reading of *The Picture of Dorian Gray* (1891) will indicate. However, homosexual sexual contact by no means exhausts the meaning of the term. The spells the mesmerizing aesthete was imagined to produce were both stranger, and queerer, than a reduction of influential attachments to a cover for homosexuality will allow. Influence, as linked with the hypnotic/vampiric powers of the fictional villains I describe, comes to stand for a nexus of 1890s fears about the porous constitution of the self and its desires. Hypnotic sway, the non-benign, terrorizing form of magically thinking one's way into the interior of another, is not simply a cover for sexuality, although it is also that. Rather, at the end of the nineteenth century, what we now think of as the realm of the sexual is being constructed amidst wide-ranging doubts about the efficacy of individual agency in relation to the invasive potential of art, literature, fashion, new technologies, mass media, political movements, and advertising.

In this chapter I examine the anxieties around, and the potential hypnotic attractions to, the *fin-de-siècle* influential villain. I argue that the rhetoric surrounding Oscar Wilde's arrest and imprisonment only marks the culminating point of a series of popular portrayals of the aesthete as a dangerous influential monster. Yet the initial motivations behind this particular portrayal of the aesthete are not immediately apparent. Why should an admiration for the writings of Ruskin and Pater, a championing of art for its own sake, a preference for certain kinds of porcelain, or an ability to sparkle at society parties come to appear as such a threat to the *fin-de-siècle* culture which wound up rejecting Wilde with such vehemence?[5] One answer to this question is that before Wilde's trials, many of these aesthetic markers may have been labelled effeminate but did not thereby imply a particular sexual object choice. After Wilde's trials, however, these characteristics came to signify homosexuality to a homophobic, and homosexually panicked culture.[6] The real threat of the aesthete lay in his sexual practices, not his porcelain collection. Anything that seemed troubling or transgressive about Wilde's image, from the popularity of his plays to the ubiquity of his appearance in the newspapers, was suddenly attributed to his aberrant sexuality; and his 'aesthetic' characteristics were permanently marked by the scandal of his sexuality. In this version of the Wilde story, Wilde was made into a dangerous influence retrospectively, his coded attributes, such as his famous green carnation, finally able to be understood for what they had always really meant: male–male love. But as we shall see, this explanation is not completely satisfying. Too many questions about the effects of influence are raised in Wilde's own pre-trial oeuvre. *The Picture of Dorian Gray,* especially centres around questions of influence over others' personalities: Lord Henry's influence on Dorian; Dorian's compelling influence over the painter Basil Hallward; the painting's influence on Dorian's life; the influence of certain books such as J.-K. Huysmans's *À Rebours* (1884) and Walter Pater's *The Renaissance* (1873). Similarly, the other 1890s novels I discuss in this chapter also raise questions about influence through their portrayal of powerfully hypnotic figures who exemplify some of the attributes of the aesthete. All of these books are written before Wilde's trials, although clearly after Wilde's presence in the press was felt. The image of the aesthete as vampiric – sucking the life out of his hapless victims and holding dangerous sway over others – pre-exists the marking moment of Wilde's trials.

The question then becomes, what is it at this time that makes the aesthete appear threatening to the boundaries of others through this peculiarly *fin-de-siècle* form of psychic vampirism? In this chapter I examine Wilde's trials and *Dorian Gray* along with two other 1890s portrayals of suggestibility run amok – *Trilby* (1894) and J. MacLaren Cobban's *Master of his Fate* (1890) (with its Salpêtrière-trained, hypnotizing, aesthete villain) – to argue that the life-sucking, vampiric aesthete encapsulated a constellation of fears and desires in the 1890s about the potentially hypnotic effects of newly visible sexual acts and identities because these newly visible acts and identities asserted themselves in relation to versions of the body, mind and soul as potentially alienable and marketable, capable of being bought, sold or stolen. The paradigm shift around male homosexuality, that Foucault and others have located in the late nineteenth century, intersects significantly with popular and scientific debates about suggestibility. The figure of the aesthete comes to embody fears about the suggestive potential of gay male sexuality, but he also raises the issue of the seductive potential of consumption, and the uncertain status of the potentially seducing, as well as the potentially enthralled mass public. Thus I argue that the hypnotic aesthete threatens an eroticized, potentially soul-sucking manipulation of his audience through style as well as sex, and through market choices, as well as hypnotic imposition.

But what precisely was hypnotic imposition? The word hypnotism originally appeared as an attempted redefinition of an earlier trance phenomenon associated with the eighteenth-century physician, Franz Anton Mesmer's magnetic salons. Mesmer's practice of 'animal magnetism' involved placing patients into a trance by making hand motions called 'passes' over their faces and bodies, sometimes to astonishing physical and mental effects. Mesmer claimed that his work was an application of Newtonian philosophy, using the body's own magnetic forces. Critics who denied that any physical agency was involved renamed the practice 'mesmerism', calling attention to the central (and, as it was often perceived, dangerously intimate) relation between the instigator of the trance and the entranced subject. As Alison Winter asserts mesmerism and animal magnetism, 'came to refer to a wide range of different techniques, each claiming to give one person the power to affect another's mind or body'.[7]

The term 'hypnotism' was coined by the surgeon James Braid in the 1840s in his attempt to clear out Mesmer's physiological, magnetic claims and make the practice of inducing trance a wholly psychological one, thereby more acceptable in medical circles. By defining hypnotism in opposition to mesmerism, Braid attempted to replace mesmerism's eroticized power dynamics with an element of individual choice – a trance state could not be forced on someone; they had to be willing. Furthermore, according to Braid, everything that happened in the hypnotic state was a product of the individual's own mind, not of a paranormal clairvoyant ability, as some supporters of mesmerism claimed. Those who championed hypnotism attempted to discard explanations which relied on magical bonds to others, instead concentrating on the workings of the inner mind, what post-Freud we would call the unconscious: 'Braid's "hypnotism" made three important changes to mesmerism. He removed from mesmerism its magnetic fluids, the sexual associations that attended the "passes", and the personal relationship between mesmerist and subject explicit in the claim that one person's body, mind or will impinged on another's.'[8] Braid's attempts at distinguishing hypnotism from mesmerism were successful enough that today the term hypnotism is more common than mesmerism for discussing trance phenomenon. However both terms are still with us, signifying, amongst other meanings, an inexplicable bond between people, what Freud in 'Group psychology and the analysis of the ego' suggestively termed 'Being in love and hypnosis'.[9] The differing meanings of hypnotism, mesmerism, and the more general 'influence' revolve around the question of what impulses come from the self's desires, what come from an influential other, and what come from elsewhere – that elusive space called variously (and vaguely) culture, the zeitgeist or the social. The specific story that I tell here, about several novels with powerfully influential characters, happens in reaction to the spread and diffusion of ideas about influence, into ways of conceiving of one's relationship to politics, literature, sexuality, culture. When the specific sources of bad influence can no longer be clearly isolated and exorcised, powerfully suggestive characters begin to appear at an increased rate in the cultural imagination, in fiction and in court-rooms; influence itself begins to seem criminal; new crimes of influence are demarcated.

These criminal connections come to the forefront in 1880s France. Hypnosis entered French newspaper headlines during the 1880s through a debate about the mysterious sources of the hypnotic trance, and what it might indicate about the human will. Medical interest in hypnotism divided into two camps, that of Charcot's Salpêtrière and Ambroise Liébault and Hippolyte Bernheim's Nancy School. The Salpêtrière position maintained that only the already hysterical (primarily female patients) were hypnotizable, and that hypnosis was a phenomenon of illness. The Nancy School challenged the notion that hypnosis was rare or pathological, claiming that everyone was hypnotizable under the right conditions, and that suggestibility was a universal human condition.[10] Jules

Liégois, a supporter of the Nancy position and a lawyer, instigated what was to become a forensic debate, enacted in the court-rooms of Paris when he suggested that people could be coerced into crimes through suggestion. Suggestion, the generalized, universal and particularly anxiety-provoking version of hypnosis, became the operative term for the Nancy school.[11]

Popular interest in hypnosis often centred around its relation to criminal activities – the complicated questions of legal and moral responsibility which emerged from a hypnotized mind and a subject literally not present to his or her self.[12] The arguments which arose from the Nancy–Salpêtrière debate stemmed from two divergent conceptions of the human will, as infinitely pliable or stably set. Questions about the nature of human agency also appeared in writings about crowds, multiple personalities and trance mediums. Was excessive suggestibility a staple of human existence or a pathological state? Did people in crowds act as if they were hypnotized? Was the 'herd mentality' which appeared to develop in rioting mobs caused by a kind of mass hypnotic effect?

In *Mesmerized: Powers of Mind in Victorian Britain*, Alison Winter traces the emergence and decline of mesmerism during the nineteenth century. She suggests that as the popularity of mesmerism retreated towards the end of the century, a new and more widespread sense of human suggestibility entered discussions of political consensus and mass movements.[13] The end of the century sees these diffuse questions about suggestibility and the formation of public opinion intersecting with specific monsters of influence; the idea that people in general are dangerously suggestible crosses with elaborate imaginings of powerful personified influences who want to do the suggesting. In many popular novels hypnosis was used by manipulative villains literally to steal the souls of their victims. Yet fears about a general suggestibility, inspired in part by a new sense of destabilizing forces at work in mass culture, modernity and sexuality, were only loosely contained by the image of the mesmerizing bad man (or, less often, woman). What interests me is the residue that escapes that containment; the suggestions which cannot be securely identified as the desires of a single demonized other, but which are neither easily translated in post-Freudian terms into the unconscious or repressed desires of the self.

France was a particular locus for anxieties about hypnosis and agency in relation to criminal acts, but 1890s Britain also found itself fascinated by a court-room scene that raised the spectre of corrupting influence – Oscar Wilde's 1895 trials for gross indecency. During the trials Wilde's writings, such as *Dorian Gray*, and his homosexuality were portrayed as substitutable for one another; both were dangerously seductive and contaminating. The prosecution and the press made Wilde out to be a monster of influence for the consumption of a public, who, a year earlier, had been thrilled by the similarly powerful effects of Du Maurier's Svengali.

The spectacle of Wilde's trials centrally staged many *fin-de-siècle* anxieties of influence. These anxieties about the potentially porous constitution of the self were not limited to the dangerous realm of sexual influence; in Wilde's trials literary influence was also seen as pernicious and corrupting. At this time, the hypnotic/vampiric aesthete is imagined as consuming other people, or life in the abstract; these acts of consumption are often pictured as extensions of the aesthete's pleasure in, and manipulation of, art. In the novels I examine here the villain figures consume others, sometimes literally, but they also come to embody methods of controlling and determining different kinds of consumption.

Many 1890s hypnotic novels aestheticize and commodify life itself, picturing it as a material and economic reality, a product you can own, lose or steal. This move is central to the storyline of a book published the same year that Wilde's *The Picture of Dorian Gray* first appeared in Lippincott's Magazine. Like *Dorian Gray*, J. MacLaren Cobban's *Master of his Fate* (1890) revolves around an economic exchange of age for eternal youth. A mysterious wave of hypnotized victims begin appearing in hospitals in London and Paris. The patients have no idea what has happened to them but appear to have literally had the life sucked out of them. In the beginning of the novel the newspaper reports of these cases are being discussed by the members of the suggestively named Hyacinth Club. The two main participants in the debate are the book's hero, Dr Lefevre and Julius Courtney, close friends, both of whom have been trained in the art of hypnosis at the Salpêtrière by a barely disguised Charcot (called 'Charbon'). Lefevre, who has invented a new science called 'psychodynamics', soon finds himself obliged to save the life of several hypnotized victims who have been brought near death by a removal of their life forces. Lefevre restores them via electrical charges. It soon becomes clear, to the reading audience although not initially to Lefevre, that his friend Courtney is the villain who has kept himself permanently youthful by hypnotically draining the life from his various victims.

Julius Courtney is an extremely appealing and attractive figure to everyone in the book, especially the admiring denizens of the Hyacinth Club: ' . . . though he had done nothing, it was commonly believed he could do anything he chose'.[14] Where Courtney has picked up his conversational style is nearly as obvious as where he's received his medical knowledge. Courtney speaks in sub-Wildean paradoxes dropping sentences such as: '" . . . it goes without saying that Art can never compete with Nature in creating human pleasure . . . I can't endure Art except in winter, when everything (almost) must be artificial to be endurable" (p. 8); "To live," said Julius, "is surely the purpose of life. Any smaller, any more obvious purpose, will spoil life, just as it spoils Art"' (p. 24). Courtney's desire for eternal youth mirrors Dorian Gray's, and both Courtney and Dorian voice the desire to experience the immediate sensations of life to their fullest, apart from ethical or teleological concerns. In his short story, 'The Portrait of Mr W. H.', Wilde defines art as ideally, 'a mode of acting, an attempt to realize one's own personality on some imaginative plane out of the reach of the trammeling accidents and limitations of real life'.[15] 'Real life' is a hindrance, but also a desperate necessity to Julius Courtney who suffers from a morbid fear of sickness and death, and an overwhelming desire to maintain his eternal youth, whatever this may entail. He is horrified when he sees Lefevre ill. Julius spouts the discourse of degeneration and eugenics in diatribes about the advantages of weeding out the sick and infirm: 'medical philanthropy, like all other philanthropy, is so overdone that the race is fast deteriorating; we strive with so much success to keep the sickly and diseased alive, that perfect health is scarcely known' (p. 27).[16] In *Master of his Fate*, as well as in *Trilby* and *Dorian Gray*, the aesthete is imagined as a vampiric villain who sucks the life out of others, treating them as objects, or storehouses of energy, from which to extract his own (artistic or material) life's blood.

Master of his Fate runs into narrative trouble trying securely to distinguish its hero from its villain; the hypnotizing doctor looks suspiciously like the vampiric mesmerizer. The good English doctor has a French surname; the sinister foreign villain has a name which sounds as English as can be. Both wield magnetic powers; both play with electricity in the service of giving and taking away life. The two men are involved in a mirroring relationship and an economic tug-of-war; Courtney sucks life from his victims and Lefevre restores it to them. Lefevre's 'psychodynamics' hinges on the fact that energy and electricity are interchangeable terms; his miraculous electrode machine 'worked on the theory that the electricity stored in the human body can be driven out by the human will along a prepared channel into another human body' (pp. 55–56).

Like *Dorian Gray* and *Master of his Fate*, Henry James's 1899 novel *The Sacred Fount* is also an economic parable. James's novel consists, in its entirety, of the narrator's speculations about various sexual liaisons at a country house party; he surmises that he can guess who is sleeping with whom according to their relative states of enervation or rejuvenation. In the world of *The Sacred Fount* there is only so much life or youthful energy to circulate. If someone is gaining it, then someone or something is losing it rapidly.

At the end of *The Sacred Fount* although the possibility of a material exchange of sexual energies still hovers out there in the world, the economic threat turns out to be most probably a delusion of the voyeuristic narrator. Some have read the novel as an allegory of James's own aesthetic practice – the speculative imagination functions to suck the life out of those whom it studies. In these earlier 1890s economic parables, *Dorian Gray* and *Master of his Fate*, the decadent artist figure actually does enervate his surroundings. What the narrator of *The Sacred Fount* does metaphorically the aesthete hypnotizer does literally; he sucks energy from life and deposits it elsewhere, in himself, or in his art.

For Julius Courtney, as for the Wilde of so many of his writings, life is the most challenging artwork imaginable. Life as art, as embodied in the dream of an eternal and incandescently beautiful youth, emerges as a fantasy within aestheticism that is potentially attractive to a nascent gay political/cultural agenda because it de-emphasizes the reproductive demand to replicate the bourgeois family. Living through the artistic imagination, or for the sensory experiences of the moment, circumvents a societal insistence upon generational reproduction.[17] As Julius Courtney puts it:

What does a man want with a family and a name? They only tie him to the earth as Gulliver was tied by the people of Lilliput. We have life and health, – if we have them, – and it is only veiled prurience to inquire whence we got them. A man can't help having a father and a mother, I suppose; but he need not be always reminding himself of the fact: no other creature on earth does. (pp. 42–43)

During the 1880s and 1890s supernatural fiction, as well as aesthetic writings, suggest that reproduction may be seductive in new and 'unnatural' forms – the vampirism of *Dracula* and its carbon paper; the mesmeric birth of the opera star in *Trilby*; the aesthetic seductions and mimetic reproductions of *Dorian Gray*. Reproduction comes to seem both queer and occult in these texts, even when that reproduction retreats finally to its oldest and most established artistic or procreative forms.[18]

Queer dynamics of influence become central to *Master of his Fate* through its hypnotic/economic system. One of Courtney's initial victims is a young soldier on a train, coming, perhaps not coincidentally, from Brighton. Courtney, in his enervated aging state, asks to share the young soldier's compartment: 'In a quarter of an hour the young man felt as if he had known and trusted and loved his neighbour all his life; he felt, he confessed, so strongly attracted that he could have hugged him' (p. 65). As the two converse, the soldier:

felt more and more enthralled and fascinated by the stranger's eyes, which as he talked, lightened and glowed more and more as their glance played caressingly about him. He was beginning to wonder at that, when with some emphatic phrase the stranger laid his fingers on his knee, upon which a thrill shot through him as if a woman had touched him. He looked in the stranger's face, and the wonderful eyes seemed to touch the root of his being, and to draw the soul out of him. He had a flying thought – 'Can it be a woman, after all, in this strange shape?' and he knew no more . . . till he woke up in the hospital bed. (p. 66)

The blatant homoerotics of a passage such as this does not require much critical exegesis. However, the newspaper response that the novel imagines to Courtney's hypnotic crimes is still more interesting than the scene of the crime itself. The exact nature of Courtney's attack is, it seems, unrelatable. *The Daily Telegraph* appeals to the police 'to find the man "who has alarmed the civilised world by a new form of outrage."' But the reading public seems unclear about precisely what this outrage consists of: 'What could the "singular railway outrage" mean? – Some – probably most – declared it was very plain what it meant; while others, – the few, – after much argument, confessed themselves quite mystified' (p. 69). The unspoken, unspeakable, plain and obscure meaning of the hypnotic crime prefigures Wilde's trials even as it takes its place next to the similarly elusive crimes of Dorian Gray.

Lefevre is particularly fascinated by this problem of how to classify the crime, reverting to it again and again. When the young and beautiful Lady Mary Fane is hypnotically vamped in a style similar to the Brighton train victim, her powerful father Lord Rivercourt insists that justice be done. A police detective promises that the Metropolitan's finest will find the villain, but Doctor Lefevre points out a difficulty:

'It rather puzzles me,' said the Doctor, 'what crime you will charge him with.'

'It is an outrage,' said Lord Rivercourt; 'and if it is not criminal, it seems about time it were made so.'

'Oh, we'll class it, my lord,' said the detective; 'never fear.' (p. 132)

Later, when Julius himself asks Lefevre what exactly this outrage is, the doctor replies: 'I don't know what the outrage can be called, but I am sure Lord Rivercourt – and he is a man of immense influence – will move heaven and earth to give it a legal name and to get it punishment' (pp. 156–157). It is difficult to read passages like this without Foucault, Wilde and the Labouchère amendment of 1885 which criminalized male homosexual acts in Britain, ringing in one's ears. (The Labouchère amendment actually labels the crimes it describes 'outrages on public decency'.[19]) The way in which *Master of his Fate* describes the law and the aristocracy as wielding 'immense influence' mirrors the influence of the hypnotizing Julius, and returns us once again to the ambiguous status of influence. Through reading novels such as *Master of his Fate* along with the transcripts of Wilde's trials it becomes clear that 'influence' at the turn of the century is a capacious word, capable of referring to seductive hypnotizers, decadent reading material, gay sex or the structures of the juridico-legal system. The power to classify, to name that particular outrage as criminal, is part of the project of pinning influence down, pointing a finger at a single source for the crime.

Chapter Four of *Master of his Fate* has a title identical to that of Edgar Allan Poe's 1840 tale, 'The Man of the Crowd'.[20] Poe's story details a night and a day in the life of a younger man following an old man who has strangely arrested him in his own voyeuristic watching of night-time city life. After following the old man through a surreal night of wandering, at the end of the story the narrator diagnoses the man of the crowd with a satisfying pathologizing flourish – '"This old man," I said at length, "is the type and the genius of deep crime. He refuses to be alone. *He is the man of the crowd*"' (p. 162, italics in original). This diagnosis cannot simply be taken at face value, for what does it then imply about the man who spends all night not allowing the man of the crowd to escape from his sight? Who is it who seems pathologically incapable of being alone, and what does it mean to be unable to be alone? (The epigraph to the story is *Ce grand malheur, de ne pouvoir être seul* – La Bruyère.) Poe's story fits into Eve Sedgwick's psycho-gothic, homo-social, paranoid genre in which the chaser and the chasee trade places and become indistinguishable during the course of the narrative. William Godwin's *Caleb Williams*, Mary Shelley's *Franken-stein*, James Hogg's *Confessions of a Justified Sinner* and Poe's own 'William Wilson' amongst others are part of this genre.[21] 'The Man of the Crowd', however, introduces the element of the crowd – the possibility that an explanation which relies on a doubling of the individual cannot fully explain the diffuser cultural dynamics of suggestion or contagion – a spreading of influence which instead of reinforcing the individual makes him or her seem obsolete and unnecessary. In Poe's tale the individual appears to be simply a frail vessel, a crowd container, even though what the crowd itself actually *is*, or signifies, remains obscure.

Cobban's book borrows explicitly from Poe's story but changes its direction. 'The Man of the Crowd' chapter of Cobban's book takes place one night after Lefevre has had a hard day at the hospital saving the life of the Brighton soldier. Lefevre finds himself, much like the narrator of Poe's story, impelled to go on a night-time sojourn in the city. The attraction of the crowded city street becomes for Lefevre the pull of the past and sends him into a reverie clearly influenced by Stevenson's *Dr Jekyll and Mr Hyde*, as well as Poe's tale:

> Insensibly his attention forsook the busy and anxious present, and slipped back to the days of golden and romantic youth, when the crowded nocturnal streets were full of the mystery of life. He recalled the sensations of those days – the sharp doubts of self, the frequent strong desires to drink deep of that life had to offer, and the painful recoils from temptation, which he felt would ruin, if yielded to, his hope of himself, and his ambition of filling a worthy place among men. (p. 104)

The lure of the crowd is the lure of unnameable sin, perhaps because in the crowd one can lose one's name, become no longer responsible for one's own actions. When Lefevre drifts through the crowd and discovers the unspeakably horrifying face of the old man he feels compelled to follow, the novel seems to relegate a more threatening generalized danger the crowd offers, the fear of 'losing oneself' (Lefevre's experience of 'sharp doubts of self, . . . frequent strong desires to drink deep of that life had to offer'), to a particular individual's dangerous influence. When Lefevre remembers his youth with its *Dorian Gray*-like desires to drink deep of life, he of course resembles the vampiric hypnotizer he finds himself following. But the juxtaposition of the Poe and Cobban versions of 'The Man of the Crowd' makes Poe's analysis of the problem of the crowd seem more radical, more uncertain than Cobban's rewriting. The anxiety in the Poe story envelops the reader – by the end if the reader recognizes that the narrator is himself the man of the crowd, she must also recognize that, by attempting to distance herself from the spectacle of the crowd by observing, or reading the story, she similarly becomes identified with the man of the crowd. The Cobban chapter simplifies this complicated dynamic, making it comfortingly vampiric. Dr Lefevre can find the real and singular villain out there in the world – Courtney is the source of the dangerous influence, the aestheticizing and objectifying threat. Lefevre can thus turn his own inner turmoil – the shady past that is brought out in the moment of entering the crowded city street and becoming a flaneur – outwards, and project it safely onto his hypnotizing aesthete alter ego. This dynamic of projection takes the fears and anxieties brought out by a constellation of potentially transgressive choices and desires available to the late-nineteenth-century urban reader/consumer, and locates them safely in the person of an abjected villain, who functions as a magnet for the diffuser consuming desires that permeate the book.

Early in *Master of his Fate*, Julius Courtney voices anti-aesthete opinions, celebrating the superiority of life over art. He associates the onset of aesthetic desire with a waning of energy, the decline of old age: 'A winter may come in one's life – I wonder if it will? – when one would rather look at the picture of a woman than at the woman herself. Meantime I no more need pictures than I need fires; I warm both hands and heart at the fire of life' (p. 8). When the fire of life diminishes, in *Dorian Gray*, *Trilby* and *Master of his Fate*, the wily and influential aesthete villain turns the humans that surround him into fodder for his own artistic and sensory life. This allegory of aesthetic power in the 1890s often relies on the mechanism of hypnotic influence. By the time of Wilde's trials the hypnotizing aesthete with ambiguous sexual and vampiric desires exists in multiple popular representations. Wilde's trials may be the most potent but are certainly not the first cultural representations to link the hypnotically powerful aesthete to homosexuality; *Master of his Fate* covered the same ground five years earlier. Influence is by no means a new form of outrage in the 1890s, when the denizens of Cobban's book are wondering how to classify it and criminalize it. But with the arrival of *Trilby* and George Du Maurier's diabolical Svengali, influence reaches new heights of popularity.

In 1894, a few years after the publication of *Dorian Gray*, and the year before Wilde's trials, George Du Maurier's *Trilby* worked its own hypnotic effects on the mass market. *Trilby* is the story of three Bohemian artists in Paris, and the beautiful artists' model who befriends them, Trilby O'Ferrall. The novel is primarily remembered for the creation of the brilliant, evil, foul-smelling, terribly-accented, Jewish musician Svengali who mesmerizes Trilby into becoming the greatest singer of her age.[22] The novel is simultaneously a celebration of the Bohemian life for men, and a damnation of its dangers for the single vulnerable woman. Trilby has 'all the virtues but one' – but as it happens, it is the only virtue that matters. She is a fallen woman – a perennially popular topic that was sympathetically revisited in the 1890s by Hardy's *Tess of the D'Urbervilles*, Wilde's hit play, *Lady Windermere's Fan*, and New Women novelists. After the British painter Little Billee falls in love with Trilby, he looks deep into her eyes and reads a layered story:

And in one of his quick flashes of intuitive insight he divined far down beneath the shining surface of those eyes (which seemed for a moment to reflect only a little image of himself against the sky beyond the big north window) a well of sweetness; and floating somewhere in the midst of it the very heart of compassion, generosity, and warm sisterly love; and under that – alas! at the bottom of all – a thin slimy layer of sorrow and shame.[23]

When Little Billee looks into Trilby's eyes, he initially sees a comforting reflection of himself – the narcissistic desire of most men who look into the eyes of their nineteenth-century beloveds. The woman should not have any sort of history – she should not reflect back anyone or anything else that has ever happened to her (since if anything has happened to her it inevitably means that something sexual has happened to her). But Trilby's palimpsestic history reveals that she has a past, a thin slimy layer of sexual knowledge beneath her apparent wholesomeness and bodily cleanliness, which Du Maurier is careful to stress. Trilby seems vulnerable to the hypnotic effects of Svengali partly because she is a barrier that has already been broken.

In a fascinating article on *Trilby* Jonathan Grossman points to the ways in which *Trilby*'s Bohemian community is part of culture's emerging concept of homosexuality which is about to be outed with Wilde.[24] *Trilby*'s Bohemian artists' colony is a place where men can be with men, where the nuclear family and the heterosexual couple are not the only models of life available. Eve Sedgwick defines Bohemia as: 'the temporal space where the young, male bourgeois literary subject was required to navigate his way through his "homosexual panic" – seen here as a *developmental* stage – toward the more repressive, self-ignorant, and apparently consolidated status of the mature bourgeois paterfamilias.'[25] In the world of *Trilby* British men can enter European Bohemia for a few years, frolic with other men, and create art which will later fetch enormous market prices (perhaps because this art is actually the fetishized and saleable sign of a desired youth), yet still return safely to the heterosexual bourgeois world of England, get married, settle down. However, the plotlines for women, *Trilby* suggests, are not so easily resolvable. There is no adolescent space for women to indulge in Bohemia safely and enjoy its privileges. There is no return to the haven of the bourgeois family for the artist's model who allows her body to be consumed for profit, and who becomes the hypnotic victim of both Svengali and the demands of the market.

Trilby's large size and her powerful singing lungs, when contrasted with the tendency towards fainting and debilitating illness of the small, infantilized and effeminate Little Billee, puts into play a fear of overwhelming femininity that is dealt with in the novel by literally pulling Trilby apart – her feet are anatomized in the pictures; her voice is literally stolen by the evil hypnotizing Svengali who also gets a sexual thrill out of imagining Trilby's dead and dissected body.[26] For him, and perhaps for the book as well, the ideal Trilby is nothing but a skeleton:

ach! What a beautiful skeleton you will make! And very soon, too, because you do not smile on your madly-loving Svengali . . . You shall have a nice little mahogany glass case all to yourself in the museum of the Ecole de Médecine, and Svengali shall come in his new fur-lined coat, smoking his

big cigar of the Havana . . . and look through the holes of your eyes into
your stupid empty skull, and up the nostrils of your high, bony sounding-
board of a nose without either a tip or a lip to it, and into the roof of your
big mouth, with your thirty-two English teeth, and between your big ribs
into your big chest, where the big leather lungs used to be, and say, 'Ach!
what a pity she had no more music in her than a big tom-cat!' And then he
will look all down your bones to your poor crumbling feet, and say 'What a
fool she was not to answer Svengali's letters!' (p. 74)

Later in the book Trilby describes how Svengali used to explain to
her the pleasure he would take in coming to view her body at the
Paris Morgue (p. 215).

Like *Dorian Gray*, *Trilby* is another terrifying story of the dangers of
influence. *Dorian Gray*, however, raises the possibility that desires that
appear to be installed in a person by an overwhelming outside
influence may actually emerge from within the self, from a subliminal consciousness such as that which F. W. H. Myers posits. The jury
remains out on the nature of influence in *Dorian Gray*. In *Trilby*,
however, there is little suggestion that the desires that are installed in
Trilby reflect her own 'real' desires. Svengali is simply the invasive
and mesmeric monster who steals her soul.[27] In fact, Svengali as a
character is a mixture of aesthetic qualities and rabidly unaesthetic
traits. His brilliance as a musician, his desire to sacrifice all (or at
least other people) to art, and his foreign exoticism are counter-
balanced by the anti-Semitic portrayal of his repulsive demeanour
and his dirtiness. Any attraction to Svengali outside of the hypnotic
bond remains almost entirely unfathomable. The terms of influence
in the novel are thus simpler than those of *Dorian Gray*, in which the
problem of influence involves a see-saw between the desires of the
influencer and the influenced. As Grossman argues:

In *Trilby*, *Dorian Gray*'s 'influence' is recast as overwhelming, rather than
inspiring, as victimizing, rather than empowering, as specific to a single
character, rather than ubiquitous, and as an evil power, rather than as a
complex reality. *Trilby* thus at once made influence itself dangerous and
framed the aesthetic movement, in all its dimensions, as a truly dangerous
influence. Whereas in *Dorian Gray* 'influence' signals both subjectivity and
subjects (art, homosexuality, developing identities), Svengali redefines
influence as the evacuation of subjectivity with his mesmeric invocation: 'Et
maintenant dors, ma mignonne!'[28]

If subjectivity is easily evacuated in *Trilby*, by the dangerous
aesthetic villain, then the body of the evacuated subject Trilby is also
literally and figuratively dismantled. In the economy of the novel

Trilby's body is aestheticized, dissected and evaluated in market terms. This dissection of Trilby the woman seems to be re-enacted in the publishing sensation that was *Trilby*. As Daniel Pick points out in his introduction to *Trilby*: 'The novel instances the ambiguity of the relationship between popular, mass and elite cultures as well as science across the period. How had the widespread popular interest in the theatrical staging of the hypnotic world come together with salesmanship, advertising, commercial exploitation, as well as with the concerns of high culture and the bastions of the medical establishment?'[29] *Trilby* as publishing sensation had its own seemingly mesmerizing influence on the market. Not only did the novel sell an unprecedented number of copies, but for perhaps the first time products were marketed en masse that had originated in a popular novel. There were Trilby sweets, Trilby hats, plays based on *Trilby*, plays making fun of *Trilby*, towns named after Trilby – you name it: 'One . . . entrepreneur on Broadway went so far as to offer ice-cream moulded in the shape of Trilby's "ever-famous foot" in the marketing mayhem which broke in 1894.'[30] By 1896 there were twenty-four productions of *Trilby* running simultaneously in the United States.[31] Because the copyright laws were unfixed and ownership of texts was heavily contested, *Trilby* inspired more than a few lawsuits. The actress Estelle Clayton who was playing Trilby in one production, applied for an injunction against a rival actress on the grounds that her impersonation of the heroine used bare feet, a device allegedly invented by Miss Clayton.[32] This anatomizing of Trilby once again foregrounds the question of what aspects of a person actually belong to him or herself. The possibility of copyrighting the act of not wearing shoes goes far towards breaking down the ownership of one's voice and one's body which the plot of *Trilby* also enacts. The plot of *Trilby* and its spread through the market raises a question: how can you know that you own yourself, your desires, your inner self, amidst the wide range of suggestive influences, from the subtle machinations of the market to the more obviously threatening dangers of hypnotic invasion?

In many ways *Trilby*'s popularity set the stage for Wilde's demonization. Wilde could be read in the light of that other 1890s degenerate Svengali as one in a series of dangerously influential high art connoisseurs.[33] Like the musician Svengali, Wilde was an artist with strict ideas about the importance of art at the apparent expense of the human. And Wilde's concerns, like *Trilby*'s, touch on questions about the commodification of the self. Owning oneself is obviously problematic in *The Picture of Dorian Gray*, the novel in which the aesthete anti-hero can only experience life to its fullest potential through a splitting of the self into body (which acts as it pleases but suffers no loss of beauty or youth) and portrait (which reflects the true debauched and aging condition of the inner self). After Trilby dies, paintings of her foot still fetch high prices. By contrast, we do not know what becomes of Dorian's portrait but the two are reunited in death when Dorian's body takes on the degenerative decay that the picture has borne for so long:

When they entered they found, hanging upon the wall, a splendid portrait of their master as they had seen him, in all the wonder of his exquisite youth and beauty. Lying on the floor was a dead man, in evening dress, with a knife in his heart. He was withered, wrinkled, and loathsome of visage. It was not till they had examined the rings that they recognised who he was.[34]

In the last line of the novel, Dorian's rings remain as the only material markers of an identity that has become fluid and strange. Art is expected to survive, while people age and expire. The ecstatic fantasy of reversing the aging process, which *Dorian Gray* enacts, has been read by critics such as Ed Cohen as part of a strategy of gay concealment, a process of 'the symbolic displacement of the erotic onto the aesthetic'; the disguising of male–male desire through the aestheticization of the perfect male body, first in the portrait and then in the ageless Dorian himself.[35] Male–male desire is undeniably central to the dynamics of Wilde's novel, but this desire is also inseparable from the question of influence – the radical making and re-making of the erotic object and the desiring subject. The process of making someone or something into an artwork, a process which is experienced in different ways by Dorian and Trilby, is couched in terms of influence in both novels. And, in a sense, something like this process is experienced by Wilde himself when his sexuality became the central spectacle of *fin-de-siècle* Britain.

In a footnote to Wilde's trial transcriptions H. Montgomery Hyde summarizes W. B. Yeats's analysis of the hysteria surrounding Wilde:

[Yeats] explained the unanimity of the mob by the fact that it had become hypnotized by a word or a notion, and showed the senseless behaviour of an individual under the effect of hypnotic suggestion. 'The rage against Wilde,' said Yeats, who was living in London at the time, 'was also complicated by the Britisher's jealousy of art and the artist, which is generally dormant but is called into activity when the artist has got outside his field into publicity of an undesirable kind. The hatred is not due to any action of the artist or eminent man; it is merely the expression of an individual hatred and envy, become collective because circumstances have made it so.'[36]

Yeats's relegating the Wilde effect to a mass hypnotic hysteria raises as many questions as it answers. What is the unspecified word or notion to which Yeats refers? Homosexuality? Irishness? European-ness? Aestheticism? The fearful group repudiation of Wilde's sexu-ality here is seen as part of the general public's jealousy of the artist; the need to scapegoat him is connected to the envy and distrust of the artist, or other eminent man, by the rabble. Hyde's glossing of Yeats finally explains very little in this passage about the relationship between the crowd's rage and the scapegoated artist. Without pretending to uncover all of the factors involved in the demonizing of Wilde, I want to try and unpack some of the connections between the threatening aesthete artist and the apparently hypnotized mob that the passage from Yeats only begins to suggest.

Many recent critics have explored the importance that Wilde's 'influence' came to take on during his trials, and the subsequent blurring of the boundaries between the sexual acts of which Wilde was accused and his written work.[37] In 'The Mesmerizing of Dorian Gray' Kerry Powell links the numerous uses of the word 'influence' in *Dorian Gray* to Wilde's interest in sensational fiction about mesmerism.[38] Wilde was enthusiastic about several pot-boilers about mesmerism he reviewed for *The Woman's World* in the 1880s. In his review of Violet Fane's *Helen Davenant*, a novel about a murder committed while under hypnotic compulsion, Wilde maintained that: 'This is the supreme advantage that fiction possesses over fact . . . It can make things artistically probable . . . [and] by force of mere style, compel us to believe. The ordinary novelists, by keeping close to ordinary incidents of commonplace life, seem to me to abdicate half their power.'[39] In this passage different forms of power and compulsion collapse into each other; extraordinary novelists, whether aesthetic stylists or writers of absorbing pot-boilers, act like hypnotists, employing their power to compel their audience to believe in the truth of their most outrageous claims. These aesthetic questions about whether and how representations can influence and compel take on criminal and legal import during Wilde's trials.

In 1895 Wilde became embroiled in the tragic libel suit against the

Marquess of Queensberry, the father of his lover Lord Alfred Douglas, that lead to Wilde's eventual arrest, trial and imprisonment for committing 'gross indecency'. In the wake of the trial, Wilde's spectacular celebrity and his aesthetic privileging of art over life were disavowed by the society which had initially accepted and applauded him. Wilde's verbal wordplay, his brilliance, his celebration of surface over depth, began to be understood as a code for his homosexuality by the wider reading public. He went from being either admired, or gently ridiculed, to being a cultural pariah. In his trials Wilde was damned as much for what he wrote (and sometimes for what someone else wrote) as for the sexual acts he committed. Whatever it was that made Wilde seem so evil to *fin-de-siècle* society was inextricable from the potential corrupting power of his words and his image – the possibility that through his rhetoric Wilde, the successful playwright, the popular figure, the homosexual man, would influence others to follow his deviant example.

The famous incident which initiated the lawsuit rested on the question of pose, rather than reality. Queensberry left Wilde a card at his club which read, in a famous mis-spelling, 'To Oscar Wilde, posing as a somdomite.' In the trials themselves the word 'pose' became key – to defend himself Queensberry had to prove that Wilde had simply posed as a sodomite, not that he had actually committed sodomy. Wilde stood accused of having a certain way of being in the world, adopting an identity, rather than committing specific acts. In the process of establishing that Wilde had posed as a sodomite, the trials turned into a battle of hermeneutics – what was the proper way to read Wilde's pose? What did Wilde signify?[40]

Because of the then current libel laws, Queensberry's lawyer Edward Carson (who was coincidentally Wilde's old schoolmate) had to prove not just that what Queensberry said was true, but that publishing his accusations was in the public interest. Here is where the question of the construction of Wilde's influence becomes key. In order to defend Queensberry from the charge of libel Carson had to establish that Wilde's pose actually itself posed a threat to the general public. To prove this Carson attacked Wilde's character by way of his writing – his aphorisms, his letters, and *The Picture of Dorian Gray*. Carson described Wilde's work, particularly *Dorian Gray*, as itself a contagious disease that could spread and affect the reading public.

The novel contains two apparently contradictory attitudes

towards the power of influence. On the one hand, Dorian seems to have been fatally influenced, both by Lord Henry Wotton and by the 'poisonous' yellow book Lord Henry gives him, which is modelled on J.-K. Huysmans's *A Rebours*. To Dorian, this book 'seemed to him to contain the story of his own life, written before he had ever lived it' (p. 97). Dorian becomes fascinated by this book which simultaneously indicates to him a new way he should live his life and tells him something he's always already known. On the other hand, Lord Henry states that there is no such thing as influence: 'As for being poisoned by a book, there is no such thing as that. Art has no influence upon action . . . It is superbly sterile' (p. 156). Like Lord Henry, during his trials, Wilde repeatedly denies that art either reveals anything about its creator or has any moral effect whatsoever on its audience. It is autonomous unto itself.

But as Wilde's person and art are imagined as powerfully influential in the discourse of the three trials, he becomes unable to maintain this position. Life leaks into art and art leaks into life. The transcripts of the next two trials alternate between testimony by the young men who slept with Wilde for money and the question of his corrupting literary influence. It is difficult to separate the issues here. Carson foregrounded the question of literary and personal influence in the first libel trial and it continued to pervade the other trials as well. In Carson's opening speech for the defence in the first trial he stressed Wilde's evil influence on Bosie, saying: ' . . . everything shows that the young man was in a dangerous position in that he acquiesced in the domination of Mr Wilde, a man of great ability and attainments.' – 'I ask you to bear in mind that Lord Queensberry's son was so dominated by Wilde that he threatened to shoot his own father.'[41] Bosie's mother Lady Queensberry also adopted the words of *Dorian Gray* to understand her son's relationship to Wilde, claiming that the effect that Wilde had had on her son, was like Lord Henry Wotton's on Dorian.[42] Prosecutors in the case read out bits of *Dorian Gray* in court, particularly one point where the painter Basil Hallward asks Dorian 'why is your friendship so fatal to young men?' The question of unhealthy influence is one at which the prosecution hammers away, although Wilde continues to deny the relevance of it, saying on the stand: 'I do not believe that any book or work of art ever had any effect whatever on morality.'[43]

During the course of the trial Wilde's influence spreads to the point that he begins to be held responsible for a number of works he didn't actually write, including Bosie's poem 'Two Loves' that concludes with the famous phrase 'the Love that dare not speak its name'. He is also held accused of authoring a short story 'The Priest and the Acolyte' that appeared in *The Chameleon*, an Oxford literary magazine that portrayed homosexuality sympathetically. Wilde's 'Phrases and Philosophy for the Use of the Young' appeared alongside the unsigned story about a priest caught in a compromising position with a young acolyte, and Wilde was held responsible for both by some outraged readers (including Queensberry).[44] The story was really written by Jack Bloxam; under cross-examination in the trial Wilde criticized the story's style but refused to judge it on moral grounds.

The idea of Wilde's unhealthy influence on the young that emerges so problematically in the trial's emphasis on the damning juxtaposition of Wilde's 'Phrases and Philosophy' with Jack Bloxam's story, is prefigured in Robert Hichens's 1894 satire of Wilde and Bosie, *The Green Carnation*.[45] In Hichens's comic novel Esmé Amarinth, the Wilde figure, holds a nearly mesmeric sway over his friend the Bosie-like Lord Reggie Hastings. Hastings is described as 'an echo' of Amarinth (p. 179). As Richard Ellmann points out, Hichens, who was a gay friend of Bosie's and an admirer of Wilde, seems to adopt Queensberry's line in his analysis of the power relations between the two men; Wilde is the villain and Bosie is the enthralled dupe.[46] But any suggestion of Wilde's particularly dangerous influence is deflated in one section of the novel in which Amarinth lectures to a group of young schoolboys about the necessity of absurdity, folly and by implication, other dangerous pursuits. When the heroine, the sensible, heterosexual, maternal young widow Lady Locke (who is briefly tempted by marriage to Hastings but refuses him because of his unhealthy relationship with Amarinth) tells her son Tommy to do the opposite of everything Mr Amarinth has told the group of boys, she discovers that Tommy has already forgotten everything he has said (pp. 176–177). In *The Green Carnation* the Wilde effect, the combined force of aesthetic drollery and homosexual suggestiveness, is pictured as paradoxically both threatening and easily resistible. The 'healthy' young boys won't hear a word, but the ones who have their own secret unnameable desires may be instantly susceptible.

If the previously barely nameable condition homosexuality seems to spread rapidly throughout Wilde's trials, then it is important to remember that the perception of influence as a problem in relation to Wilde pre-exists his trials, both in *The Green Carnation* and in his own work. The initial critical reception of *Dorian Gray* when it first appeared in 1891 was steeped in the discourse of contagion and influence. The *Daily Chronicle* called *Dorian Gray* 'unclean and leprous'. Wilde's words were accused of 'defiling' those they touched. The *Scots Observer* claimed that the novel would 'taint every young mind that comes in contact with it'.[47] In the debates that surround Wilde from the early 1890s there is something evil, unnameable and capable of spreading that he exudes – the vice which, once the trials have served to make it more explicit will then be understood as that which had always defined him.

In his final trial Wilde was asked a question about the limits of influence, a question about the working class boys with whom he had continually dined and to whom he had given expensive presents: 'Did it not strike you that in your position you could exercise a considerable influence over these lads for good or ill?' Wilde responded: 'No, I am bound to say I don't think it did. The only influence I could exercise on anybody would be a literary influence. Of course in the case of these young men that would be out of the question. Otherwise I don't see what capacity I have for influencing people.' [48] In this passage Wilde insists that he can not have any influence over these men, because in point of fact they do not appreciate the high cultural figure that is Wilde; they don't read. They have no reason to be influenced by him because any influence he has is in the realm of the literary. One underlying point here seems to be that they are not influenced by him because he pays them for their services – or at least gives them expensive presents and dinners for their company. The exchange is monetary rather than a meeting of minds and souls, or an invasion of one mind (or body) by a stronger one. At the end of the nineteenth century, it is difficult to portray the construction of male same-sex relationships outside of one of these two models – either there is a money/blackmail exchange or a hypnotic, mesmerizing spell exerted by one party over the other. Love and hypnosis come together in images of homo-sexuality at the turn of the century, when love and money do not.[49]

The question of Wilde's dangerous influence continued to haunt him, even into prison. In October 1895, after Wilde was transferred from Pentonville to Wandsworth prison, he collapsed from illness and exhaustion. Regenia Gagnier writes:

As he improved in the infirmary, which because of staff limitations did not have continuous supervision, he was caught entertaining other convalescents. The secretary of the Prison Board immediately reprimanded the governor and ordered that a guard be present at all times, day and night, in the infirmary room Wilde inhabited. The secretary especially stressed that the guard himself not be susceptible to Wilde's conversation.[50]

Wilde's danger appears to inhere as much in his capacity to entertain as in any specific sexual threat. The correct prison guard for him must be protected from his dangerous influence by having no sense of humour. But this also points to a specific discourse of contagion that emerged through the prison. The Victorian value of one man, one prison cell actually stems from something a little less pleasant than the right to privacy. It was an outgrowth of the idea that if prisoners were kept in solitary confinement they could not contaminate one another.[51]

Dorian Gray is steeped in questions of influence defined variously as love, contamination and absorption. When the painter Basil Hallward first encounters Dorian he is terrified that Dorian will absorb him. He says: 'I knew that I had come face to face with some one whose mere personality was so fascinating that, if I allowed it to do so, it would absorb my whole nature, my whole soul, my very art itself. I did not want any external influence in my life' (p. 21). If Basil is overwhelmed by Dorian's influence, then it seems that Dorian is overwhelmed by Lord Henry's. The question of influence is continually canvassed between Dorian and Lord Henry:

'Have you really a very bad influence, Lord Henry?'
    'There is no such thing as a good influence, Mr Gray. All influence is immoral – immoral from the scientific point of view.'
    'Why?'
    'Because to influence a person is to give him one's soul. He does not think his natural thoughts, or burn with his natural passions. His virtues are not real to him . . . He becomes an echo of some one else's music, an actor of a part that has not been written for him' (p. 28).

In this passage influence is imagined as dangerous because of its tendency to do away with the 'natural': when under the influence a person is separated from their real nature. But knowing Wilde's propensity to invert the natural and the artificial, and his fondness for posing, it is difficult to know how to interpret this. On the one hand Wilde idealizes the artist who pours out his strong personality into perfect autonomous artworks, uninfluenced by the requirements of a restrictive culture or morality. On the other hand, whenever Wilde begins to talk about the natural it may be dangerous to try and read him straight, so to speak.

Perhaps the clearest picture of the problem of influence in the novel comes when Dorian Gray listens to Lord Henry speak while Basil is painting him. Lord Henry's mesmerizing words are para-doxically about the very necessity of living for oneself – realizing one's own nature perfectly through living out one's every fantasy and desire. However, in the process of exhorting that creed, he claims to know Dorian's wishes and fantasies – he seems to be inside his mind, moulding his desires. He says: 'You, Mr. Gray, you yourself, with your rose-red youth and rose-white boyhood, you have had passions that have made you afraid, thoughts that have filled you with terror, day-dreams and sleeping dreams whose mere memory might stain your cheek with shame —' (p. 29). Whose fantasies and desires are they which stop Dorian dead in his tracks? How can we know where one mind ends and the next begins, the book seems to ask? The passage continues:

He was dimly conscious that entirely fresh influences were at work within him. Yet they seemed to him to have come really from himself. The few words that Basil's friend had said to him – words spoken by chance, no doubt, and with wilful paradox in them – had touched some secret chord that had never been touched before, but that he felt was now vibrating and throbbing to curious pulses.

. . . Words! Mere words! How terrible they were! How clear, and vivid, and cruel! One could not escape from them. And yet what subtle magic there was in them! They seemed to be able to give a plastic form to formless things, and to have a music of their own as sweet as that of viol or of lute. Mere words! Was there anything so real as words?

Yes; there had been things in his boyhood that he had not understood. He understood them now. Life suddenly became fiery-coloured to him . . .

With his subtle smile, Lord Henry watched him. He knew the precise psychological moment when to say nothing. He felt intensely interested. He was amazed at the sudden impression that his words had produced, and, remembering a book that he had read when he was sixteen, a book which had revealed to him much that he had not known before, he wondered whether Dorian Gray was passing through a similar experience. (p. 29)

This is a passage precisely about the difficulty of mapping the workings of influence. If we read that what Dorian is uncovering is his own pool of desires, queer desire, perverse desire, or just socially unsanctioned desire – we can see how complicated a model of influence is actually in place here. Although Dorian believes that Lord Henry's words are entirely fresh and new to him, he simultaneously sees his influence as waking up something that was dormant in himself. Do words work performatively to create desire, or do they just give a name to what is already there? What is the power of language? Lord Henry seems to speak words by chance; like Wilde he speaks the language of the aphoristic paradox, the word puzzle that should exist ideally in itself, and for itself with no relation to real life. Yet, for Dorian it is these contingent and paradoxical phrases which enter into him and make him 'vibrate to curious pulses'. The clever paradox, paradoxically, seems to be at the very source of the self at this moment when influence takes its effect.

When Dorian thinks 'there had been things in his boyhood that he had not understood that he understood now' this retrospective understanding of the past reads now like a coming-out moment. The coming-out moment is often couched in such a way as to make sense of a past that couldn't be properly understood before, that is only experienced for what it actually was (the dawning of desire for the same sex) after the fact, retrospectively. When Dorian suddenly understands things in his childhood that he had never understood before he seems to endorse a model of influence that is both entering from the outside and uncovering something that is already present in himself – making sense of a past he has experienced but never properly understood. This model of retrospective understanding of the past is not limited to gay identity. It is a model that is similar to the one Freud employs when he formulates a theory of the traumatic installation of childhood sexuality – the seduction theory. In Freud's famous theory of the 1890s an event – a sexual attack – happens to a child at an age when he or she does not have the ability to understand it. That event is later retriggered by a second event which retrospectively makes sense of the first one – it is a moment in which one says, oh that was sex.[52] Freud later discards this theory, but his question remains, the hypnotic question par excellence: was that my desire or someone else's? Who seduces whom, the parent or the child? Or to put it another way, what is at issue – an outside invader or the subject's inner psychic imaginary?[53] This question is central to the spate of horror fiction of the *fin de siècle*. In late-nineteenth-century supernatural fiction questions about the nature of influence and the boundaries of what makes for the individual's identity manifest themselves repeatedly in supernatural scenes of invasion and projection, see-sawing desires.

Dorian's experience reminds Lord Henry of his own similar awakening scene inspired by a book he read when he was sixteen, presumably Walter Pater's *The Renaissance* which inspired Wilde's generation of aesthetes. The political goal of aestheticism as Wilde lays out in his essay 'The Soul of Man under Socialism' is to enable its proponents to 'know the meanings of the words, and realise them in free, beautiful lives.'[54] Aestheticism implies a radical freedom – the word can be realized in and of itself and for itself – it is not about its moral effects or its social construction. But at the same time words as they are imagined in *Dorian Gray*, and in Wilde's trials, travel to the heart of identity, and influence the people who hear them to an astonishing and powerful degree. Words become invasive. As in Freud's then current model of the installation of sexuality, words seduce, enter and work mysterious changes on what the self then wants. The tradition of the poison book, such as Huysmans's *À Rebours*, or Pater's *The Renaissance*, which infects its reader is one way of tracing this within the world of *Dorian Gray*. And, of course, *Dorian Gray* itself becomes the poison book during Wilde's trials. Both words and the sexually enthralling character begin to seem equally dangerous; both can install desire where none seemed to exist But both also suggest that those desires were already in place, simply dormant and waiting to emerge.

By 1895 fictional portrayals of hypnotic influence reflect general anxieties about the limits of suggestive influence that emerge in a plethora of sites comprising the familiar stomping ground of the late-nineteenth-century aesthete. Fears about influence cluster centrally around the mesmerizing potential of transgressive sexualities, but they also emerge through the suggestive potential of linguistic wordplay, literature, art and the fluctuations of an expanding marketplace that helps set the terms for all these things. During Wilde's trials, influence is redefined as dangerous reading and homosexual sex, so that the two become intertwined in the public imagination. If Wilde, like Svengali, is a hypnotic figure for the 1890s it is perhaps because he acts as a magnet for so many different fears about the possibility of different kinds of influence – whether those influences are imagined as homosexual sexual contact, decadent reading matter or the compelling effects of a new and expanding marketplace of commodities, in which everything, including human beings may be up for sale. As imagined by novelists of the 1890s, the magically vampiric, hypnotically consuming, late nineteenth-century aesthete had an astonishing range of outlets for new forms of outrage, but of course, the press and the law were also waiting in the wings, to classify influence as crime.

CHAPTER 3

Henry James's lives during wartime

> One doesn't give up one's country any more than one gives up one's grandmother. They're both antecedent to choice – elements of one's composition that are not to be eliminated.[1]

Henry James officially gave up his country and became a British citizen on 28 July 1915. At the same time he was working on his final unfinished ghost novel, *The Sense of the Past*, that he had begun in 1900 but had soon abandoned. He took it up again in 1914, in the process stopping work on *The Ivory Tower.* According to Leon Edel, 'that novel was too actual; the war seemed to make it obsolete. Instead he turned to the unfinished *The Sense of the Past* . . . The story of an American walking into a remote time seemed more possible to James in the midst of headlines and casualty lists.'[2] The standard critical take on the return to *The Sense of the Past* is that it was a retreat for James away from the overwhelming and unbearable sense of the present, the War. But I want to maintain that *The Sense of the Past* in fact resembles James's wartime writings – his posthumously published book of propagandistic essays *Within the Rim* – as well as letters and biographical anecdotes about James's relationship to the war effort, all of which negotiate the psychoanalytic process of identification.

According to Laplanche and Pontalis, identification is a 'psychological process whereby the subject assimilates an aspect, property or attribute of the other and is transformed, wholly or partially, after the model the other provides. It is by means of a series of identifications that the personality is constituted and specified.'[3] In this definition the agency of identification – 'assimilation' – provokes uncertainty: is it volitional (a product of a conscious choice) or non-volitional (antecedent to choice, as Ralph Touchett would have it)? When Freud maintains that identification precedes desire, he posits identification as primary and mimetic, that which constitutes the personality rather than that which the already-constituted personality chooses to adopt.[4] The identifications I examine in this chapter that James and his character Ralph Pendrel adopt are secondary, chosen identifications. In fact, as is indicated by the repetitive failures and subsequent embarrassments which dog them, they are clumsily chosen ones – identifications which spectacularly display the gap between identifier and identified, allowing for no smooth transitions or easy interpellations into new symbolic communities.

James's boundless faith in the potential for stretching identificatory limits is an outgrowth of his expansive view of 'the great extension' of consciousness.[5] Consciousness for James, as many critics have argued, takes on the power of magical thinking. At crucial points in James's fictions an individual consciousness, such as Maggie in *The Golden Bowl*, makes a subjective desire into an objective reality apparently through the force of will alone. Whether this faith in the omnipotence of thought is desperate, beating back its own recognition of inevitable failure, or triumphant, it is undeniable that James's writing continually pushes the metaphoric towards the real, and the desiring consciousness towards the determining one.[6] James's late identificatory performances participate in the pleasures, dangers and embarrassments of magical thinking. When he sheds his country, or has his character Ralph Pendrel shed his century, James celebrates the ways in which consciousness can perform itself, can create, can make things happen.

Recently Christopher Nealon has pointed towards the ways in which Willa Cather's fictions deploy identifications which cross racial, national and sexual divides in order to construct genealogies apart from patriarchal, heterocentric models of inheritance and lineage. James's exuberant faith in the potentially magical powers of consciousness participates in what Nealon has labelled, 'the complex of shame and exhilaration that comes with the act of affiliation'.[7] At the end of his life, James employs complicated, convoluted, sometimes violent strategies of identification and affiliation, in order to force his way into symbolic communities which are otherwise closed or inaccessible.

James's final ghost novel suggests that one of the most inaccessible barriers to community is that of history. The American hero of *The Sense of the Past*, Ralph Pendrel, inherits a house in England from a distant relation who leaves it to him after being impressed by an article Ralph has written called, 'An essay in aid of the reading of history'. Ralph's relative 'had nowhere seen the love of old things, of the scrutable, palpable past, nowhere felt an ear for stilled voices, as precious as they are faint, as seizable, truly, as they are fine, affirm a more remarkable power than in the pages that had moved him to gratitude'.[8] The house Ralph inherits eventually gives him access to the past which he desires – he finds himself thrust back nearly one hundred years, trying to pass himself off as an inhabitant of 1820. The problem of passing is the major dynamic of the novel as it stands – will Ralph be unmasked as an intruder from the future, or will he be able successfully to seize and be seized by the past, to become completely immersed in it? What Ralph wants is a total identification with the past, 'for the old ghosts to take him for one of themselves' (p. 49). In a sense, both 'Within the Rim' and *The Sense of the Past* are spy stories about passing – either openly, adopting a new national identification as when James takes on British citizenship, or covertly, as in Ralph Pendrel's attempt to reinvent himself as someone from 1820.

James's official adoption of and by England is pictured in most biographies as part of his profound war fervour.[9] According to a letter to his nephew Harry, the discovery that, because of the war, he would have to register as an alien under police supervision, inspired James to 'rectify a position that has become inconveniently and uncomfortably false, making my civil status merely agree not only with my moral, but with my material as well, in every kind of way'.[10] James felt that for all intents and purposes he was already 'naturalized' as British, but the war provided an urgent reason to make his status public and official. He writes: 'Let me repeat that I feel sure I shouldn't in the least have come to it without this convulsion, but one is *in* the convulsion (I wouldn't be out of it either!) and one must act accordingly.'[11] The spatialized conception of war as a 'convulsion' that one could somehow be 'in' without necessarily being on the front lines, emerges in a different way in the title of one of James's war essays 'Within the Rim,' in which Britain as an island seems to promise a protected space from which to view the violence that is devastating Belgium and France. Being *in* 'the convulsion' suggests that war makes communities of those who experience it, either firsthand or from a distance, and that war also creates new imperatives towards community, towards imagining oneself as necessarily 'in', together with others who are also 'in'.

When Violet Hunt asked him why he became a British citizen James replied, 'my dear Purple Patch, chiefly because I wanted to be able to say *We* – with a capital – when I talked about an Advance.'[12] According to Hunt in her memoir *The Flurried Years*, at the end of his life James 'talked Army, thought Army, and died Army'. Hunt claims, 'he said *We* so hard, took the affairs of *Us* so much to heart, that it gave him the stroke from which he died'.[13] Here Hunt intriguingly posits death as the result of an out-of-bounds, apparently unsustainable national identification. Death from saying 'we' seems apropos, because, for the later James, there is clearly no way of saying 'Us' simply, no way of constructing community in a defined and goal-oriented way. A novel such as *The Golden Bowl* is about the attempted enforcing of the ability to say 'we' in the face of the unsustainability of any possible 'we,' the repeated failure of alliance or communication.[14] I want to suggest that in some of James's other late writings the dynamic between the threatened breakdown of the performative, community-enforcing 'we', and its repeated phantasmatic reinstallation creates a space for queer identifications to play themselves out in the process of shoring up a national wartime identity.

James's attempts to say 'we' in *Within the Rim* and *The Sense of the Past* are complicated by his sense of the often shaming failure of these attempts. Eve Sedgwick has suggested that shame is a particularly important affect for James and for queer theory. In developmental terms shame is part of a dynamic of identification. For Sedgwick, following the work of the psychologist Sylvan Tompkins, '[s]hame floods into being as a moment, a disruptive moment, in a circuit of identity-constituting identificatory communication.'[15] Shame appears when the mutual gaze between care-giving adult and the infant who is looking for support for its own emerging identity, who is being 'given face', is interrupted – when recognition fails. In the Lacanian mirror stage, the infant misrecognizes itself as more autonomous, more complete than it really is, provoking a jubilant assumption of selfhood, a mistakenly optimistic leap into differentiation, language and identity. In shame's version of this story, that jubilation is embarrassing as well as empowering. When you experience yourself as standing up you also experience yourself as standing out.[16] Shame exposes one to the uncomprehending and potentially judgemental gaze of the other by making it impossible to make wholly successful identifications – to 'blend in with the crowd' – but it also exposes the process of identification as inevitably performative and therefore liable to failure. Shame is a performance gone wrong, a communicative disaster. As Joseph Litvak puts it: '. . . – the experience of making a spectacle of oneself – presupposes one's lack of complete cognitive control over one's own signifying power, whose subsequent "excesses" become available for identification, interpretation and supervision by others'.[17]

Shame is ubiquitous in James's presentation of the vicissitudes of identification in his wartime work, as well as in an earlier passage from his autobiography, the 'obscure hurt' scene in which the young James suffers an unlocatable wound while helping to put out an uncertainly referential fire: 'I had done myself, in face of a shabby conflagration, a horrid even if an obscure hurt.'[18] I will return to this scene of wounding in greater detail later, but for now I simply want to stress its centrality to James's self-fashioning in his auto-biography. James's mysterious wound is retrospectively identified as that which kept him from fighting in the Civil War.[19] The relations of simultaneous shameful and spectacularly self-aggrandizing identi-fication which James sets up between his own wounds and the wounds of the country in that passage re-emerge in his later prose. This Jamesian 'theater of embarrassment' as Joseph Litvak calls it in his book, *Caught in the Act: Theatricality in the Nineteenth-Century English Novel*, becomes, in James's vision of the European theatre of war, specifically eroticized – a queer version of what national community formation might look like.

The shame associated with attempting to love, have, encompass, sympathize with, be, a larger collective parallels the identificatory embarrassment and thrilling self-exposure that Ralph Pendrel ex-periences in relation to his only partially successful immersion in the past. Both Ralph Pendrel's and James's wartime scenes of identifica-tion are failures in instructive ways. One might say that Ralph Pendrel also tries to say 'we' so hard he nearly dies from it. Despite Ralph's desire to experience the past as it actually was, to be taken for one of the ghosts, the past is, as James presents it, completely inaccessible to Ralph except as an aestheticized object: 'It was when life was framed in death that the picture was really hung up' (*SP*, p. 46). When Ralph makes a particularly incomprehensible speech, he creates 'a rupture of relation' with his 1820 audience, reducing them to silence so that they seem like 'some mechanic but consum-mate imitation of ancient life, staring through the vast plate of a museum' (p. 210). It seems as if Ralph's 'very care for them had somehow annihilated them' (p. 210).[20]

But the annihilating, aestheticizing process is not complete; the Midmore family threatens to stare back at Ralph and see through him. When Sir Cantopher nearly exposes Ralph by suggesting that his knowledge of the family, his entire sensibility, in fact, seems as if it were born just three minutes ago, Ralph reacts with mixed emotions:

> . . . but if he felt the tears rise he couldn't for his life rightly have apportioned the weight of shame in them against the joy of emotion just as emotion. The joy was for the very tribute itself of Sir Cantopher's advance upon him, whereas the shame was ever so much more vague, attaching as it did at the most to its being rather ridiculous to be so held up for transparent. *They* had seemed to him transparent, even with dim spots – he had been fairly on his way, hadn't he? to reduce Sir Cantopher to it; so he panted a little, after his fashion, . . . He was what he was, of course, and with the full right to be; but hadn't he half-seconds as of a push against dead walls, a sense of that dash at them in the dark? – so that they were attested as closely near without the fruit of it, since for one to call people reachable they had really to be penetrable. (p. 232).

The threat of being transparent, of being penetrable, provokes both joy and shame in Ralph. The ability to penetrate is necessary for Ralph's disguise, as is shown by his telepathic collecting of information which he should know nothing about, and the ways in which he literally seizes the past by, for instance, reaching in his pocket and pulling out a miniature of Molly Midmore which he knows, in the same second that he is called on to do so, will be there. In *The Sense of the Past*, to know someone's milieu, as well as the inside of someone's mind, is to imagine 'reducing' them to a helpless, conquered, expectant transparency. To penetrate another's mind means simultaneously to be in communion with them and to have colonized them. Penetration – that which makes people 'reachable' – in this passage conflates the dynamics of identification and desire. The 'push against dead walls', the 'dash at them in the dark', and Ralph's 'panting' sexualizes, as well as militarizes, the act of communicative reciprocity necessary for Ralph to achieve fully the sense of the past. This suggests one reason why the threat of being read by another human being might be a source of shame.

James's war propaganda may seem like an odd place to look to shed more light on Ralph Pendrel's ghost story dilemma, but James's experience of the war turns on similar dynamics: the desire for complete immersion in a perceived community from which one is excluded, the worry that that immersion is impossible, the shame which ensues from this fear, and the excitement which ensues from the negotiation of a new and unusually eroticized community. In his essay 'Within the Rim', James describes his relationship to England as a sort of 'sensual' immersion which overtakes him, the American outsider:

I was not then to the manner born, but my apprehension of what it was on the part of others to be so had been confirmed and enriched by the long years and I gave myself up to the general, the native image I thus circled around as to the dearest and most precious of all native images. That verily became at the crisis an occupation sublime; which was not, after all, so much an earnest study or fond arrangement of the mixed aspects as a positive, a fairly sensual bask in their light, too kindled and too rich not to pour out by its own force. The strength and the copious play of the appearances acting in this collective fashion carried everything before them; no dark discrimination, no stiff little reserve that one might ever have made, stood up in the diffused day for a moment.[21]

The identifying James who gives himself up to the native image is also the removed, aestheticizing James who circles around it. James's sensually pleasurable 'occupation sublime' relies on the loss of individuality, the letting go of the 'stiff little reserve' which there is no place for in the diffused erotics of the passage. Yet, as James continues on the next page of the essay, it is clear that his relationship to the collectivity which makes up England at war is not one of simple immersion. He continues to speak of 'they' (in quotation marks) rather than the 'we' that he and Hunt both posit as his wartime desired pronoun: 'they didn't know how good they were, and their candour had a peculiar lovability of unconsciousness; one had more imagination at their service in this cause than they had in almost any cause of their own; it was wonderful, it was beautiful, it was inscrutable, that they could make one feel this and yet not to feel with it that it at all practically diminished them' (WR, p. 33). James, it seems, cannot entirely identify with this particular collective, as much as the eroticized thrill of doing so makes it a desirable activity. Ralph Pendrel's desires oscillate between a wish to identify wholly with the past, to be penetrated by it, and an aestheticizing urge to penetrate it wholly, to see through people and objectify them as museum pieces. James also occupies contradictory positions in relation to the mass, but he finally hangs on to his own stiff little reserve of artistic, removed selfhood. For a writer of propaganda, this is a problem, for to whom is the propaganda addressed but the lovably unconscious 'they'? Propaganda, by its very nature, is a specific kind of community-building performative speech act – its goal to create a public which will then feel addressed by it and rally to its cause.

For obvious reasons, James's relationship to audience-building is never a comfortable one. By the end of his life, with the disasters of his theatrical career and the New York Edition behind him, James was acutely aware of the problem of how to define his audience. Violet Hunt relates the following anecdote about James's (un-doubtedly well-founded) fears about the inaccessibility of his style, and how or if it will translate into effective propaganda. James asks Hunt to read an article he has written for Winifred Stephens's *Book of France*: '"Perhaps you would be kind enough to tell me if I am comprehensible? They tell me" – he turned his head away – "that I am obscure . . ."'[22] He reads aloud his essay to Hunt who listens, astonished at the '[e]motion, in Henry James! It was all perfectly clear, and of a poignancy! That was because he was in love with his subject, France, *la belle France* . . . intensely feminine, a bit of a cat, as I always saw her. She stood there personified. No real woman could have resisted a real lover pleading in such a voice as that for *le don de l'amoureuse Merci*.'[23] Hunt responds, 'Mr. James! . . . I did not know you could be so – passionate!' What then transpires: 'He turned on me an eye, *narquois*, reflective, stork-like, a little devilish, calmly wise – the Henry James eye, in fact and with a pompous little laugh . . . the male warding off any attack that the persevering female might possibly be contemplating against his supreme bachelordom: "Ah, madam, you must not forget that in this article I am addressing – not a Woman, but a Nation!"'[24]

Hunt's knowing anecdote proceeds along a number of fascinating paths.[25] If, as Sedgwick suggests, shame plays out the disruption of an assumed circuit of communication and identification, then James's famous obscurity takes on a new valence in the context of writing war propaganda which, possibly, no one might understand. Sedgwick ties the general significance of shame into James's specific fears about his audience, how or if he can communicate with anyone in his Prefaces, how or if he can expose his entire corpus of works to a potentially uncomprehending public. Both Sedgwick and Joseph Litvak relate this structure to a particular closeted yet constantly exposed gay content, both in James's writing and in the writings of James's critics and biographers. In the scenario of the closet, shame and obscurity go hand in hand – this is the paradoxical status of homosexuality as an open secret, that which is constantly displayed but never precisely named. Hunt's giggle at James's expense participates in the dynamic of exposure which Joseph Litvak calls the critical propulsion towards embarrassing Henry James. Yet, Hunt simultaneously tells a triumphant story of James's overcoming his own obscurity. James's self-fashioning as committed, and crucially comprehensible, war propagandist allows patriotic, nation-building communication to become the specific answer to the obscured question that cannot quite be asked about homosexuality.

The moment that Hunt recollects of James's worrying about his style's adequacy for the task of propaganda begins with embarrassment, but mutates into a scene of spectacular and seductive success. Hunt's reading of the scene of James's surprising passion tries to transform it into a heterosexualized flirtatious scenario in which Hunt herself seems to stand in for the seduced English public, another female seduced by James's passion on behalf of the victimized beloved France. But James refuses this heterosexualized scenario. Addressing a nation, not a woman, is by no means refusing sexual passion. It is, however, maintaining the existence of another object, apart from the implied heterosexual one. Fervent nationalistic passion during wartime is ideally patriotic and unshameful, – it is the passion of identification, the 'deep horizontal comradeship' which Benedict Anderson postulates in his book *Imagined Communities*,[26] rather than the questionable passion of (heterosexual) desire which Hunt playfully tries to ascribe to James. Two assumptions of this book are that identification and desire, which come together for Freud in the question of what constitutes homosexuality, are not easily separable, and that the passions of the homosocial fraternal ideal of the nation state are impossible to keep separate from more explicitly homosexual desires.[27] But the question of whether James's ostensible object in this anecdote is a man or a nation is not the main issue. Rather, according to Hunt, the significance of James's passion here is that it does communicate. He triumphs over his initial shame at his own obscurity through a passionate address to a collective, because, it seems, this type of address gives him the licence to display a passion which is absent from his other work.

The exchange with Hunt centres around James's article 'France,' which attempts to muster up support for the 'idea of what France and the French mean to the educated spirit of man' (WR, p. 83). In fact, not to understand this, not to rally around the supreme monument to civilization which is France – that, according to James, would be shameful: 'We should understand and answer together just by the magic of the mention, the touch of the two or three words, and this in proportion to our feeling ourselves social and communicating creatures – to the point, in fact, of a sort of shame at any imputation of our not literally understanding, or our waiting in any degree to be nudged or hustled' (p. 83). James constructs a community – the civilized sociality – around the common understanding of France as 'the cause uniting us most quickly in an act of glad intelligence, uniting us with the least need of any wondering why' (p. 83). Ideally, the propagandist performatively creates instinctual unthinking passion in 'our' response to the long-suffering France. Shame lies in the imputation that this does not happen instantly, that 'we' could hesitate, or fail to understand the imperative. If hesitation and non-comprehension are two potential, indeed, likely, outcomes of any encounter with a James text at this point in his career, then James seems to be gesturing, once again, in 'France', towards his own failure as well as trying to ward off that of his audience.

Here is the breathtakingly Jamesian final sentence of the article:

It takes our great Ally, and her only, to be as vivid for concentration, for reflection, for intelligent, inspired contraction of life toward an end all but smothered in sacrifice, as she has ever been for the most splendidly wasteful diffusion and communication; and to give us a view of her nature and her mind in which, laying down almost every advantage, every art and every appeal that we have generally known her by, she takes on energies, forms of collective sincerity, silent eloquence and selected example that are fresh revelations – and so, bleeding at every pore, while at no time in all her history so completely erect, makes us feel her perhaps as never before our incalculable, immortal France. (pp. 92–93)

In this passage's ambiguous play of connotation, France under attack turns from being a wasteful artist/aesthete, perhaps prostitute – a signifier of unanchored symbolic exchange – into a new nation, both 'collectively sincere' and 'completely erect'. James, constructing the necessary nation out of the previously diffuse France, seems to reflect his own process of turning himself from what some might label a splendidly wasteful novelist, into a propagandist. But, in point of fact, the free play of identificatory aesthetic exchange is never left behind. The 'forms of collective sincerity' which describe what it means to be constituting oneself as part of a nation under siege instead allow for a new arena for subversive identifications and desires to play themselves out in James's simultaneously shameful, patriotic and achingly empathic writings around the war.

In his wartime letters as well as in his essays, James constructs a multiplicity of sites for passionate identification with the war effort, and makes that passion practically into an ethical imperative. 'I am so utterly and passionately enlisted', James writes to his nephew, 'up to my eyes and over my aged head in the greatness of our cause that it fairly sickens me not to find every imagination not rise to it.'[28] In a letter to Clare Sheridan about the departure of her husband Wilfred to the front, he says:

I . . . but express in rather a ragged way perforce my intimate participation in your so natural sense of violence done you. I enter into that with all my heart and I wait with you, and I languish with you – for all the good it will do you; and I press the mighty little Margaret to *my* aged breast, and tell her fifty things about her glorious Daddy – even at the risk of finding her quite *blasé* with the wonders you have already related. All this, dearest Clare, because I am really very nearly as fond of Wilfred as you are, I think – and very nearly as fond of you as Wilfred is, and very nearly as fond of Margaret as you both are together! So there I am, qualified to sit between you and hold the massive Margaret in my lap. All of which means that I utterly measure the wrench from which you are suffering and that there isn't any tender place in any part of you that some old bone of mine doesn't ache responsive to.[29]

Here James seems to take on all parts in the family Oedipal triangle, actually inserting himself bodily, if phantasmatically, between husband and wife, and even metaphorically enveloping the mass by holding the massive Margaret. This desire for complete sympathetic communion with the soldiers at the front and the suffering of the family at home is a staple of James's war letters. He writes to Edward Marsh about reading Rupert Brooke's sonnets: ' . . . I have been reading them over and over to myself aloud, as if fondly to test and truly try them; almost in fact as if to reach the far-off author, in whatever unimaginable conditions, by some miraculous, some telepathic intimation that I am in quavering communion with him'.[30] James's expressed desire for sympathetic, even telepathic, experience of the war in all its multiple subject positions, leads towards endlessly exposing scenarios of passionate identification – that Jamesian need to 'get into relation' with others, here portrayed as 'quavering communion'. A repeated scenario of James's which occurs first during the Civil War and then again during World War I, is one in which he visits and talks to wounded soldiers. This affectively charged site of identificatory and homoerotic possibility emerges first in his autobiography when he remembers making a 'pilgrimage' to 'a vast gathering of invalid and convalescent troops, under canvas and in roughly improvised shanties, at some point of the Rhode Island shore that figures to my memory, though with a certain vagueness, as Portsmouth Grove' (*A*, p. 421). The site of this vagueness is revisited in his essay 'The Long Wards' written in 1914 for Edith Wharton's *Book of the Homeless*. In it James compares his visits to the wounded in St Bartholomew's Hospital to his earlier experience in the American Civil War.

In his autobiography James discusses his visit to the Civil War soldiers as a hazy, yet significant, memory. Typically for the auto-biography, the importance of specific details of recollection recedes in the face of James's concentration on his own consciousness. He experiences the visit as 'simply . . . an emotion – though the emotion, I should add, appeared to consist of everything in the whole world that my consciousness could hold' (*A*, p. 422). James doesn't know exactly who the troops were; he is not even sure that they were actually wounded, but whether they were or not is finally unimportant. It is his perception of their woundedness, their vulner-ability, their sadness, that invests them with phantasmatic signifi-cance. He says:

Discrimination of the prosaic order had little to do with my first and all but sole vision of the American soldier in his multitude, and above all – for that was markedly the colour of the whole thing – in his depression, his wasted melancholy almost; an effect that somehow corresponds for memory, I bethink myself, with the tender elegiac tone in which Walt Whitman was later on so admirably to commemorate him. (*A*, p. 422)

James, identifying with Whitman visiting the soldiers, identifies the position of soldier as that which is disabled, threatened, potentially missing something – a figure of loss, and, simultaneously, a figure needing the input of the artist to tease out his full potential for meaning. Putting himself into relation with soldiers for James here means observing their pain from a pleasurable, hazy, aestheticized distance. In 'The Long Wards' he again recalls his 'confused' impressions of the Civil War troops:

If I speak of the impression as confused I certainly justify that mark of it by my failure to be clear at this moment as to how much they were in general the worse for wear – since they can't have been exhibited to me, through their waterside settlement of tents and improvised shanties, in anything like hospital conditions. However, I cherish the rich ambiguity . . . I may not pretend now to refer it to the more particular sources it drew upon at that summer's end of 1861, or to say why my repatriated warriors were, if not somehow definitely stricken, so largely either lying in apparent helplessness or moving about in confessed languor: it suffices me that I have always thought of them as expressing themselves at almost every point in the minor key, and that this has been the reason of their interest. (*A*, p. 421)

The 'rich ambiguity' which James cherishes allows him to see every soldier as wounded, languid, prostrate.[31] In contrast to what soldiers are supposed to be, James admires, 'the note of the quite abysmal softness, the exemplary genius for accommodation, that forms the alternative aspect, the passive as distinguished from the active, of the fighting man whose business is in the first instance formidably to bristle' (WR, p. 99). Of course, James himself was famously passive during the Civil War. But what he finds in these scenes of supine male bodies, I want to suggest, is more than an arena in which he can desire, care for and get 'into relation' with formerly active, formerly 'bristling,' young men (simultaneously getting into relation with a literary precursor, Whitman, who presumably had similar desires and identifications), although this is clearly one crucial aspect of the dynamic of identification involved in this scenario.[32] What I am concerned with primarily, are the ways in which James's delighted assumption of his desire is worked out in terms of his ability to communicate with the wounded soldiers. The soldiers' collective significance shifts from their being an active destructive force to their being a passive receptive vessel, ready to receive, amongst other things, the words of Henry James. Describing the troops in Bart's he says: '. . . I *am* so struck with the charm, as I can only call it, of the tone and temper of the man of action, the creature appointed to advance and explode and destroy, and elaborately instructed as to how to do these things, reduced to helplessness in the innumerable instances now surrounding us . . . I find its sugges- tion of vast communities of patience and placidity, acceptance and submission pushed to the last point, to be just what makes the whole show most illumination [sic]' (pp. 105–106). I want to argue, only half facetiously, that the 'charm' James finds in the community that the wounded soldiers signify, has something to do with the fact that they represent a captive audience. They don't get up and leave, as the audience for *Guy Domville* did. They give him the opportunity to work out his various relations to them.

In a letter to Hugh Walpole of 1914, James writes:

> I have been going to a great hospital (St. Bart's), at the request of a medical friend there, to help give the solace of free talk to a lot of Belgian wounded and sick (so few people appear to be able to converse in the least intimately with them), and have thereby discovered my vocation in life to be the beguiling and drawing-out of the suffering soldier. The Belgians get worked off, convalesce, and are sent away, etc; but the British influx is steady, and I have lately been seeing more (always at Bart's) of *that* prostrate warrior, with whom I seem to get even better into relation. At his best he is admirable – *so* much may be made of him; of a freshness and brightness of soldier-stuff that I think must be unsurpassable. We only want more and more and more and more, of him, and I judge that we shall in due course get it.[33]

James's desire for the figure of the soldier is, as we have seen before, bound up with what 'may be made of him'. The ways in which the wounded men present themselves as grist for a devouring artistic consciousness – 'soldier-stuff' rather than individual separate soldiers – momentarily overshadow the material tragedy of how they got to the hospital in the first place. As with Ralph Pendrel's difficulty in distinguishing between wanting the past as aesthetic object and wanting to be 'in' and 'of' it, James's avowed desire for 'more and more and more and more' wounded, a veritable call for the escalation of casualties, sits uneasily with his discovery of his true vocation, his ability to comfort, 'beguile' and 'draw out', to get into relation with the suffering soldier. The long wards of St Bartholomew's Hospital, which recall the Civil War tents of distant memory, are a site for James to display his voracious desire for communication with people who might not ordinarily sit down with a Henry James novel.

If James sees the war at least partially in terms of the urgent need it sets up for passionate shared sympathetic communion, then by contrast, by the end of his life James is popularly identified (and self-identified, as the Violet Hunt story shows) with an emblematic obscurity. As Henry James, he stands for obscurity.[34] Allon White has pointed out that James's obscurity veils desire.[35] As F. M. Colby writes in a 1902 article called 'The Queerness of Henry James': 'Never did so much vice go with such sheltering vagueness.'[36] If Jamesian obscurity usually veils sexual meaning, then there are several reasons why James's writing would appear especially out of place in the context of the war; the assumption of a public/private divide dictates that a concern with sexual desire is detrimental to the public effort of war. Furthermore, James's linguistic obscurity – his endlessly refined chartings of the vicissitudes of upper-class consciousness – seems to allow for little of the quick, decisive action which war requires. Obscurity, however, does not only veil one sort of desire. For James, rather, obscurity masks homosexual desire with a more safely obscured heterosexual desire.[37] In his autobiography, James's obscure memories of the Civil War function to link the (presumably) public arena of war with the (presumably) private space of desire through his creation of the figure of the 'prostrate warrior' with whom he can then establish relations.

The public spectacle of James's obscurity in relation to the later war enacts different scenarios of shame and exposure. In 1915, James gave a newspaper interview to the *New York Times* in order to talk about the work he was doing as chairman of the American Volunteer Motor Ambulance Corps in France.[38] The dynamic of the article consists mostly of the interviewer, who refers to James as his 'victim,' trying to get James to talk about something other than the war, and James insisting that he will only talk about the war.[39] Interestingly, what the interviewer wants him to speak about is the way he uses language: 'there are many people who are eloquent about the war, who are authorities on the part played in it by the motor ambulance, and who take an interest in the good relations of Great Britain and the United States; but there is nobody who can tell us, as Mr James can, about style and the structure of sentences, and all that appertains to the aspect and value of words.'[40] James is explicit that he wants to control the content and form of the interview, insisting that 'his punctuation as well as his words . . . be noted'.[41] At this point James's precision is difficult to separate from his obscurity. His desire to be accurately portrayed is inseparable from the sense that the war is the last thing Henry James should be discussing. He is more at home with punctuation than ambulances, and ergo, he is gently attacked by the genially mocking, as well as admiring, interviewer who wishes to expose the 'real' Henry James behind the determined patriot. But James eventually winds up indicating why the war is a war which also affects words – why punctuation and ambulances are not so easily separated:

One finds it in the midst of all this as hard to apply one's words as to endure one's thoughts. The war has used up words; they have weakened, they have deteriorated like motor car tires; they have, like millions of other things, been more overstrained and knocked about and voided of the happy semblance during the last six months than in all the long ages before, and we are now confronted with a depreciation of all our terms, or otherwise speaking, with a loss of expression through increase of limpness, that may make us wonder what ghosts will be left to walk.[42]

James portrays language as world-weary, a casualty of war. In the wake of the war James's desire to control the punctuation of the interview seems tragically futile, or alternatively, encouragingly heroic, in that James will fight on to keep his words from limping. However, the interviewer's response to James's statement is deflating: 'This sounded rather desperate, yet the incorrigible interviewer, conscious of the wane of his only chance, ventured to glance at the possibility of a word or two on the subject of Mr. James's present literary intentions.'[43] It is as if he doesn't believe what James has just said about the impossibility of extracting language as an aesthetic realm separated out from the rest of the destruction, and it is as if he does not believe that James believes it either. Preston Lockwood assumes that James will continue writing novels in the same way he always has. When James places himself in the spotlight on the subject of the war, he is inevitably portrayed as embarrassingly out of place, as needing to be put back in his place, which is that of the obscure but precise artist, concerned with the minutiae of language and intimate human relations, but not with politics.

Undoubtedly Henry James on a battlefield is an unlikely person in an unlikely setting, yet, as I have shown, James consistently and emphatically places himself 'in' the war, 'in' Britain as a citizen, 'in' the convulsion, making himself into a figure of mild bemusement at the time. When the *New York Times* ran a sympathetic editorial responding to James's announcement that he had switched citizenship they picked up on the wording of his formal statement from his application for citizenship. The statement read in part:

Because of his having lived and worked in England for the best part of forty years, because of his attachment to the Country and his sympathy with it and its people, because of the long friendships and associations and interests he has formed there these last including the acquisition of some property: all of which things have brought to a head his desire to throw his moral weight and personal allegiance, for whatever they may be worth, into the scale of the contending nation's present and future fortune.[44]

The *New York Times* editorial of 29 July 1915 said: 'Henry James has long been most at home in England. Most of his friends live there. As to his desire . . . to throw his "moral weight and personal allegiance" . . . in the scale of the contending nations; his brother William might have smiled a little, but we shall not smile. The war is too grave a matter to stir much smiling, even if it is responsible in part for the loss of James's American citizenship, long lightly held.'[45] It is the idea that James's moral weight could be useful, or anything but almost totally ineffectual in this particular context, which inspires the smiling projected onto the presumably weightier (decisive, pragmatic, masculine) William. If the joke is that the moral weight of someone who spends his time writing about adulterous liaisons amongst upper class Europeans could hardly make much difference to the war effort, then the implication is that Henry James is taking himself a little too seriously. The editorial misses out the fact that James himself refers self-mockingly to the smallness of his own contribution with his 'for whatever they may be worth'. But in another sense the *New York Times*'s analysis seems correct. James's construction for himself of a space for participation in the war is partly based on taking himself too seriously, on exposing himself to the dangers of outrageous identifications and fantastic claims.

According to H. Montgomery Hyde, Edith Wharton recalls James bursting into a luncheon party at the height of the discussion about the war:

'My hands, I must wash them!' he cried. 'My hands are dripping with blood. All the way from Chelsea to Grosvenor Place I have been bayoneting, my dear Edith, and hurling bombs and ravishing and raping. It is my day-dream to squat down with King George of England, with the President of the French Republic and the Czar of Russia, on the Emperor William's belly, until we squeeze out of it the last irrevocable drops of bitter retribution.' Mrs. Wharton, who shared Henry's patriotic feelings, said that she must have a seat with the others, 'No, Edith,' was the stern reply. 'That imperial stomach is no seat for ladies. This is a war for men only: it is a war for me and poor Logan.'[46]

The astounding spectacle of James and various heads of state bumping up against each other on the exclusive men's club of the

Kaiser's belly, squeezing out drops of retribution, hardly requires much explication. Its jubilantly over-the-top rhetoric (whether James's or assigned to James by his jubilantly over-the-top biographer H. Montgomery Hyde is not really my concern here) allows James phantasmatically to 'be a man', create a thrilling homoerotic community from the homosocial links which war instantiates. This passage allows James to participate in the war effort, in a way which he did not in his previous experience of the American Civil War.[47] It is to that war as James describes it in his autobiography that I now turn.

In a famously obscure incident from his autobiography James sustains some sort of unspecified injury while helping to put out a barn fire with a number of other men: 'I had done myself, in face of a shabby conflagration, a horrid even if an obscure hurt' (*A*, p. 415). Paul John Eakin has shown that the chronology James sets up which indicates that the wound was his reason for not entering the army is not verified by the facts.[48] Hence the incident seems to be satisfying some need apart from autobiographical 'truth.' Critics have interpreted the hurt variously as a compensatory excuse for his non-participation in the Civil War, as a symbolic castration, as an identification with a similar wounding of his father, and as the scene of the young James's initiation into the aesthetic life.[49] Adrian Poole has indicated the linkages that the wound constructs for James: 'This hurt became a means of establishing the war's "presence for me." It was for the writing, remembering James, no less symbolic than real, a way of insisting that war takes place for bodies off the battlefield as well as on it, and that it assails something other than the body.'[50] I want read the analogy that James constructs between his wounds and the wounds of the country, as an element of James's 'theater of embarrassment' which functions as an enabling device – a queer entry into wartime community formation.

In James's scenario, both he and America experience wounds simultaneously:

Two things and more had come up – the biggest of which, and very wondrous as bearing on any circumstance of mine, as having a grain of weight to spare for it, was the breaking out of the War. The other, the infinitely small affair in comparison, was a passage of personal history the most entirely personal, but between which, as a private catastrophe or difficulty, bristling with embarrassments, and the great public convulsion that announced itself in bigger terms each day, I felt from the very first an association of the closest, yet withal, I fear, almost of the least clearly expressible. (*A*, pp. 414–415)

There's an obscure connection between James's obscure wound and the wounds of the nation at war. The private catastrophe and the public catastrophe are hard to hold together when one seems like a shameful excuse for avoiding the other, but James's insistence upon the linkage between the two is, amongst other things, an insistence upon his shame – an exposure of himself in his impossible relation to his first nation at war. Shame becomes a method of exposing the strange relationship between his attacked individual body and the attacked social body – a relation James refers to as 'the queer fusion or confusion established in my consciousness' (*A*, p. 414). Here James uses his own obscurity to both finesse and create the connection between the psychic and the social, which can also be identified with the connection made in the *New York Times* interview between words and the war. Ambivalence defines this analogy in its insistence upon its truth simultaneously to its utter lack of confidence about its validity:

. . . the interlaced, undivided way in which what had happened to me, by a turn of fortune's hand in twenty odious minutes, kept company of the most unnatural – I can call it nothing less – with my view of what was happening, with the question of what might still happen, to everyone about me, to the company at large: it so made of these marked disparities a single vast visitation. One had the sense, I mean, of a huge comprehensive ache, and there were hours at which one could scarce have told whether it came from one's own poor organism, still so young and so meant for better things, but which had suffered particular wrong, or from the enclosing social body, a body rent with a thousand wounds and that thus treated one to the honour of a sort of tragic fellowship. The twenty minutes had sufficed, at all events, to establish a relation – a relation to everything occurring round me not only for the next four years but for long afterward – that was at once extraordinarily intimate and quite awkwardly irrelevant. (*A*, pp. 414–415)

A 'company of the most unnatural' establishes itself between that posited synchronicity – James's body identified as the social body – and the embarrassment about the outrageousness of this claim, the gap in proportion between James's small hurt and the savage wounds of the country. The extraordinarily intimate and quite awkwardly irrelevant relationship between the two events can be seen as pointing to a rift which exists within any individual's identification with a larger social body. If there is an unbridgeable gap between the psychic and the social, between the individual's experience of history and History with a capital H, we may have no real choice but to make these dangerous, potentially irresponsible, often embarrassing analogies between what I spy with my little eye and what transpires out of sight on the world stage. James continues: 'Interest, the interest of life and of death, of our national existence, of the fate of those, the vastly numerous, whom it closely concerned, the interest of the extending war, in fine, the hurrying troops, the transfigured scene, formed a cover for every sort of intensity, made tension itself in fact contagious – so that almost any tension would do, would serve for one's share' (A, pp. 415–416). This 'cover' reads as both an excuse for taking on an unjustifiable identification ('any tension would do'), and a closet-like structure in which transgressive 'intensities' – desires for other men, for the nation's body – can be expressed under the sanction of shared fears, shared patriotism. But to turn that excuse around, contagious tension is also one plausible way of thinking about what it might mean to construct a nation during wartime – what sorts of shared identifications, desires, and fears go into building the necessary bridges between the mass and the individual experience which war so urgently requires.

Like James's tension, shame is also contagious. Sedgwick says, 'Shame – living as it does, on and in the capillaries and the muscles of the face – seems to be uniquely contagious from one person to another. Indeed, one of the strangest features of shame (but also, I would argue, the most theoretically significant) is the way bad treatment of someone else, bad treatment *by* someone else, someone else's embarrassment, stigma, debility, blame or pain, seemingly having nothing to do with me, can so readily flood me . . . with this sensation whose very suffusiveness seems to delineate my precise, individual outlines in the most isolating way imaginable.'[51] Shame makes the person in the process of making her stand out from the crowd, yet paradoxically shame is also a disease of the crowd – mimetically transmissible, easily shared without obvious cause. Think of the phrase 'a nation's shame', and the difficulty in trying to chart out what share any given individual holds in it. Through its potential transmissibility shame emerges as a successful identification with a failed identification – a blush that spreads across the face and across the mass.

James's magical faith in the efficacy of his own consciousness is sometimes painful to witness. Inevitably, the reader of James's autobiography finds herself at times treating James, like the doctor who looks at him after he sustains his obscure hurt, to a 'comparative pooh-pooh'(*A*, p. 416). In his difficult, embarrassing identification with an America torn apart by civil war, James takes on a martyrdom which is arguably not his to take on, but in exposing his own 'intimate and quite awkwardly irrelevant' relationship to national events, he participates in nation-constructing, homoerotically charged stagings of dilemmas of identification, dilemmas he will later restage in his World War I propaganda and in *The Sense of the Past*. There may be no secure way of diagnosing the relation between the social convulsion and the individual body. This is not to claim that these two things are identical but that we, with James rather than against him, should take their connection seriously, and that we should take his embarrassment seriously. The problem, which only becomes more visible and acute during wartime, is that identifying with one's country, as a whole, or through the separate bodies which appear to constitute it, is as vexed a process as desiring it. James's unsatisfiable desires at the end of his life to identify with the mass, or, as in *The Sense of the Past*, to take on and enter into history, seem to re-enact the obscure-hurt scene from his auto-biography – provoking scenes of intense shame and exposure but also of triumphant overcoming through jubilantly pleasurable col-lapses of desires and identifications. James's attempts to say 'we' may have failed, may have embarrassed him, may even have killed him, but perhaps, they also moved him, and us, further towards the recognition of what was always already a queer nation.

CHAPTER 4

On the typewriter, In the Cage, *at the Ouija board*

Twenty million young women rose to their feet and said 'We will not be dictated to' and immediately became shorthand typists.[1]

In 1897 Henry James began dictating to an amanuensis (his preferred word for secretary or literary assistant) who typed his works, and sometimes his letters, directly into a Remington typewriter. In his entertaining biography of James, *Henry James at Home,* H. Montgomery Hyde devotes some pages to describing James's relationship with his various secretaries, from his first assistant William MacAlpine, who typed stoically through *The Turn of the Screw* without, according to James, betraying the least frisson of fright or interest, to his replacement Mary Weld, who used to crochet during James's pauses in dictation, to her replacement, Theodora Bosanquet, who went on to make her mark as a Bloomsbury feminist and author. Theodora Bosanquet's relationship to James was more lasting than that of her predecessors – she began as a fan of his and worked for him until he died. James was apparently relieved to finally have a kindred spirit at his typewriter, saying to her: 'Among the faults of my previous amanuenses – not by any means the *only* fault – was their apparent lack of comprehension of what I was driving at.'[2] One might argue that that particular lack of comprehension isn't specific to James's long-suffering secretaries. It could be levelled at a good portion of James's audience, then and now. But it does bring up the question of how knowledgeable the ideal secretary should be. Must one know to record? What sort of relationship does the act of dictation beget between author and recorder?

In this chapter I will consider two accounts of how intimacy comes to be mediated through teletechnology around the turn of the century, and how new communication technologies such as the

86

telegraph and the typewriter are instrumental in creating transgressive fantasies of access to others who would be otherwise inaccessible to the fantasizing operators of these technologies, because of gender and class barriers, or that even more difficult to negotiate barrier between the living and the dead. The occult significance of tele-technologies, established through the structuring analogies I discussed in my first chapter, manifests itself both in a story such as James's *In the Cage,* his 1898 novella about a telegraph office, and in his relationship with his principal secretary Theodora Bosanquet, both during James's life and after his death. In both cases mediumship extends its boundaries; lines are crossed; relationships which are primarily instrumental when seen from the message senders' perspectives may become intimate, occult and powerfully invasive when seen from the perspective of the mediators. Both *In the Cage,* and the story told by Theodora Bosanquet's archive, culled from piles of her automatic writing and unpublished autobiographical material, are stories of mediums exploring the potential pleasures and dangers of carrying the words of others. Both stories suggest how simultaneously intense, erotic and distancing mediation, at its most material level, can be. Both stories enact complicated power dynamics of class and gender between a male message composer and a female medium. Both lead back towards telepathy and contact with the dead through the question of what it means to have secretarially sanctioned access to the inside of another's mind, and both bring up the vexed question of economics – the question of who pays for whose words.

Entering the emerging secretarial profession at the turn of the century meant negotiating and establishing that profession's boundaries. The typewriter has often been portrayed as a tool for women's emancipation and entrance into the workforce: 'apart from Freud, it was Remington who "granted the female sex access to the office"'.[3] From its inception the typewriter was imagined as a technology that would be especially liberating for women. Christopher Sholes, the designer of the first commercially produced typewriter, claimed, 'I do feel I have done something for the women who have always had to work so hard. This will enable them more easily to earn a living.'[4] Although the truth of this claim is debatable – Morag Shiach and others have challenged the notion that the entry of women into the workforce and the development of the typewriter are related in obvious causal ways – it is clear that New Women and typewriting were associated at the time.[5] Neither was the typewriter necessarily emancipating for women. The eventual association of women with typewriting was probably inevitable considering that they could be paid significantly less than men for the same work. Henry James shares the joy of this discovery, as he exclaims in a letter, 'Mac-Alpine's lady successor is an improvement on him! And an economy!'[6]

MacAlpine's successor, Mary Weld, was trained at Miss Petheridge's Secretarial Bureau, one of many schools for typewriting and related skills which were springing up at the time.[7] Businesses such as Miss Petheridge's clearly sold certain expectations of class respectability along with the typing skills of the women they trained. After Miss Weld left his employ James returned to the same bureau to find her replacement. At the time Henry writes to his brother William:

My pressing want is some sound, sane irreproachable young type-writing and bicycling 'secretary companion,' the expense of which would be practically a 100 fold made up by increased facilitation of paying work. But though I consider the post enviable, it is difficult to fill. The young typists are mainly barbarians, and the civilized here are not typists.[8]

When James characterizes the potential typing pool in 1898 as 'mainly barbarians' he may be referring to their working-class origins, or their inability to get what he was driving at. However the mediating messenger pictured as barbarian also would not be an entirely arbitrary linkage because of the Cleveland Street Scandal of 1889–1890. In 1889 the police interrogated a fifteen-year-old telegraph messenger boy who had been selling his services from a brothel in the West End at 19 Cleveland Street. The ensuing scandal implicated a large number of aristocratic men including the second in line to the throne, Prince Albert Victor.[9] The roving telegraph boy, the working-class boy on the streets travelling from 'good' home to 'good' home, in possession of private potentially scandalous information about the upper classes, became a locus for fears of contamination, blackmail and homosocial panic, as Cohen amply shows. An 1890 *Scots Observer* review of *Dorian Gray* suggested that, 'Mr Wilde has brains, and art, and style, but if he can write for none but outlawed noblemen and perverted telegraph boys, the sooner he takes to tailoring (or some other decent trade) the better for his own reputation and the public morals.'[10] In James's own *What Maisie*

Knew, telegraph boys 'haunt' Maisie's dubiously moral father Beale Farange's door, 'kick(ing) their heels while, in his room, answers to their missives took form with the aid of smoke-puffs and growls'.[11]

James's uncivilized typists may partake of the taint of Cleveland Street, but the scandal of typewriting is of a somewhat different nature from the scandal of telegraphing, perhaps because the typical typist is of a somewhat different gender than the typical telegraph boy. Rather than being out and about, spreading words and lord knows what else, the typist is enclosed with his or her author in a potentially sexualized private space. When Mary Weld first became James's secretary, the unfamiliar familiarity of the secretary/author relationship made the establishment of proper codes of dress and behaviour a necessity, as did the gender shift from a male to female secretary. As Weld recalled, 'a certain woman in Rye came to Lamb House to make sure that everything was "respectable" – since so young a lady was working for an elderly bachelor'.[12] Much had to be negotiated in the process of becoming Henry James's secretary: 'they discussed what she should do during the long pauses that sometimes occurred during dictation. MacAlpine had smoked; it was settled that she should crochet. James escorted her into Lamb House proper for lunch where she met the William Jameses. There was a long discussion at table as to what an amanuensis should wear for such duties. Mrs William agreed that a "suit" – that is a dark coat and skirt – would be appropriate.'[13] For James, Mary Weld clearly differed from her predecessor MacAlpine in ways that relate to the question of why and how women were imagined as being better secretaries than men. James described the difference between the two in a letter to the Duchess of Sunderland, 'he had too much Personality – and I have secured in his place a young lady who has, to the best of my belief, less, or who disguises it more'.[14] For James the constitution of the perfect secretary shifts. After MacAlpine's apparent excess of personality, perhaps figured through his smoking and stoicism, an empty vessel seems like a relief; yet after Weld a comprehending reader is James's greatest desire. With Theodora Bosanquet James finally has found what he's looking for – a civilized typist.[15]

When Bosanquet began working for James in October 1907, James wrote to his brother William expressing his satisfaction with his new 'excellent amanuensis, a young boyish Miss Bosanquet, who is worth all the other (females) that I have had put together and who confirms me in the perception afresh – after eight months without such an agent – that for certain, for most, kinds of diligence and production, the invention of an agent is, to *my* perverse constitution, an intense aid and a true economy! There is no comparison!'[16] The psychic and economic investments in such a vessel, the perverse eroticism of the boyish Miss Bosanquet as well as her salary – make intimacy with one's secretary the product of a complex of medium-istic and economic relations which are simultaneously imagined as distancing techniques that fend intimacy off. The 'agent' invented is first and foremost a tool. The word typewriter originally meant both the machine itself and the person who worked it. But what then might the invention of an agent look like from that agent's perspective?

Rudyard Kipling's story 'Wireless' suggested some of the ways in which analogies between technological mediums and spiritualist ones were being deployed by the cultural imaginary of the early twentieth century. In this chapter I will consider the ways in which the place of the primarily female deployers of these new technologies becomes more than just analogically significant for fantasies about mediation, economics, language and intimate knowledge of others' minds. Secretaries are, on the one hand, tools – ideally meant to function as unmediating recorders of another's thoughts, like the dictating machines they themselves employ. On the other hand, secretaries are, as mediums, never themselves unmediating. When information travels it changes – it becomes open to reinterpretation and negotiation, it is cathected and de-cathected in new ways. Language is both the medium for and the content of this circulation. During the process of the exchange of information, language takes on new valences. Words can be, and constantly are, quantified and valued in terms of market requirements, yet they simultaneously retain their privileged position as the medium of affective communi-cation, intimacy and relations in the world.

Mary Weld recorded in her diary that *The Wings of the Dove* was begun on 9 July 1901 and finished on 21 May 1902, and that the work involved 194 days of dictation.[17] In her memoir of James, *Henry James at Work*, Theodora Bosanquet recalls their first interview in somewhat different terms: 'He invited me to ask any questions I liked, but I had none to ask. I wanted nothing but to be allowed to go to Rye and work his typewriter.'[18] If Mary seems only to count words, and Theodora seems only to lust for access to James's mind and machinery, then these two versions of mediation meet in Jacques

Lacan's psychoanalytic theory of the quantification of desire in language. Lacan's seminar on 'The Circuit' indicates that Mary Weld's and Theodora Bosanquet's attitudes towards James's words are not necessarily at odds with each other, that a language of quantification (and the quantification of language) coexists with a language of desire, and that the telegraphist's entrapping cage in James's novella, is in part constructed by this very fact.

In *In the Cage*, language is imagined as quantifiable and material. The nameless heroine of the story works in a telegraph office where her job is to count words and put a price on them: 'Her function was to . . . more than anything else, count words as numberless as the sands of the sea, the words of the telegrams thrust, from morning to night, through the gap left in the high lattice, across the encumbered shelf that her forearm ached with rubbing.'[19] The words thrust through the high gap and the telegraphist's perpetually rubbed and aching forearm represent counting words as a form of sexualized drudgery, converting the potential for desire in language into a prostitution-like business proposition.

Jacques Lacan imagines a similarly quantitative and unerotic fate for desiring language in his seminar 'The Circuit'. In Lacan's allegory of the Symbolic, a telephone system rather than a telegraph office is made into a metaphor for how language works and how communication takes place. For Lacan, telephonic communication takes place within a limited system where structure takes precedent over content. The Bell Telephone Company's need to 'pass the greatest possible number of communications down one single wire' suggests that information is both material and quantifiable.[20] Further, within this system, the success of the telephone connection '. . . (has) nothing to do with knowing whether what people tell each other makes any sense' (TC, p. 82). What is said on the phone, Lacan suggests, never makes any sense:

But one communicates, one recognises the modulation of a human voice, and as a result one has that appearance of understanding which comes with the fact that one recognises words one already knows. It is a matter of knowing what are the most economical conditions which enable one to transmit the words people recognise. No one cares about the meaning. (TC, p. 82)

On the telephone one only hears what one already knows and this is always within the limited number of things one could possibly be hearing. The structure of the Symbolic, or the telephone connection, creates the illusion of communication in the absence of any firmly transmissible content. The limiting powers of this circuit system create the conditions necessary for what Lacan says Freud misla-belled telepathy:

Think back on what we said in preceding years about those striking coincidences Freud noted in the sphere of what he calls telepathy. Very important things, in the way of transference, occur in parallel in two patients, whether one is in analysis and the other just on the fringes, or whether both are in analysis. At that time, I showed you how it is through being links, supports, rings in the same circle of discourse, agents integrated in the same circle of discourse, that the subjects simultaneously experience such and such a symptomatic act, or discover such and such a memory. (TC, p. 89)

Lacan here assimilates telepathy to coincidence, coincidence which is more likely to happen the smaller and more limited the system you are working in is. In a sense Lacan's schema, this 'coincidence,' becomes the basis on which depends all intersubjectivity (the enabling illusion that we understand what others are saying); we can communicate because we share the fact that we are all links in the same 'inhuman' system, the Symbolic:

This discourse of the other . . . is the discourse of the circuit in which I am integrated. I am one of its links. It is the discourse of my father for instance, in so far as my father made mistakes which I am absolutely condemned to reproduce – that's what we call the *super-ego*. I am condemned to reproduce them because I am obliged to pick up again the discourse he bequeathed to me, not simply because I am his son, but because one can't stop the chain of discourse, and it is precisely my duty to transmit it in its aberrant form to someone else. (TC, p. 89)

Lacan's version of transmission invokes a phylogenetic fantasy, a Lamarckian inheritance, a swallowing and passing on of stories which create the possibility of substitution, identification, and understanding. Absolutely condemned to inherit the sins of the father, the son becomes a link in the chain of the signifier. Unable to process and assimilate the information which structures him, he is condemned to a blind, mimetic repetition of a past which isn't properly his, which can't properly be said to belong to anyone, but which grounds all subjectivity in language and desire. For Lacan the Oedipal structure and the Symbolic work, machine-like, repetitively churning out subjects of desire.

Derrida's critique of Lacan points out that Lacan's limited system

and the material and quantifiable nature of language is the product
of a metaphysics of presence, a system which centres around the
phallus.[21] Once Lacan has installed a closed circuit centred around
the phallus, then a letter always arrives at its destination; then at
least the illusion of communication is always possible; then, since we
are all implicated in the Oedipal structure, we inherit a big problem
from our parents.

The logic of Lacan's circuit may be suspect, but the fantasy his
logic engages is worth thinking about further, especially because it
manages to interlock two apparently opposed ways of thinking about
communication. One pole might be labelled telepathy – the fantasy
of total communication, from mind to mind without interference
(and with this version of telepathy I would include love or intimacy –
an emotional tie which might be pictured as, if not beyond language,
a place where language between two people would not be necessary).
The other pole to this is the idea of language as material, quantifiable – words as things to be counted. Both in Lacan's 'Circuit' and
in *In the Cage* this pole turns out to be inextricable from and
sometimes indistinguishable from the first pole.

At times *In the Cage* lays out these two versions of language as
incompatible. When the telegraphist complains to her friend Mrs
Jordan that she hates her wealthy customers, Mrs Jordan replies:

'Ah, that's because you've no sympathy!'
   The girl gave an ironic laugh, only retorting that she wouldn't have any
either if she had to count all day the words in a dictionary. . . (pp. 145–146)

Here, it seems that sympathy and sympathetic imagination, the
ability to enter into other people's minds and lives, is set against the
deadening task of counting words – breaking down sympathy into its
component linguistic parts. Words are drained of meaning and
subjects are demystified and drained of affect when words become
calculable objects. Yet this desire to separate language into its
sympathetic (human, meaning-filled) use and its object-like
(inhuman, deadening) use falls apart during the course of the story.

The story begins with the paradoxically powerful position of the
aspiring lower-class heroine: 'It had occurred to her early that in her
position – that of a young person spending in framed and wired
confinement, the life of a guinea pig or a magpie – she should know
a great many persons without their recognizing the acquaintance'
(p. 119). The telegraphist may be trapped but she is also in the

position of the Foucauldian panopticon surveyor – she sees (into minds at least) without being seen. Yet, there is another sense in which her position in the cage puts her on a perversely simultaneously sexualized and desexualized display. In *Discourse Networks*, Friedrich Kittler maintains that around 1900 the image of woman as sexual object and woman as mother (in other words the image of woman as sex worker) is in essence replaced in the cultural imagination by woman as information worker – typist, telegraphist, relayer of others' information. Kittler points out that these new information worker jobs are rapidly devalued and coded female; women as secretaries, like Mina Harker in *Dracula*, become the 'central relay station(s)' for vast networks of usually male-manipulated information.[22] Kittler pictures this as a replacement of older images of female sexuality with a new one – sex (or the lack of it) in the age of mechanical reproduction: 'In the discourse network of 1900– this is its open secret – there is no sexual relation between the sexes.'[23] Kittler's thesis is compelling but I am not sure he entirely takes into account the ways in which the sorts of desexualization of woman he points to often work in tandem with an instant resexualization or rematernalization of women. The typewriter can be imagined as bringing the comforting female presence into the male sphere. The angel in the house becomes the angel in the office:

. . . at this point [the publication date of *In the Cage*] in both Britain and America the presence of women in office and clerical jobs was burgeoning. Where even twenty years previous to the 1898 date of publication only a miniscule percentage of office workers were women by the 1890s secretarial and clerical work was firmly gendered. Part of this impetus derived from the technology of the typewriter – not entirely obvious as a specifically 'feminine' mechanical instrument, but designed as an amalgam of the sewing machine and the piano to allow women to confidently enter the work force, familiar with these devices from domestic techniques, and there to receive less money than had formerly been paid for hand copying to men. The ameliorative presence of the woman in the office sphere is lauded in these ways by an anonymous male employer in the *Phonographic World* for 1890: 'They carry with them an air of refinement and a sense of fidelity that is comforting to a busy, worried man. They seem to belong to the place somehow to fit in deficiencies. A girl, such as I have in mind, has her eyes about her, she is full of sympathy, constantly on the alert for unpleasant things which she may avert or turn to good account. She anticipates the wishes of her employer and gratifies them almost before he has them.'[24]

As this quote indicates women are still expected to act like women even in the mechanized workplace. New forms of technical mediation, and the markets in which these forms take place, have their own erotics which can be, but are not necessarily, tied to older versions of feminine sexuality. For instance, in *In the Cage* the heroine is on display, both for the men who work around her, her grocer fiancé, Mr. Mudge, and the counter clerk, whose desire for her she manipulates in order to get the customers she wants; and for her wealthy customers, specifically Captain Everard once he has 'noticed' her outside the cage. Initially the cage may be a place where the telegraphist, as the invisible medium of communication between others, can see without being seen. But when the frame of that relationship is broken, as it is with Everard, the telegraphist becomes a target of the desiring male gaze which will always know where to find her. She sees this when she imagines herself in the cage, as a 'picture of servitude and promiscuity' to the outside world (p. 142).

The heroine who counts words all day also imagines herself (and rightly so, as the story eventually indicates) in close contact with the people whose messages she relays. In this story commodification quantifies things which we often like to imagine as part of the realm of affective or non-market relations, for instance words and flowers. The heroine's friend Mrs Jordan, the impoverished widow of a clergyman, 'had invented a new career for women' (p. 122). She arranges flowers for the houses of the wealthy. Both careers, telegraphing and flower arranging, set up the fantasy of crossing class lines for the two women by allowing them a certain fantasized intimate access to the privileged lives of their clients. Yet both of these careers are also viewed by the heroine as being about quantifiable market relations. Fantasies of power and access: 'combinations of flowers and green-stuff, forsooth! What *she* could handle freely, she said to herself, was combinations of men and women' (p. 123) both merge and conflict with questions of economics: 'a thousand tulips at a shilling clearly took one further than a thousand words at a penny' (p. 142).

At times it seems that when intimacy (either the intimacy the telegraphist imagines existing between herself and her customers, or the intimate relations between people that she views by dispatching their telegraphs) is quantified, it loses its appeal: 'The only weakness in her faculty came from the positive abundance of her contact with the human herd; this was so constant, had the effect of becoming so cheap, that there were long stretches in which inspiration, divination and interest quite dropped' (p. 123). Too much intimacy makes that sort of knowledge of others' minds 'cheap'. Her knowledge participates in a market economy in which the over-availability of goods sends the price down. The unique relationships between people to which the telegraphist has access are shown to be commodified and quantified from the perspective of the cage. And, as the perspective of the cage ends up determining the marriage between Lady Bradeen and Everard (the telegraphist's fateful intervention seems to force them into a blackmail-induced marriage neither of them may have wanted), it becomes clear that the 'intimate' relation the heroine sees as existing between those two is both determined by her action, and already, initially and finally, a money matter. Intimacy is inseparable from information flow which is inseparable from economics.

The telegraphist's own consciousness seems uneasily affected by her job, which both gives her access to the world of other consciousnesses and simultaneously cheapens that world through its sheer quantifiability: 'She had surrendered herself moreover, of late, to a certain expansion of her consciousness; something that seemed perhaps vulgarly accounted for by the fact that, as the blast of the season roared louder and the waves of fashion tossed their spray further over the counter, there were more impressions to be gathered and really – for it came to that – more life to be led' (p. 124). The vulgar way of accounting for expansion of consciousness would be to say that consciousness could be counted. The telegraphist expands her own consciousness, makes herself more herself and makes more of herself, through her 'relations' with her customers, which increase or decrease depending upon the season, and which finally break down into the words of the messages that she counts and charges them for. For James the potential vulgarity of consciousness seems to lie in the possibility of locating it so precisely. As Sharon Cameron indicates, consciousness in late James seems to exist between people, in relations, rather than 'inside' them in any sense.[25] Whether a particular sentence is thought or spoken in late James is often impossible to determine, and who is doing the thinking or speaking is sometimes similarly occluded. Instead of mystifying the Jamesian sense of consciousness, or even just psychologizing it (Cameron points out that whatever consciousness means for James, it cannot be contained by what we normally think of as psychology), *In the Cage,* because of its, for James, unusually explicit portrayal of class relations and commercial exchange, allows the reader to think about how questions of communication and consciousness in other works by James might also be related to economics and technology. The ways in which consciousness in late James is externalized are in a continuum with the externalizing impetus of new communication technologies and the fantasies about communication that these technologies inspire at the turn of the century.

This model of exteriorization is made manifest in *In the Cage* where the telegraphist's expansion of consciousness resides wholly outside herself in the information she collates, counts and crucially commits to memory. The development of an information-based, service-oriented society sets the grounds for the sense of intimacy between the telegraphist and Everard. From one perspective, the real basis of this intimacy is the threat of blackmail. Blackmail, as Alexander Welsh points out, 'is an opportunity afforded to everyone by communication of knowledge at a distance. The communications are exposed – more so by the electric telegraph than by the post – to agents who have no personal relation to the sender or receiver and hence no personal reason to guard their secrets.'[26] The Cleveland Street telegraph boys with their personal/impersonal (economically mediated) sex and their personal/impersonal (economically mediated) information were the frightening harbingers of a new age of blackmail. Eric Savoy says of *In the Cage*: '. . . the ways in which its upper-class subjects come to represent themselves as at risk of scandalous humiliation are governed entirely by juridical deploy-ment of the working-class person who knew too much to ensure the conviction of transgressive aristocrats in sensational court trials of the 1890s'.[27] This scenario culminates of course with Oscar Wilde's trial in 1895. However, foregrounding the Foucauldian 'juridical deployment' of the working class mediator/blackmailer ignores his or her probably constrained, but still complicated, motives. *In the Cage* shows that intimacy – the Jamesian 'personal relation' – is constructed from the same material as blackmail. James's heroine creates a personal interest, her sense of 'relation' to Everard, precisely from her knowledge of him. She transforms impersonal, unattached, collatable and, when translated, valuable (in blackmail terms) knowledge, into intimacy, just as she translates Everard's banal exchanges with her, the 'Oh yes, hasn't it been awfully wet?'

(p. 155), into a different sort of utopian–arbitrary economics of
language, one in which 'everything . . . might mean almost anything'
(p. 155).

When the telegraphist fantasizes an intimate scene between herself
and Everard she can only picture it as a scene of blackmail. She
imagines herself saying, '"I know too much about a certain person
now not to put it to you – excuse my being so lurid – that it's quite
worth your while to buy me off. Come, therefore; buy me!" There
was a point indeed at which such flights had to drop again – the point
of an unreadiness to name, when it came to that, the purchasing
medium. It wouldn't certainly, be anything so gross as money, and the
matter accordingly remained rather vague, all the more that *she* was
not a bad girl' (p. 158). Money or sex are set up here as the only two
imaginable purchasing mediums. As Wicke says of Everard and the
telegraphist: 'Their relation is so transparently a commercial transaction that to suffuse it with the erotics of knowledge the text employs
the vocabulary of prostitution to suggest its singularity.'[28] Yet, to
imagine the 'erotics of knowledge' as simply a cover for the real
modes of exchange (prostitution and other commercial transactions)
which determine the 'real' relations of this story seems to me like
substituting one fantasy of what it means to be in relation to someone
(the fantasy of what happens when people exchange money) for
another (the fantasy of what happens when people exchange knowledge or when one person has access to another's knowledge). The
heroine of *In the Cage* replaces a potential sexual or money relationship with a sense of intimacy which springs from her knowledge of
Everard, and culminates in her desire, not for sexual contact but to
do something for him (to help him and to put him in her debt) by
means of sending or receiving information: 'As yet, however, she
could only rub along with the hope that an accident, sooner or later,
might give her a lift toward popping out with something that would
surprise and perhaps even, some fine day, assist him' (p. 156). The
triumphant moment in which she recalls from memory the words of
his encoded message shows that she, in her position as storehouse of
information, may actually know more about him than he knows
about himself, even if that knowledge is for her unreadable because
encoded. At the end of the nineteenth century owning or having
access to one's own life is a tricky business when new forms of
information technology are making storage and retrieval of things
like memory recognizably a matter of exteriorization.

In *In the Cage* that overloaded Jamesian word, 'relation' relies on mediation through technology, or its human equivalent – the new, primarily female, human storehouse of information as exemplified by the telegraphist in *In the Cage* or Mina Harker in *Dracula.* It is impossible for the telegraphist to imagine intimacy outside of this definition of 'relation', because the two apparently conflicting definitions of language – as the vehicle of human contact (meaning, reference) and as words to be counted (materiality) – actually coincide: 'the flood of longing coexists with the language of quantification: what James's text spells out is a calculus of desire performed in words, on the page'.[29] The complicated commercial and emotional negotiations of *In the Cage* indicate that we have to imagine this as happening both 'in' language and in the sphere of commercial transactions in ways in which one does not entirely determine the other. The intimate relation, or it might be more accurate to say the perception and/or invention of intimacy in James, is a product of this paradoxical, often voyeuristically enjoyed, layering of relations mediated through sex, economics and the limits of language.[30]

The telegraphist in *In the Cage* manufactures a sort of telepathic intimacy from a commercial transaction, in the process blurring the boundaries between money, mediation and love. Yet, for someone embroiled in a similar set of circumstances, *In the Cage* hardly represents a triumph of possibility for the expansive secretarial-class spirit. On Tuesday, 29 October 1907, Theodora Bosanquet wrote in her diary: 'Mr. James away in town so I had a free day. Went round to his house however & carried off an armful of books & spent most of the day reading Turgenev's "Smoke" and "In the Cage" by Henry James. It's just the right length for its subject – really awfully good. It makes me feel desperate though.'[31] To understand why *In the Cage* might make one's secretary feel desperate we need to think further about the constructions and/or failures of possible relationships between author and mediator. How do we determine the status of mediators' intimacies as fantasy or reality? Critics have argued about the level of the narrator's delusion in *In the Cage,* and James's intentions towards her, some becoming downright hostile. E. Duncan Aswell refers to 'the feeble fantasies of her worthless fiction'.[32] It is to the construction of Bosanquet's and James's similarly intimate and mediated relationship that I now wish to turn, a relationship which could also easily be labelled deluded by those unsympathetic to the goals of spiritualism and psychical research. Yet this relationship is also one I want to take seriously.

After James's death in 1916, Theodora Bosanquet moved on from secretarial work to other forms of literary activities: 'in her work for James she was submerging her distinct personality and cultivated literary tastes. She was in every way a true hand-maiden to the Master. When he was dead, she was able to enter on her own career.'[33] Bosanquet refused an offer from Edith Wharton to work for her and went on to an active and varied career. She wrote books on Paul Valéry and Harriet Martineau, as well as a memoir of what it was like to work for James, *Henry James at Work*, which was published by the Hogarth Press in 1924.[34] She acted as secretary to the International Federation of University Women and was the literary editor of the journal *Time and Tide* for nine years, for which she wrote reviews and poetry. She also became an active member of the Society for Psychical Research, editing its journal during World War II.

Bosanquet describes herself and her developing interest in psychical research in an unfinished manuscript for a book on the immortality of the soul:

A training in science (biology, geology, elementary physics), a profound admiration for the life and opinions of Thomas Henry Huxley, a genuine feeling for poetry, a fair knowledge of nineteenth century English literature. To that equipment I added a persistent interest in psychical research. Not a burning interest but enough to produce a guinea a year out of a slender income as the subscription of an Associate member of the Society for Psychical Research.[35]

Her interest in psychical research was already active when she was working for Henry James. She discussed her enthusiasm with William James, who, although a dedicated psychical researcher himself, was sometimes sceptical in return:

'*10 September 1908*: Saw Professor James and told him of my interest in the Society of Psychical Research report [on automatic writing]. He said I evidently had a logical mind! He found it hard to keep the threads clear! Horrid sarcasm.' On another occasion, seeing that Miss Bosanquet was reading a book on spiritualism, he told her a 'new era' was dawning in these matters.[36]

Bosanquet was to become intensely engrossed in sittings with mediums and her own experiences of automatic writing, living out the similarities between her secretarial position and the spiritual world. She took careful notes at her live-in companion the Viscoun-tess Rhondda's sittings with mediums, and eventually became heavily involved in automatic writing which she engaged in consis-tently during the 1930s and 1940s. According to her notes, on 15 February 1933 she anonymously attended a sitting with Mrs Hester Dowden, a medium who was known for her ability to contact literary figures.[37] Mrs Dowden's spirit guide Johannes relayed a message through a Ouija board, spelling out the name of Henry James, and then proceeded to answer correctly various questions about the gardener's name at Rye, etc.[38] James, it turned out, wanted to re-engage Theodora as his secretary, saying through the Ouija board, 'I have come because I, with many others, have felt that a literary circle should endeavour to add to the evidence you have of our world. It has been discussed here and it is felt that we should try to give something to the world that is at least in a sense literary work.'[39] There is, it seems, a dearth of good secretarial help on the other side. A posse of recently and not so recently deceased writers require her services:

Johannes: (in answer to a question about how and when an attempt should be made to assist H.J. to communicate) 'I should like you to wait until the Rilke book is finished, then devote an evening to the attempt to get these people to communicate. I believe the idea is to write (each) a characteristic essay through the hand of your sitter.'
   (By the ouija we were told that in addition to Henry James, Meredith, Hardy and Galsworthy wanted to try. Mrs. Dowden thought it was hardly likely that Galsworthy would be ready to communicate so soon after his death).[40]

The negotiations with James (William appears later on) continue for some time. When the sitting is resumed a week or so later James makes the following statement:

HENRY JAMES: I have been summoned somewhat peremptorily but it is a pleasure to me to feel that my very urgent request has been so kindly attended to. I have a most sincere desire to begin the experiment of which I spoke the other day. The atmosphere here, I mean in this house, is of a nature that lends itself to what I want to do and I should like to make it clear that this is not a collaboration of four persons but four separate experiments. I propose to make mine first. And now I should like to explain that even using the brain that I am using at this moment I must accustom myself to this communication with the Earth before it will be natural to me to set down words in the order I should wish. It will be a process rather of the nature of sharpening a knife before it is used. Therefore I must ask for your kind patience. You remember my methods when I was dictating to you. The hesitation before the word chosen was preferred to subsequent correction and I shall hope to be as definite and precise now that I am dictating from a different condition.[41]

A few weeks later the ever-verbose James puts it this way:

If I may be permitted to thank the friends who are making such a valiant effort to help me to speak I shall put it this way. There is the intention enabled by kindness and a desire to return to relations that existed in a distant past between me and the lady who kindly acted as my secretary. I will draw her attention to the similarity between the past and the present. In the past she acted to a great extent as a mouthpiece for me, recorder perhaps might define the relationship still better now, although we have not entered into what might be described as fluent cooperation her efforts suggest the past relationship. A lending of the mind to follow mine, or should I say a willing perception of my work and intention . . . (What is the plan?) Just to produce an instrument and when that instrument is as efficient as my secretary's typewriter to proceed with either a short tale or an essay whichever pleases her best.[42]

James's post-death musings on 'producing an instrument' recall his desires for the 'invention of an agent' in his letter to William. In James's laying out of their new relationship, Bosanquet herself is the instrument to be produced, the typewriter incarnate. But, James indicates, some effort is required on her part. There is no seamless movement of transparent mediation from James's spirit's words through to Bosanquet's automatic transcription. 'A lending of the mind to follow mine . . . a willing perception of my work and intention' is required. Bosanquet is an active participant in this scenario even if it is only to the extent of a loan. This willing perception of James's intention also recalls the perfect prescient and feminine secretary of the 1890 *Phonographic World* who 'anticipates the wishes of her employer and gratifies them almost before he has them'.[43]

Friedrich Kittler and Mark Seltzer have argued that the spread of the typewriter helped dislodge a nineteenth-century reliance on a seamless continuity between eye, hand, and paper that supported the fantasy of a natural and self-present creative process:

The linking of hand, eye and letter in the act of writing by hand intimates the translation from mind to hand to eye and hence from the inward and invisible and spiritual to the outward and visible and physical, projecting in effect 'the continuous transition from nature to culture.' The typewriter, like the telegraph, replaces, or pressures, that fantasy of continuous transition with recalcitrantly visible and material systems of difference:

with the standardized spacing of keys and letters; with the dislocation of where the hands work, where the letters strike and appear, where the eyes look, if they look at all.[44]

Machine culture and the typewriter bring a new recognition of disruption, differences, arbitrariness in the deployment of the symbolic in the act of artistic creation. However, as Seltzer has also pointed out, for James these dislocations accompanied a new sense of the immediacy of writing – the instant translation from speech to writing through dictation.[45] Bosanquet describes her sense of James's liberation through dictation, and her own sense of the meaning of mediumship, in her memoir, *Henry James at Work*:

The business of acting as a medium between the spoken and the typewritten word was at first as alarming as it was fascinating . . . The practice of dictation was begun in the nineties. By 1907 it was a confirmed habit, its effects being easily recognisable in his style, which became more and more like free, involved, unanswered talk . . . 'It all seems,' he once explained, 'to be much more effectively and unceasingly *pulled* out of me in speech than in writing.' Indeed at the time when I began to work for him, he had reached a stage at which the click of the Remington acted as a positive spur.[46]

For James the technologized instrument – the automatic, repetitive sound of the typewriter enhances the ability to create. Yet this creation is still pictured along the lines of speaking through; some form of alterity exists inside James which can be 'pulled out' with the help of speech and a technological spur. The new technologies of machine culture paradoxically serve to imbue writing with a sense of presence, and the author with a corresponding prolixity; while for James the old trope of poetic inspiration flowing from hand to pen in fact hinders articulation:

Once or twice when he was ill and in bed I took down a note or two by hand, but as a rule he liked to have the typewriter moved into his bedroom for even the shortest letters. Yet there were to the end certain kinds of work which he was obliged to do with a pen. Plays, if they were to be kept within the limits of possible performance, and short stories, if they were to remain within the bounds of publication in a monthly magazine, must be written by hand. He was well aware that the manual labour of writing was his best aid to a desired brevity.[47]

One's own hand hinders writing, but somebody else's hand, especially somebody else's hand attached to a typewriter, enhances it, makes for what amounts to an unstoppable flow.[48]

Bosanquet as, and along with her, typewriter creates a specific sort of intimacy between herself and James. The relationship of the medium to his or her living or dead dictator is one that requires a 'fluent' apparently intersubjective cooperation usually imagined as absent in the relationship between human and machine. But at the turn of the century a new recognition of the ways in which bodies and machines are similarly things which can be made creates new ways of imagining intimacy with machines, especially 'prosthetic' machines such as the typewriter.[49] Equally, newly technologized ways of understanding intimacy with other minds invade old versions of romance, as well as other apparently intersubjective relationships, such as that between employer and employee. Bosanquet's lending of her mind both to follow and anticipate James replicates the quandaries of *In the Cage*'s telegraphist, caught up in a desired but also unavoidable back and forth movement from pure mediumship as pure instrumentality through a sort of telepathic and prescient communion with one's dictator. Because the mind that is lending itself has its own desires, the invention of an agent, in these cases, is also the invention of a new spatialized, externalized, intimate knowledge of the other/employer.

This is perhaps why Theodora Bosanquet's forays into a secretarial afterlife come equipped with erotic prohibitions. Shortly after the early sittings Bosanquet left off using Hester Dowden as the medium for James's messages and began transcribing her own automatic writing.[50] It is at this point that the negotiations for the literary project take a somewhat sinister turn. It appears that the spirit guide Johannes, who also migrates from Hester Dowden's sittings to hers, has strict notions of what is expected in a secretary chosen for the task of automatically recording literary works from the other world. Vows of poverty, chastity and obedience:

JOHANNES: . . . We want you to make yourself a little more like a nun for the rest of your life on the earth because you have to be the instrument of a great work of wonderful and appealing beauty and you must be the first to realise that this work will need all your faculties to make it a little bit of what we want it to be for the world of lower planetary influences and on the lower mental levels. And we want to make you an offer very definitely today. Will you be contented with the reflected glory of the new work towards the heavenly hosts . . . and of the mighty dead or must you insist on being taken care of in the way of financial worries to be turned(?) . . . But I want to know if you insist on being wealthy or not in the least . . . [51]

Johannes's expectations for her point towards the inextricability of the financial and the sexual. The 'offer' he makes her, using the language one might expect from someone engaging secretarial help, is really an insistence upon her self sacrifice. The choice is between her desire to write something of her own (and earn her own living) or agreeing to Johannes's demands and giving up both a steady income and the satisfaction of earthly sexual desires. Although Johannes claims he is not damning her to total poverty:

JOHANNES: George Meredith is here but will not interrupt the conversation we are having. No, I do not mean that you will be too poor to buy plenty of books for I know that you enjoy that form of spending and it is the right way to spend your money but if you insist on the help to be given for other things that you may want to do in the world there will be no real peace of mind for you in the world at all until you die to it and its vanities.[52]

But Bosanquet does not just want to be able to afford to read books, she wants to write them. While James was alive her diary more than once expresses a desire to exchange the position of secretary for that of author: 'I positively loathe the thought of going back to write to Mr. James's dictation tomorrow, and on for months and months. Why can't one live by writing?'[53] Now, she admits to a wish for recognition in her own right for writing 'a good book or a good play'. Johannes is unrelenting: 'You must be quite clear in your desires. Are you going to be a mere writer of good books of critical understanding or think that you belong to the other world entirely for us to do what we like with you?'[54] In a question that strikes at the heart of every literary critic, Johannes asks whether she wants to be a mere critical parasite or an inspired medium. Is she willing to sacrifice her own self interest and critical understanding, in order to make herself into the perfect bearer of the undistorted word? Theodora replies, 'This is so immense. Do you wonder that I ask myself sometimes if I'm qualified for a lunatic asylum?'[55]

It turns out the corollary sacrifice of her sex life is a contested issue. It appears that Johannes is playing bad cop to Henry and William James's good cops, who seem to expect no such total sacrifice from her:

(Who is writing?) William James the medium for his brother . . . We are the last people in the world to make you nunlike or make you take any kind of vow of chastity or of the least . . . All we want from you may be understood in a very few lines for your conduct . . . [56]

But Johannes continues to insist that good mediumship involves total energetic control. Theodora should not be wasting herself and her energy on earthly desires:

. . . William James has to be very careful of his mediumship for the present and nunlikeness is the essential thing . . . Now be of good courage. Nothing will be the worse for your change of controlling force. Never be the least bit afraid of the future life that lies before you in the next world where you will be the very best kind of medium to the earthbound . . . Until you never think of yourself at all there will be the most awful difficulty in getting through to you. (Then it isn't really worth your while, is it?) Yes it is because you have a very good brain for the new men to work with, but whenever you make a new contact anything may happen.[57]

The emerging pattern in the dialogues of Bosanquet's automatic writings is a see-saw between desires to extinguish her own personality in the service of some great work of literary and cultural transmission, also bringing knowledge of the other world to the living, and her desires to write for herself and her livelihood, desires which are seen as psychically equivalent to and bound up with sexual desires.[58]

Here, I encounter what may be an unavoidable difficulty in reading and interpreting the transcripts of séances as literary and/or historical texts. To relegate the psycho-secretarial dynamics I have been discussing to the level of Bosanquet's personal psychopathology would be to internalize and psychologize what I am trying to analyse as a crossing of certain specific social, literary and cultural phenomena. Of course individuals internalize and pathologize 'outside' forces, but the interest of automatic writing and mediumship as Bosanquet uses it seems to me precisely in its existing on the cusp between inside and outside. Is it self-help? A form of therapy? Is it like email? Is it more like talking to oneself or talking to another? And what difference does it make if that other, or others, turns out to be most of a literary period?

One nineteenth-century tradition had no problem interpreting female mediumship as either charlatanship or mental illness. Scientists such as Henry Maudsley believed that spiritualism lead to insanity and only appealed to those who were incipiently crazy. The American physician Frederic Marvin dubbed the belief in spiritualism 'mediomania,' a female problem: 'If the womb was only slightly off-balance the woman would be liable to "embrace some strange ultra ism – Mormonism, Mesmerism, Fourierism, Socialism, often Spiritualism."[59]

The enlightened version of this diagnosis tended to render mediumship as a misinterpretation of what was actually multiple-personality syndrome.[60] Théodore Flournoy's 1899 best-seller *From India to the Planet Mars: Observations of a Case of Sleepwalking with Glossolalia* was a record of his sittings with the medium Hélène Smith who, in trance, spoke in Sanskrit and Martian. After pulling in Saussure to confirm the authenticity of her speech (Were they languages? Maybe. Were they Sanskrit or Martian? No.), Flournoy diagnosed his subject's trance speeches as the products of separate personalities.[61] Automatic writing, initially the stuff of the séance, also became early on central to the psychological experiment. The medium was the first and perhaps best experimental subject for the early interests of subliminal psychology such as that of F. W. H. Myers.[62] The Freudian eclipse of these early studies succeeded in sweeping mediumship under the umbrella of sexuality. Clearly the séance was a space in which sexually transgressive desires could be enacted, but the collapse of the medium into the hysteric, and the apparent historical disappearance of them both, does a disservice to the complicated dynamics of mediumship.

When Theodora Bosanquet sat down at her table to write automatically, as her archive indicates she apparently did often three or four times a day during the 1930s, she was engaging in a practice that should not be mistakenly reduced to a simplistic Freudian psychodynamics (i.e. Johannes, the prohibitive super-ego assigns Theodora to her proper repressed and self-annihilating secretarial place, because the force of her desires for sex, selfhood, money, authorial fame, recognition by the Jameses, is so strong they must be punished). Much of the interest of reading Bosanquet's SPR archive would vanish with this interpretation, just as the reading of *In the Cage* which labels the telegraphist nuts simply misses the point of the story. In fact the line between the intersubjective séance – in which an out-of-body, post-death James really does speak – and an intra-subjective one – in which Bosanquet voices her own repressed desires for what she always hoped James would say – is not a line that James's own accounts of consciousness necessarily allow one to draw.[63] Bosanquet's own view of the status of herself, and the 'self' in trance is similarly complicated. In her Christian trance writings (which make up a large portion of the automatic scripts) she sometimes sounds a lot like Myers writing on subliminal consciousness. In one automatically written dialogue with 'O', her spirit guide, she asks:

T. Who is 'I'?
O. In psychic trance 'I' appears.
    'I' is not to be confounded with ɪ or i
    'I' is single, is separate – is double, is fused.
    'I' pursues its *own* purpose, speaking through the peeping fracture, Dream, vision, all that pertains to a state of somnambulance belongs strictly speaking, to *dis*-conscious 'I'.
T. What will happen?
O. You will be *invaded*.
T. By what?
O. Solitude consciousness expanded. Various Rites explained. The Book of Books underlined. Perfections approached.[64]

The 'I' of the trance resembles the problematic 'I' of the secretary who cathects her employer and his words. Whether this dynamic appears as a religious invasion or a literary one, it does reflect back on her secretarial past. But it also reflects current scientific understandings of the self as medium and container, which are irreducible to a Freudian schematic of repression and release.

    Friedrich Kittler calls the final chapter of his book *Discourse Networks*, 'Queen's Sacrifice', equating the Lacanian disappearance of the woman (*La femme n'éxiste pas*) with the subsumption of the Romantic equation of woman with nature into the modern equation of wom*en* with denaturalized recording media. In modernity's masculinist dream, as described by Kittler, the other can be built to order, respond, record, repeat, mirror.[65] The boyish Miss Bosanquet – whose sexual othering of James may have been played out in complicated but difficult to trace dynamics between a lesbian secretary and a gay male author – finds herself, after her boss's death, still subject to his words and his dictation. The disembodied Henry and William James suggest to her, however, that the secretarial sacrifice is not necessarily the sacrifice of passion, that in fact the relationship requires an act of love on both sides:

(Can I do anything to help?) Nothing but take the trouble to make a little time every day for the practising of the hand. Now I must go to my other medium on this new plane of the . . . . fondest love from William and Henry. Until you can love us a little we don't think that we can do much for the work that my medium will try to help make for us, but the new plans will bring love. New plans will make your life a very different thing and nobody can do more for you than that. Now, Miss Bosanquet, take the greatest care – are you taking care to make a glad and happy surrender of your own personal . . . New plans will be a very great pleasure to me Henry James . . . gladly and happily surrender your own personal . . .[66]

William and Henry insist upon the necessity of Theodora loving them a little. Mediumship may require surrender of one's personality towards a spiritual make-over, making one's life 'a very different thing', but in order for authors to begin to dictate both their works and her life, here it seems that their recording machine must agree to love them. It is yet another stipulation of the secretarial contract.

In *In the Cage* the telegraphist finds herself unwilling to name or unable to imagine a purchasing medium which would cement her relationship to Captain Everard, binding them together through simultaneously commercial and intimate transactions. To do so would be vulgar. What emerges in Bosanquet's writings as binding her to James is an erotics of exchange, not simply of money, information or sex, but rather of recognition, specifically recognition through *reading*. She and Henry engage in a dialogue about her memoir on him which he has not read (presumably since it was written after his death):

HENRY JAMES is here now just to wave you his friendly blessing. Yes, he knew you would recognize the words that he used to use so often in his letters to his friends but he means it with a very different kind of love and greeting now for he loves you now and he did not in the least then, for he thought that you were a very uninteresting young woman who had a marvellous gift for transcribing his words correctly, but he now, . . . finds now that all the time you were observing his style and taking mental notes and that afterwards you wrote a little book about him which he has never had the courage to look at, but he thinks he will have to now if you don't mind. Yes (in answer to a mental demur on my part) he agrees that it is not the best kind of beginning for a new relationship but he would like to know what you thought of him in the old days. (Here my mind flashed to what M.R. told me about Elizabeth Robins having said it was a book that would make H.J. turn in his grave) He knows what you are thinking but he never knew that Elizabeth Robins would know what sort of book would make him turn in his grave. ('Mrs. Wharton liked it') Yes he knows that and he things [sic] that in that case it must have been a good little book but he must read it for himself and he asks you to leave a copy unopened on the table by the window tonight when the sitting is going on for he will be in the room most of the time and he can read through the covers of any book in the world quite easily but he can't make out what is locked away in a cupboard as this book is. Now go and prepare your supper my dear child . . .[67]

How does one begin a new relationship with an old secretary? On the one hand, this is a fantasy of recognition – James finally reads what she has written – no longer just his voice coming through her but her speaking to him, her perceptions of him. But of course the only reason this master/slave dialectic reversal can take place is because he is currently speaking *through* her. Or else, those of us who do not believe in ghosts demur, she is speaking *as* him. Either way, the possibility of a new relationship emerges from acts of reading as mutual recognition.

Style is a key term in the development of this new relationship. Bosanquet's James discovers that Bosanquet is not such an uninteresting young woman after all because she has observed his style: she writes critically of it and imitates it. What is at stake here is not just whether or not Bosanquet somehow got James right in her book, but how or whether she has correctly inhabited him, just as he has continued to inhabit her even more vividly after his death.

Before I return to the mimesis of the secretarial relation I would like to explore some ways in which inhabiting one's own or another's writing style can also be played out in ghostly and coercive ways between brothers. William and Henry had a long-standing dispute about how the 'country' of the James family could have begat two such different practitioners of the English language.[68] William's comments on Henry's late style grow increasingly more exasperated: 'I have read *The Wings of the Dove* (for which all thanks!) but what shall I say of a book constructed on a method which so belies everything that *I* acknowledge as law? You've reversed every traditional canon of story-telling (especially the fundamental one of *telling* the story, which you carefully avoid) and have created a new *genre littéraire* which I can't help thinking perverse, but in which you nevertheless *succeed*, for I read with interest to the end (many pages, and innumerable sentences twice over to see what the dickens they could possibly mean) and all with unflagging curiosity to know what the upshot might become.'[69] *The Golden Bowl* was even more disturbing to William:

It puts me, as most of your recenter long stories have put me, in a very puzzled state of mind . . . the method of narration by interminable elaboration of suggestive reference (I don't know what to call it, but you know what I mean) goes agin the grain of all my own impulses in writing . . . Your methods and my ideals seem the reverse, the one of the other – and yet I have to admit your extreme success in this book. But why won't

you, just to please Brother, sit down and write a new book, with no twilight
or mustiness in the plot, with great vigor and decisiveness in the action, no
fencing in the dialogue, no psychological commentaries, and absolute
straightness in the style? Publish it in my name, I will acknowledge it, and
give you half the proceeds.[70]

A thematics of ventriloquism and stylistic rivalry runs throughout
the exchanges between the two most famous Jameses.[71] It is
interesting to note here that it is not just secretaries and employers
who dispute the question of who is licensed to speak for whom and
who gets paid.

Later, in an aesthetic power play, Henry reverses his brother's
desire to impose his own 'straight' style on Henry's work. Henry
edited a selection of William's letters for publication after his death.
For Henry, entrenched in the massive revisions of the New York
Edition, this process involved not only selecting but revising William's letters, as if they were one of his own similarly defenceless
novels.[72] More radically still, Henry revised not only the letters he
published, but, in the course of dictation, letters he did not publish,
making for a particularly acute collapse of the public and private
archive of an enormously public family, with an enormously exclusive private family world. William's son Harry, not surprisingly,
objected to Henry's changes, and Henry mounted an elaborate and
fascinating defence of his motives, claiming that Harry could not
possibly understand his position,

. . . – in the absence of your entering into the only attitude and state of
feeling that was possible to me by my mode of work, and which was one so
distinct, by its whole 'ethic' and aesthetic (and indeed its aesthetic, however
discredited to you in fact, *was* simply the ethic) from what I should have felt
my function in handling my material as an instalment merely of the great
correspondence itself, just a contribution, an initial one, to the long
continuity of that. Then the case would have been for me absolutely of the
plainest – my own ethic, with no aesthetic whatever concerned in the
matter, would have been the ideal of documentary exactitude, verbatim,
literatim et punctuatim – free of all living back imaginatively, or of any of the
affects of this, into one's earliest and most beguiling, and most unspeakable
(for actual justifyings) contemporaneities with the writer.[73]

James's method at this point, which seems inseparable from both his
aesthetic and his ethic, is the practice of dictation; not crossing out
words on a previously authored page but speaking old words anew
to another. The acting out of the past to a live audience seems to
help create the possibility of a visible, audible, ghostly speech.

'Living back imaginatively' *is* the stake of James's claim to taking liberties with his brother's writing, as he goes on to try to explain to Harry. Through a sort of ghostly interaction with William, Henry feels compelled to revise his words:

And when I laid hands upon the letters to use as so many touches and tones in the picture I frankly confess I seemed to see them in a better, or at all events in another light, here and there, than those rough and rather illiterated copies I had from you showed at their face value. I found myself again in such close relation with your Father, such a revival of relation as I hadn't known since his death, and which was a passion of tenderness for doing the best thing by him that the material allowed, and which I seemed to feel him in the room and at my elbow asking me for as I worked and as he listened. It was as if he had said to me on seeing me lay my hands on the weak little relics of our common youth, 'Oh but you're not going to give me away, to hand me over, in my raggedness and my poor accidents, quite unhelped, unfriended, you're going to do the very best for me you *can*, aren't you . . . ?' . . . These were small things, the very smallest, they appeared to me all along to be, tiny amendments in order of words, degrees of emphasis etc., to the end that he should be more easily and engagingly readable and thereby more tasted and liked – from the moment there was no excess of these *soins* and no violence done to his real identity. Everything the letters meant affected me so, in all the business, as of *our* old world only, mine and his alone together, with every item of it intimately known and remembered by me, that I daresay I did instinctively regard it at last as all *my* truth, to do what I would with.[74]

Henry's revisions are part of a re-enacting of an intimate old world in which documentary truth takes second place to a subjective, but as Henry aggressively asserts, shared version of the past which, it seems, William could only be called upon to verify or deny through a Ouija board.[75] Clearly the fact that the living William felt that the 'best thing' for Henry's style would have been for him to have written more like his pragmatic brother was immaterial. In the process of creating this shared, private fraternal world, this passage layers its images through a sort of synaesthetic effect: Henry lays his hands on the letters, feels William in the room, hears him speak, feels compelled to make him more tasted and liked. It is possible to understand how this process might be enabled by the presence of an amanuensis, who becomes a living embodiment of the possibility of ghostly speech, of the archive as human being, of dictation as dialogue and dialogue as dictation – our necessary set of illusions about alterity and intersubjectivity: the belief, fear, hope that when you are talking to yourself you are really talking to another, and vice versa; or that when you are listening to another you are really only listening to yourself, and vice versa. When James feels William at his elbow, there is in fact another person in the room. When he insists that the language of the letters refers to a private world which only he and Harry's father share, there is still another person in the room. James's late style, as well as his developments of the limits, expansiveness and dictatorial powers of consciousness are transformed by this fact.

Style, the ability to express things in a proper, individual way; to make words live through one's own individual signature (or as in the previous example, the contested sign of a shared but private world) literally seems like a life-or-death matter for James at the end of his life. And this too is necessarily filtered through Miss Bosanquet. After James's second stroke Theodora writes to Edith Wharton telling her that he's regaining his alertness: 'James assured them that he did not quite feel paralyzed, that there must be a better word for his condition. He asked for a thesaurus to help him find it.'[76] James must *write* (which means dictate), and write precisely, his own sense of himself in illness:

He was very sleepy all this morning, and didn't send for me till nearly luncheon time, when I was very sorry to find him quite oblivious of everything but the effort to give expression to the sensations of illness and convalescence. That isn't very clear. What I mean is that he was intent on dictating several laboriously composed sentences, quite long and punctuated, describing his state of mind at the moment in regard to his illness. That seems to me to be about the worst thing possible for his brain, but it isn't possible, nor indeed desirable, to stop him, for he only goes on worrying about the phrases and it must be some relief to have them spoken and taken down and done with.[77]

To read James's death through Bosanquet's continuous resuscitation of him, as well as through his own radical revising of himself and his brother, is to know that phrases are never done with even when they are taken down. Through the enormous responsibilities and demands of her psychic secretarihood Bosanquet negotiates a terrain that is also negotiated by James's own explorations of the potentially determining powers of consciousness, and the uncertain barriers between consciousnesses. Maybe Bosanquet, like the telegraphist, parlays a primarily economic relationship into a spectacularly intimate, if not, as in *In the Cage,* explicitly sexualized one. But maybe taking the dictation of the other, negotiating a salary, and counting words per minute are all in fact the material bases for that shifty superstructure, love, or for the hyper-cathected symbolic coincidences I spoke of in my first chapter as telepathy. If the effects of this relationship are perceptible in Bosanquet's writings they may also be visible in James's (the ones he did when he was alive). And if this is the case then what seems to be made manifest in the secretarial relation is a constitutive inability to disentangle the imposition of meaning from a genuinely intersubjective formation of it. But of course, at this point, whether we are talking about *The Golden Bowl* or Theodora's automatic scripts, the genuinely intersubjective might encompass talking to the dead or to or through a machine. Just as long as there's love, and payment.

CHAPTER 5

Freud, Ferenczi and psychoanalysis's telepathic transferences

We must never let our poor neurotics drive us crazy. I believe an article on 'countertransference' is sorely needed; of course we could not publish it, we should have to circulate copies among ourselves.[1]

In the abridged version of the *Freud/Jung Letters* edited by William McGuire, the first mention of Sandor Ferenczi refers the reader to the following footnote which I quote in full: 'Sandor Ferenczi (1873–1933), Hungarian ventriloquist; introduced by Jung, he became Freud's close friend and psychoanalytic collaborator.'[2] Since there is no evidence to suggest that Ferenczi was ever employed as a ventriloquist, or that he even practised puppetry as an identity-defining hobby, it seems likely that the footnote is simply a joke at Ferenczi's expense. Unlike some other early analysts Ferenczi was never one of Freud's puppets. He stirred up far too much trouble. However, the title of Ferenczi's final paper, 'Confusion of Tongues between Adults and the Child', suggests that the label ventriloquist might adhere to Ferenczi for another reason.[3] Contra Freud, Ferenczi's late theories and practice radically problematize the question of whose desires speak through the subject. In 'Confusion of Tongues', Ferenczi returns to Freud's earliest ideas about the traumatic effects of childhood sexual abuse to insist that the child's material experience of abuse and invasion could result in her identifying with, introjecting and even speaking in the voice of the attacking adult. This confusion over who speaks can be seen to result from a confusion over where tongues literally are: in whose mouths, in relation to whose bodies.

Ferenczi's final thoughts on psychic and physical invasion have been read as the ghost story of psychoanalysis. Detractors of Freud, such as Jeffrey Masson, have resurrected Ferenczi as the unsung hero of the seduction theory – the analyst who dared to speak the truth about the frequency of child abuse, and whose work was finally suppressed for its apostasy. But if this is one version of a ghost story of psychoanalysis it is not the only one. The occult's incompletely excavated place in the history of psychoanalysis may lead to other ghosts, and more interesting connections between fantasy, history and the individual psyche, than Masson's reading of Freud's 'assault on truth'. (The title of Masson's book indicates his absolute certainty about both what constitutes assaults and what constitutes truth.) Masson's version of psychoanalysis's relationship to the 'real event' oversimplifies both Freud's and Ferenczi's engagement with the seduction theory. Contrary to Masson's assertions, Freud does not suggest that child abuse does not occur; rather he argues that real occurrences are not the only possible trigger for fantasized relations. Violent, invasive relations occur in fantasy as well as in reality, and the psyche can not automatically distinguish between these two realms. Freud never discards the structure and logic of the seduction theory, which he returns to again and again.[4] Nor does he ever deny the reality of child abuse. But psychoanalysis, as Freud conceives it, concerns itself with the realm of fantasy. Events may happen, or they may not, but fantasized relations to these events and non-events always *do* happen, and it is in this realm of relations that the work of psychoanalysis takes place.

Ferenczi's psychoanalytic work, like Freud's, relies on this re-working of the seduction theory through fantasy. However, by the end of his life, in his *Clinical Diary* and in his radical practices, Ferenczi, more so than Freud, seems drawn towards the inextricability of fantasy and a brute, material reality. Ferenczi's practices push at the borders of psychoanalysis; he is willing, even eager, to dispute the separation between practice and theory, the personal and the professional and the psychic and the physical. His writings tell a series of disturbing and provocative stories about the contingent outside world and the psyche's functioning to process it, stories that have helped foster a critical unease about Ferenczi's place within the institutional history of psychoanalysis.

A comprehensive explanation of Ferenczi's comparative neglect in the history of psychoanalysis would involve an understanding of the anxieties (both theoretical and personal) his experiments in the interpenetration of the theoretical and the personal raised, for other analysts, and for the institution of analysis. Whether he was finally ventriloquist or rebel, Ferenczi's contributions undoubtedly have been downplayed in the official history of psychoanalysis. Martin Stanton's reasons for resuscitating Ferenczi's reputation are convincing:

his position as founder and former President of the IPA [International Psycho-Analytical Association]; his pioneer role in formulating training programmes for psychoanalysts; his innovative role in reforming psycho-analytic technique and proposing more flexibility and 'active' intervention by the analyst; his contribution to the debate on possible psychoanalytic treatment of victims of child sex abuse; his subtle defence of 'lay', or non-medical psychoanalysis against powerful and vociferous opposition in the United States; finally, his close friendship and co-operation with all the founders of psychoanalysis, especially Freud and Jung, with whom he traveled to the United States in 1909.[5]

What has been described as a systematic character assassination began with Ernest Jones's biography of Freud. As Martin Stanton puts it in his book about Ferenczi, '[t]he circulation of pernicious rumours that Ferenczi was deranged and seduced his patients hardly encouraged serious study of his work'.[6] Here I want to argue that Ferenczi's most innovative technical and theoretical speculations are inseparable from the fact that he was 'deranged' and seduced his patients. Or, to be more temperate, Ferenczi's active technique, in which the analyst may actually take on the roles his patient suggests, to the extent of giving the patient the physical affection that he or she craves, grew out of his desire to stretch the limits of psycho-analysis in order to reach his most seriously disturbed patients. Similarly, what Jones saw as Ferenczi's psychosis – for instance, his belief 'that he was being successfully psychoanalyzed by messages transmitted telepathically across the Atlantic from an ex-patient of his' – was connected to this same desire to break down mental and physical barriers.[7]

Ferenczi was fascinated by the occult for the very reason that it might contribute to an understanding of psychoanalysis's own mysterious and intimate transmissions. He tried to make occult matters an integral part of psychoanalytic theory and technique; he went to mediums, gave lectures on thought transference, and even planned a book on it which he never wrote.[8] For Ferenczi thought transference made fantasy sharable, material, objective – it helped bring him back around to the seduction theory at the end of his life because of the questions of intimacy in analysis – the ways in which models of physical invasion of children by abusive parents could shed light on the potentially unbearable nature of psychoanalytic intimacy.

Freud's attempts to keep psychoanalysis's boundaries distinct from those of the occult have been well documented.[9] One reason for Freud's concern is that psychoanalysis's ostensible object, sexuality, is not easily and obviously understood under the new terms for it which psychoanalysis proposes. No longer viewed as a biological drive, desire emerges from a complicated layering of infantile experiences, memories, scenes and structures. Sexuality becomes the primary source of the psychological disorders which create uncanny effects in the subjects who are governed, and produced, by desire. In its effects desire resembles the demonic. Adam Phillips claims: 'From the extraordinary correspondence between Freud and Ferenczi, which radically changes the way we read psychoanalysis . . . it is clear that sexuality and the unconscious were the new, scientifically prestigious words for the occult, of that which is beyond our capacity for knowledge, for the weird, unaccountable effects people have on each other. In psychoanalysis the supernatural returns as the erotic.'[10] As Freud's and Ferenczi's interest in thought transference and the potentially invasive nature of others' minds and bodies attests, what the supernatural and the erotic have in common is the ways in which fears, anxieties, desires – the meat and potatoes of psychoanalysis – emerge from questions of proximity and distance. Are the dead ineradicably distant/other to us? Or can they invade our very selves? What if they speak through us? What if other living minds are closer to us than we like to think; what if they too invade us? What if we are sexually invaded, if our bodily boundaries are violated at an early age, or what if we only fantasize about this taking place? *How close is too close?*

As I have shown in my first chapter, turn-of-the-century psychical researchers also explored this breaching of sense boundaries, developing hopes and fears for newly proximate relations to other minds. Psychical research borrows from, and trades its structuring analogies for transmission with, new forms of teletechnology. Both psychical research and these teletechnologies work to make the reality of thought transference acceptable to late nineteenth-century culture, rendering the concept of contact with the dead at least potentially plausible to some. Hence, psychoanalysis, working through the same themes – i.e. the dead live on in us and continue to have effects;

thoughts are shared in ways which are unpoliceable between analyst and analysand – finds itself alternately mirroring and disavowing psychical research.[11]

In this chapter I investigate several interrelated aspects of Freud's and Ferenczi's fraught engagement with the idea of material transmission, focusing first on the possibility of thought transference, what Freud refers to at one point as 'the physical equivalent of the psychical act'. Freud's correspondence with Ferenczi, and the *Clinical Diary* Ferenczi kept in the final years of his life indicate that Ferenczi's interest in telepathy and mediums, his overt transferential desire for Freud, and his turn back to the seduction theory are all aspects of a fascination with dangerous intimacy – bodies and minds which overlap in ways which are too close, too inextricable. Ferenczi's work brings certain themes which have been seen as anxiety-provoking for Freudian psychoanalysis – thought transference, psychosis, homosexuality and the seduction theory – to the forefront. He embodies the ways in which psychoanalysis cannot leave the occult behind, and the ways in which the desire for the 'physical equivalent of the psychical act' – a turn-of-the-century scientific, cultural and literary longing for explanations for transmission – becomes the disavowed but necessary building block for the new psychoanalytic economics of the mind, and for new ways of imagining intimate connections to others.

FREUD AND TELEPATHY: BETWEEN THE PHYSICAL, THE PSYCHICAL, AND THE PSYCHOTIC

Like suggestion and the seduction theory, thought transference has been seen as one of many encroaching outsides to psychoanalysis.[12] Freud's volatile relationship with telepathy, a systematic wavering between embracing it and refusing it, covers most of his career. The ever sceptical Ernest Jones devotes one chapter of his biography of Freud to 'Occultism' and is forced to admit the master's fascination with the topic:

There is no doubt that (telepathy) is by far the most 'respectable' element in the field of occultism, and therefore the one that has gained the widest acceptance. In Freud's opinion it probably represented the kernel of truth in that field, one which the myth-making tendencies of mankind had enveloped in a cocoon of phantastic beliefs. The idea of a 'kernel of truth' specially fascinated Freud and cooperated with more personal motives in his unconscious to incline him toward accepting a belief in telepathy. He had more than once had the experience of discovering such a kernel in the complicated beliefs of mankind, beliefs often contemptuously dismissed as superstitions; that dreams really had a meaning was the most important element. So he felt intuitively that telepathy might be the kernel of truth in this obscure field.[13]

In his biography Jones appears to apologize for Freud's folly. Jones reiterates his own desire to keep psychoanalysis as far away from the occult as possible in anxious letters to Freud. Freud replies in a letter of 7 March 1926: 'If someone should reproach you with my Fall into Sin, you are free to reply that my adherence to telepathy is my private affair like my Jewishness, my passion for smoking, and other things, and the theme of telepathy – inessential for psycho-analysis.'[14]

I will leave aside the intriguing question of just how private Jewishness and smoking are in relation to psychoanalysis in order to further explore Freud's differing reactions to telepathy.[15] Freud's opinion about occultism wavers. When Ferenczi reports that he has been experimenting with thought transference by correctly guessing strangers' names on buses, Freud responds that he cannot go along with Ferenczi's and Jung's 'dangerous expeditions' into the realm of mysticism, although he is apparently not too perturbed by their desire to experiment.[16] In the mode of indulgent mentor, Freud signs off, 'Regards to you, uncanny one.'[17] However, Freud seems happy to court the scientific face of occultism. When nominated as a member of the Society for Psychical Research, he writes to Jung: 'The Society for Psychical Research has asked me to present my candidacy as a corresponding member, which means I presume, that I have been elected. The first sign of interest in *dear old England*. The *list of members* is most impressive.'[18] He appears to believe that psychoanalysis will soon make inroads on the Society, and England, rather than the Society making inroads on psychoanalysis.[19]

Generally Freud remains cautious of anything which could associate psychoanalysis with occultism. In his memoir *Memories, Dreams, Reflections*, Jung indicates that Freud's fear of the occult sometimes verged on the histrionic. Jung writes:

I can still recall vividly how Freud said to me, 'My dear Jung, promise me never to abandon the sexual theory. This is the most essential thing of all. You see, we must make a dogma of it, an unshakeable bulwark.' He said that to me with great emotion . . . In some astonishment I asked him, 'A bulwark – against what?' To which he replied 'Against the black tide of mud' – and here he hesitated for a moment, then added – 'of occultism.'[20]

The potentially muddying incursion of occult knowledge into psychoanalysis would make it difficult to see psychoanalysis as a science, something that cures through a proven and repeatable methodology – the discovery of repressed sexuality, the removal of symptoms, etc. – rather than through a mystical faith in a healer–analyst. If analysts were prophets or mind-readers, then, as François Roustang has pointed out, the transference would never end.[21] The analyst as subject who, in Lacanian terminology, is supposed to know, would really know, and the patient would be caught in a psychotic bind in which the analyst would dictate the patient's terms. Prophecy, a belief in a determined or determinable future, appears to threaten a cure that wishes to restore a better informed, somewhat self-willing, somewhat self-knowing subject back to a contingent world in which choices might be made apart from the tyranny of the neurotic unconscious.

But of course, prophetic dreams do interest Freud. Early on he entertains the idea that dreams might foretell the future, although he almost immediately withdraws this supposition.[22] In *The Psychopathology of Everyday Life*, the apparent predictive power of dreams is entirely assimilated to the fact that dreams are wish fulfillments, and it just so happens that sometimes things turn out the way we want them to.[23] Freud wants to avoid endorsing prophecy as a possibility for reasons which become evident after Jung's break with him. According to Freudians, Jung's redemptive version of psychoanalysis replaced Freud's non-judgemental emphasis on the amoral workings of the libido with a Christianized, biologistic and teleological account of human psychic life.[24] Through his insistence upon the importance of sexuality and early psychic life, Freud maintains that psychoanalysis should be able to interpret the past, and understand the causes of present psychic illnesses, but not predict a future. Yet, as John Forrester points out, the interpretative claims of psychoanalysis make the analyst resemble the fortune teller: 'However abstemious Freud aimed to be in his claims as to the ability of psychoanalysis to read the future, let alone write it, and however sceptical in an Enlightenment tradition he might have been, he was well aware that psychoanalysis owed its vitality to its epistemic neighbours – the occult, the prophetic, the promisers of all kinds.'[25]

One of the most disturbing moments in which psychoanalysis explores the possibility of foretelling the future occurs in *Beyond the Pleasure Principle* in Freud's speculations on the repetition compulsion. In the course of puzzling over the fact that people seem to repeat phenomena and dreams which are unpleasant, he describes people, 'all of whose human relations have the same outcome.'[26] He then argues that this phenomenon is still assimilable to a psychoanalytic model. Desire can be for repetition and mastery, as the fort/da game shows. But if someone repeats patterns of which they can have no foregone knowledge, conscious or unconscious, then that is puzzling: 'We are much more impressed by cases where the subject appears to have a *passive* experience, over which he has no influence, but in which he meets with a repetition of the same fatality. There is the case, for instance, of the woman who married three successive husbands each of whom fell ill soon afterwards and had to be nursed by her on their deathbeds.'[27] Freud tries to assimilate fate neurosis to desire – the woman must have wanted, on some level, to be in that tragic position – but in cases like this one it seems that paradoxically, the compulsion to repeat that which has not yet been determined (the future) somehow works through the subject in ways that are irreducible to individual desire. Fate neurosis implies that we must all foresee the future in order to take the actions that condemn us to repeat it.

With fate neurosis psychoanalysis finesses the differences between desire and fortune telling in order to hold on to its own sense of mastery, in its own game of fort/da.[28] Desire merges into magical thinking, and it is only the analyst who can separate out the strands of each. As will become clear later in the chapter, fate neurosis acts as the prophetic mirror of Freud's and Ferenczi's belief in a shared archaic past – the phylogenetic scenes which Freud finds reinscribed at the level of the individual psyche. Fate neurosis and phylogenesis both install a structural template that appears to override or determine the individual's desires.

Apart from his interest in fate neurosis, Freud generally disavows fortune telling. After Ferenczi complains that at a séance, he didn't get a chance to ask the medium Frau Seidler to predict the future, Freud responds: 'You really don't need to regret that you didn't ask about the future. That always forms itself anew; even the dear Lord doesn't know it in advance. But the transference of *your* thoughts in incomprehensible ways is the strange thing and possibly something new. Keep quiet about it for the time being; we will have to engage in further experiments.'[29]

In their correspondence Ferenczi and Freud discuss in detail the mediums Ferenczi has been seeing. Of Frau Scidler, Freud says:

I also cannot exclude the probability that she can do something, namely, reproduce your thoughts, whose visual representation in her mind she herself does not understand. All other explanations, like enhanced sensitivity for mimicry and the like, seem to me first of all inadequate, and second, they presuppose a special psychic ability in this woman. The assumption of thought transference alone does not require this but rather the opposite; she may be quite an imbecilic, even inactive person who makes images of what would otherwise be suppressed through her own intellectual activity. In her intention to swindle and to play the magician, she then has the courage and the attentiveness to perceive what has come into being purely physiologically in her . . . Should one now, as a result of this experience, commit oneself to occultism? Certainly not; it is only a matter of thought transference. If this can be proved, then one has to believe it – then it is not [psychoanalytic] phenomenon, but rather a purely somatic one, certainly a novelty of the first rank. In the meantime, let us keep absolute silence with regard to it. . . .[30]

While repeatedly calling for psychoanalytic silence and secrecy around thought transference, Freud also attempts to limit its scope. He carefully distinguishes thought transference from more occult powers such as prophecy, and then distinguishes thought transference from psychoanalysis by making it a purely physiological phenomenon. He suggests that some people may be particularly sensitive to others' thoughts and capable of the immediate somatic process of thought transference because they have empty minds which can pick up on, and not distort, the images of others by an unfortunate turn for interpretation. For Freud thought transference is definitely not a psychoanalytic phenomenon, but its content can be analysed through psychoanalytic methods, as Leon Chertok and Isabelle Stengers indicate:

In Freud's view, the phenomenon of thought-transference does not put psychoanalytic technique into question. On the contrary, it is precisely this technique that is capable of elucidating the phenomenon in a rational way even if it cannot explain precisely how thoughts are transferred. The task of psychoanalysis is, on the one hand, to avoid being fascinated by telepathy, and, on the other, to elucidate the materials of thought transference just as it elucidates fantasies, ordinary dreams, and other subjective productions.[31]

Like dreams and fantasies, transferred thoughts require psychoanalytic interpretation to be properly understood. Freud can interpret the information that the thought-transferring fortune teller
receives because he can read (psychoanalytically), while the fortune
teller is simply an illiterate medium.[32]

Ferenczi also reduces thought transference to a physiological
effect, supporting Freud's belief that the best medium of thought
transference may be unthinking, and therefore unable to discrimi-
nate between her own thoughts and another's:

It seems to be indisputable that *Frau Seidler* can do things heretofore
thought impossible, and, very probably, that she recites the thoughts of
others . . . mixed with her own thoughts and unaware of the abstract or
concrete meanings of the images that she sees (probably also without
knowing what belongs to her and what to her partner).[33]

If Freud finally answers no to the possibility of prophecy it is because
he answers yes to the possibility of thought transference, much like
the members of the Society for Psychical Research who settled on
thought transference as the less occult explanation for the apparent
persistence of life after death. Freud is only able to exclude thought
transference from the domain of psychoanalysis because he sees its
causes as bio-mechanistic. Thought transference is not really about
reading another's thoughts, rather it is about directly experiencing
another's thoughts without the mediating representational step.

Jung's dangerous occultism threatened to lead towards one
problem for psychoanalysis – that of the all-knowing prophetic
analyst. But Freud's somatic explanations of telepathy may be
covering up another difficulty – the apparent similarity between
psychoanalytic transference and thought transference. Freud's insistence upon the physiological nature of thought transference should
distinguish it from psychoanalytic transference. Psychoanalytic transference – the keystone of the psychoanalytic method – takes place
through the inevitable substitution of objects. The patient responds
to the analyst (and others) with emotions and reactions that refer
back to earlier stages of the patient's life, and that were aimed
originally towards other people. But both psychoanalytic transference and thought transference depend on the potential separability
of thought from thinker, and of emotion from the object that it is
directed towards; both kinds of transference bring up questions
about the mysterious nature of the transmissibility of psychic life:

'The telepathic question par excellence, one which immediately reveals its kinship to psychoanalysis is: "Whose thoughts are these, inhabiting my inner world?"'[34] Freudian psychoanalysis attempts to answer this question by working within and through the transferences between analyst and patient, a process that involves both interpretation and affective immediacy, recalled memory and relived emotions. By contrast, professional telepaths, according to Freud, work only with physiological responses. They may be a 'novelty of the first rank', but no more.

Yet, this physiological novelty appears to hold a particular fascination for Freud. When he allows himself to speculate on the existence of telepathy at the end of 'Dreams and Occultism', his interest in the physical explanation of the phenomenon comes to the forefront:

The telepathic process is supposed to consist in a mental act in one person instigating the same mental act in another person. What lies between these two mental acts may easily be a physical process into which the mental one is transformed at one end and which is transformed back once more into the same mental one at the other end. The analogy with other transformations, such as occur in speaking and hearing by telephone, would then be unmistakable. And only think if one could get hold of this physical equivalent of the psychical act! It would seem to me that psychoanalysis, by inserting the unconscious between what is physical and what was previously considered 'psychical', has paved the way for the assumption of such processes as telepathy. If one accustoms oneself to the idea of telepathy, one can accomplish a great deal with it – for the time being, it is true, only in imagination. It is a familiar fact that we do not know how the common purpose comes about in the great insect communities: possibly it is done by means of a direct psychical transference of this kind. One is led to a suspicion that this is the original, archaic method of communication between individuals and that in the course of phylogenetic evolution it has been replaced by the better method of giving information with the help of signals which are picked up by the sense organs. But the older method might have persisted in the background and still be able to put itself into effect under certain conditions – for instance, in passionately excited mobs. All this is uncertain and full of unsolved riddles; but there is no reason to be frightened by it.[35]

Telepathy appeals to Freud in this passage as a mechanism of transmission which refers back towards an original, archaic communication – language as inseparable from biology. For Freud, as for other theorizers of telepathy at the turn of the century, modern examples of thought transference were atavistic remnants from an earlier evolutionary state.[36] When Freud enthusiastically imagines getting hold of the physical equivalent of the psychical act he imagines a physical precursor to representation. The material transformations of the telephone, and the mysterious communication methods of insects, provide him with comparisons on which to ground his speculations.

In this passage, both telepathy and the unconscious are defined as formations which exist somewhere between the physical and what once was labelled the psychical – the uncanny world of ghosts and possession. But this space between the physical and the psychical is difficult to define. When Freud rejected biologically determinist explanations for the origins of neurosis and hysteria he found himself exploring various ways to explain transmission (of mental illness, but also of sexuality, of the inner psychic life of the parents to the inner psychic life of the children, of history, etc.). One possibility his clinical practice led him towards was that of a shared evolutionary inheritance of humanity – a storehouse of primal memories.

Freud's conception of humanity's evolutionary history and pre-history shares with Lamarckian evolutionary theory a belief in the inheritance of acquired traits. In Freud's phylogenetic schemas an ancestor witnesses or participates in a scene – such as the primal murder – and that scene is then mysteriously passed down through the generations. As Martin Stanton maintains:

The problematic relationship between biological and psychological 'origins' has therefore generated a hybrid narrative space in psychoanalysis. Laplanche and Pontalis have drawn attention to the peculiar 'middle ground' occupied by scenes that are supposed to transcribe the biological development of the species in the cultural development of the individual: the primal scene, the seduction scene, the castration scene and the return to the mother's breast. Clearly it is the status of fantasy in these that renders their 'reality' problematic.[37]

It is the uncertain reality of inherited scenes that grounds the subject's sexuality (the primal scene) and morality and socialization (the primal murder). In 'The Wolfman,' and in his *Introductory Lectures*, Freud tentatively endorses a phylogenetic bedrock to fantasy:

It seems to me quite possible that all the things that are told to us to-day in analysis as phantasy – the seduction of children, the inflaming of sexual excitement by observing parental intercourse, the threat of castration (or rather castration itself) – were once real occurrences in the primaeval times of the human family, and that children in their fantasies are simply filling in the gaps in individual truth with prehistoric truths.[38]

This Lamarckian psychic inheritance of an ancestor's real action is something like the insertion of the ghostly into the social. An event happens in archaic time which is then inherited and installed in the psychic structure of the human race.

Freud's and Ferenczi's investment in thought transference is related in complex ways to their mutual fascination with Lamarck. They began planning a book on Lamarck together in 1917:

Our intention is to place Lamarck entirely on our basis and to show that his 'need' which creates and transforms organs is nothing other than the power of unconscious ideas over the body, of which we see relics in Hysteria; in short, the 'omnipotence of thoughts'. Purpose and usefulness would then be explained psychoanalytically; it would be the completion of psychoanalysis.[39]

'Need' (*besoin*) was Lamarck's term for the stimulus for evolutionary change and adaptation in animals: 'The drive to adapt was so strong that animals responded automatically to stimuli from the outside world, and from inside their own bodies, like thirst or hunger.'[40] There are two elements of Lamarckian thought that particularly intrigue Freud and Ferenczi – one is the inheritance of acquired traits, already discussed; the other is this somewhat opaque idea of 'need', a term which is already in Lamarck's terminology caught somewhere between conscious desire and automatic response.[41] It is clear why the readings (and misreadings) of Lamarck's 'need' might resonate with psychoanalytic ideas. All of Freud's early work with hysterics indicated that the unconscious mind worked upon the body to create physical symptoms. One of Freud's most radical moves was to collapse any easy distinction between the physical and the psychical. For psychoanalysis, desire can indeed transform the body, the world, reality.

If, in the quotation given above, Freud and Ferenczi seem initially intent on explaining Lamarck psychoanalytically, by subsuming Lamarck's evolutionary theory into their psychoanalytic one, then the reference to hysterical symptoms as 'relics' serves to indicate the persistence of a Lamarckian phylogenetic residue built into the very structure of psychoanalytic theories of transmission. Hysterical symptoms signify the power of unconscious thought over the body and gesture towards an atavistic re-emergence of primitive, imprinted traits – for Freud, those pre-historic moments when primal scenes of desire became embedded in the human psyche in a transmissible way. It is in this imprinting that biology seems to beckon towards Freud once again, but then psychoanalysis also beckons towards biology, suggesting that what is sometimes imagined as the purely physiological is never immune from the transferential dynamics of history and the psyche.

What is at stake in these knotted questions about the theorization of transmission in psychoanalysis? In one sense, simply more than I can begin to approach in the space of this chapter, even if I thought that I could do justice to the topic. But I do want to suggest that Freud's enthusiastic speculations about thought transference at the end of 'Dreams and Occultism' are related to his desire to write a book on Lamarck. Lamarck and his interpreters (and misinter- preters) provide Freud with a theory of transformation that imbues the material with a kind of psychic volition and allows for the inheritance of acquired history. In his speculations in 'Dreams and Occultism' Freud pictures thought transference as a mechanism of transmission that can negotiate that fraught arena with which psychoanalysis is so centrally concerned, in which the material, the psychic and the historical are interwoven.

Laplanche and Pontalis have indicated how Freud's movement from phylogeny to ontogeny – from pre-historic reality to psycho- logical reality – can be read as a prefiguration of Lacan's Symbolic order. What endures as psychical reality are the structures of fantasy which are universal, such as the Oedipal structure that grounds the Symbolic.[42] Freud's wish to 'get hold' of the physical equivalent of the psychical act opens up the possibility for understanding language itself as a phylogenetic inheritance – a structure, developed at some originary pre-historic point, and passed mysteriously from gener- ation to generation. Shared structures of fantasy create the possi- bility of thought transference because we all inherit the same structural forms. Lacan speculates that the transferential effects of analysis, and the symbolic coincidences that Freud labels telepathy, appear because of these shared structures.[43]

In one sense, these shared structures simply create the possibility of identification with others. Helene Deutsch, in her article, 'Occult Processes Occurring during Psychoanalysis', suggests that a version of this limited symbolic is what makes empathetic identification possible between analyst and patient. It is this connection, taken to an extreme, which becomes telepathy:

. . . intuitive empathy is precisely the gift of being able to experience the object by means of an identification taking place within oneself . . . The intuitive attitude, i.e., the analyst's own process of identification, is made possible by the fact that the psychic structure of the analyst is a product of developmental processes similar to those which the patient himself has also experienced. Indeed, the unconscious of both the analyst and the analysand contains the very same infantile wishes and impulses.[44]

Since we all share the same structures and developmental processes, all unconsciouses hold the same material and the same infantile wishes. It is our subsequent identifications across these shared desires which enables analysis, empathy and telepathy.

Deconstructive theory has taken up the paradox of these limited structures, pointing out that psychoanalysis simultaneously presents two different versions of the symbolic. On the one hand, according to Freud, psychoanalysis is not a system.[45] The psyche's phantasmatic flexibility (which, in structural and poststructural versions of psychoanalysis, rests on the arbitrary relation between signified and signifier) makes it impossible to securely predict responses to the raw contingencies of outer life – such as someone's death, or a sexual attack. Lacanian influenced psychoanalytic theories of reading stress the endless chain of the signifier, the movement of meaning, the loss inherent in language which makes it impossible to alight on a single fixed interpretation for any event. On the other hand, psychoanalysis simultaneously holds out a hermeneutic promise. It offers interpretation by offering a limited range of possibilities from which to choose. For psychoanalysis, as it is practised by Freud and his followers, 'no' usually means 'yes' – it rarely means 'blue'; dreams inevitably contain wishes and childhood sexual material. There are most definitely rules making for, as I pointed out in my previous chapter through Lacan's analysis of the Circuit, a limited psychoanalytic field of symbolic play.

The deconstructive reading of Freud on telepathy suggests that telepathy is a figure which embodies both of these possibilities. The fantasy of telepathy engages both the potential failure of communication (in Lacanian terms, a letter's uncertain ability to successfully reach its destination) and the inevitability of communicative leakage, the impossibility of owning oneself and one's thoughts in absolute privacy (the sense that we are all part of the same circuit, that the Symbolic suggests that keeping one's thoughts to oneself is as difficult as communicating them successfully).[46] In his article 'Telepathy' in which Jacques Derrida thematizes the difficulty of non-communication, as well as communication, by speaking largely in the voice of Freud, he says:

The truth, what I always have difficulty getting used to: that non-telepathy is possible. Always difficult to imagine that one can think something to oneself [*a part soi*], deep down inside, without being surprised by the other, with the other being immediately informed, as easily as if it had a giant screen in it, at the time of the talkies, with remote control [*télécommande*] for changing channels and fiddling with the colours, the speech dubbed with large letters in order to avoid any misunderstanding.[47]

Derrida points out with his analogizing of the psyche (already spatially imagined as 'deep down inside' – '*dans son for intérieur*' in the original[48]) to a giant television screen through which we are already invaded by the other, that our ways of representing intimacy have adapted to modern technics, although the basic binary of immediacy/distance rehearses the problem of language he finds at work in Plato. Telepathy, despite (because of) its apparent yearning for immediacy is inseparable from the dynamics of mediation:

. . . it is because there would be telepathy that a postcard cannot arrive at its destination. The ultimate naivety would be to allow oneself to think that Telepathy guarantees a destination which 'posts and telecommunications' fail to provide. On the contrary, everything I said about the postcard-structure [*la structure cartpostalée*] of the mark (interference, parasiting, divisibility, iterability . . .) is found in the network. This goes for any tele-system – whatever its content, form or medium.[49]

The deconstructive use of telepathy stresses both the phantasmatic desire for complete presence and an inevitable participation in mediation: 'I hope for complete presence [*la toute présence*] from it, fusional immediacy, a parousia to keep you, at a distance, in order to keep myself within you . . . *Fort: Da, tele*pathy against tele*pathy*, distance against menacing immediacy, but also the opposite, feeling [*le sentiment*] (always close to oneself it is thought), against the suffering of distancing [*la souffrance de l'éloignement*] that would also be called telepathy.'[50] The paradox is in the linking of tele (distance) with the pathos of presence. Or as Marc Redfield puts it: 'Telepathy communicates a fantasy of unmediated communication, and at the same time records, in its very name, an irreducible distance within self-presence. It promises an escape from the technology of the signifier, but in doing so imports *techne* into the heart of pathos. For whose pathos is it, once tele-pathy has begun?'[51]

Derrida, like Roustang, suggests that telepathy is a site of over-invested desire for Freud because of its threatening closeness to psychoanalysis. Thought transference must be kept to the outside of psychoanalysis in order for psychoanalysis to establish the boundaries of its discipline. Transference in psychoanalysis is based on the fact that the patient reacts emotionally to the analyst only as a substitute for other more primary affective bonds. If psychoanalytic transference really resembled thought transference, then this would put it in the realm of suggestion, that threatening suggestion which Freud exorcized from psychoanalysis when he broke with Breuer and hypnosis. Psychoanalysis requires a (at least somewhat) stable subject which telepathy's horizon of shared thought problematizes.

Derrida's useful reading of Freud on telepathy teases out the metaphysical fantasies around communication – of closure, completion and presence to the other – that psychoanalysis both desires and disavows. However, Derrida disregards the historical context of the materiality of thought transference as Freud and turn-of-the-century psychical researchers imagine it. Thought transference represents immediate affective and substantial (physical) transference for Freud and Ferenczi in ways which become enmeshed with the proximity of minds, thoughts and bodies in analysis. The development of psychoanalytic theory is inseparable from this fact, and from the affective and rivalrous investments of the early analysts in Freud and in each other.

Sharing thoughts, of course, opens up the possibility of stealing them. It is perhaps not surprising, therefore, that the history of psychoanalysis reveals an excessive concern for questions of originality and plagiarism. As François Roustang has shown, the rivalrous relationships between Freud's followers replicate Freud's own theories of the primal horde.[52] Freud, the father, is always finally the hated, feared and desired original source of psychoanalytic theory. Anyone who seems to come upon psychoanalytic ideas along with, or in advance of, Freud threatens his position. Although he repeatedly disavows the desire to be original, Freud claims that he avoids reading Nietzsche because he is afraid that he might have prefigured his own ideas: 'Nietzsche, another philosopher whose guesses and intuitions often agree in the most astonishing way with the laborious findings of psychoanalysis, was for a long time avoided by me on this very account; I was less concerned with the question of priority than with keeping my mind unembarrassed.'[53] An unembarrassed mind is one which, Sam Weber has indicated, has no debts to pay or no coincidence of thought to acknowledge.[54] Yet, at other times, Freud breezily acknowledges his own indebtedness. In a letter to Ferenczi of 8 February 1910 he writes: 'You should not be surprised if in my Nuremberg lecture you again hear your thoughts and even some of your formulations. It will be the way it was with my last lecture in Worcester; I have a decidedly obliging intellect and am very much inclined toward plagiarism.'[55]

'Inclined toward plagiarism' reveals a whole spectrum of concerns for psychoanalysis and its duplicitous mediator, the unconscious. Freud is more than a little worried that others might steal his ideas, but simultaneously tries to deter Georg Groddeck from 'the trivial ambition of claiming originality and priority . . . Could you have absorbed the main idea of psychoanalysis in a cryptomnesic way? In a way similar to my discoveries relating to my own originality? What's the use of struggling for priorities against an older generation?'[56] One might ask what sort of self-blinded question is this from the man who discovered the Oedipus complex? Freud suggests that we always struggle against an older generation, killing the father, and taking his ideas for our own, in order to carve out a mythical individuality in a shared and crowded terrain. Cryptomnesia allows us to believe the myth of our own originality and hold on to our desire to be 'unembarrassed' by the incursion of others' thoughts, by forgetting selectively. But of course the unconscious always knows the truth – that we inevitably borrow and steal. Working through the same psychic material we tread the same paths, fall into the same traps. Freud and his analytic followers systematically uncover and repress this repetitive schema. In her autobiography Helene Deutsch helpfully points out that even her anxieties of influence are not her own: 'Thus I became interested at one time in the problems of plagiarism, only to learn much later that these had once weighed very heavily on Freud.'[57] What emerges from these early analytic disputes is a series of mistaken, often comic, and sometimes tragic encounters around suggestibility and ownership of thought in psychoanalysis.[58]

The landscape of permeable minds that thought transference suggests can seem like a psychotic staging of these charged negotiations between Freud and his followers. One key dispute occurs between Freud and Ferenczi on a trip they take together, relatively early in their relationship, to Palermo. Bad feelings erupt when the two attempt to collaborate on an article about the famous psychotic judge, Daniel Paul Schreber. Ferenczi later described the incident:

[Freud] was too big for me, too much of a father. The result was that in Palermo, where he wanted to do the famous work on paranoia (Schreber) in collaboration with me, right on the first evening of work when he wanted to dictate something to me, I rose up in a sudden burst of rebellion and explained that it was not at all a collaboration, if he simply dictated to me. 'So that's the way you are?' – he said, astonished. 'You perhaps wanted to take the whole thing?' Having said that, he worked alone every evening from then on.[59]

Ferenczi, refusing to be dictated to, stages a secretarial rebellion that both Theodora Bosanquet and Schreber himself would recognize. Schreber's delusions literally enact the dangers of suggestion, thought transference, and taking dictation, in catastrophes upon his body and mind. Compulsively forced to think thoughts that are not his, he is invaded by foreign interlocutors (talking birds, rays made out of language) and believes himself to be the focus of an elaborate dictation plot. All of the words he utters and thinks are recorded by lackeys who send down rays saying 'we have already got this' when he dares to repeat a thought.[60]

When Freud finally writes up his solely authored treatise on Schreber he still finds himself embroiled in a plagiarism/identification problem. Schreber's ideas resemble his own a little too closely:

Schreber's 'rays of God', which are made up of a condensation of the sun's rays, of nerve-fibres, and of spermatozoa . . . are in reality nothing else than a concrete representation and projection outwards of libidinal cathexes; and they thus lend his delusions a striking conformity with our theory. His belief that the world must come to an end because his ego was attracting all the rays to itself, his anxious concern at a later period, during the process of reconstruction, lest God should sever His ray connection with him, – these and many other details of Schreber's delusional structure sound almost like endopsychic perceptions of the processes whose existence I have assumed in these pages as the basis of our explanation of paranoia. I can nevertheless call a friend and fellow-specialist to witness that I had developed my theory of paranoia before I became acquainted with the contents of Schreber's book. It remains for the future to decide whether there is more truth in Schreber's delusion than other people are as yet prepared to believe.[61]

Schreber's delusional system 'concretely' enacts Freud's theories of paranoid libidinal processes. Freud, analysing the paranoid ideas of the psychotic judge, finds himself pleased by Schreber's conceptual conformity with his own ideas of libidinal cathexes. The difference between Schreber and Freud should be that the psychotic, Schreber, lives *through* his delusional systems, while the doctor, Freud, analyses them. However, in this passage, Freud appears to compete with Schreber as theorist, foregrounding his own paranoia by calling on a friend and fellow specialist to testify to his priority and independence over the already persecuted madman Schreber. Not surprisingly, this friend and fellow specialist turns out to be the mortified secretary Ferenczi.[62] In the midst of analysing paranoid delusions of grandeur and uniqueness Freud still defends his priority as the source of ideas. If he is not himself Schreber, then he is in the position of the rays saying 'we already have that one'.

As is evident in Schreber, psychosis is a disease that depends on magical and material forms of psychotic transmission. Psychotics believe that the contents of their minds are being manipulated by strangers. According to François Roustang, psychosis is an annihilating and complete invasion by the other, an unassimilable symbolic attack which creates and destroys the subject in its wake. In 1939 the psychiatrist Kurt Schneider proposed the following list of the symptoms of schizophrenia. The patient:

(1) hears voices speaking the patient's own thoughts out loud; (2) or is the subject about which voices are arguing; (3) or is the subject of commentary by the voices, who comment on what the patient is doing or has done; (4) has normal perceptions followed by delusional versions of them; (5) is the passive recipient of body sensations coming from outside; (6) feels thoughts being extracted from the mind by external forces; (7) believes thoughts are broadcast to others; (8) or complains of thoughts being inserted into the mind from outside. Or has the sense that (9) feelings and affects, or (10) sudden impulses, or (11) motor activities, are controlled from outside the patient's own body.[63]

Every one of these symptoms with the exception of 4 concerns the inability to distinguish one's inside from one's outside, the confusion of world and psyche, the expropriation of thoughts or the self. Psychotics, Roustang argues, are incapable of entering the transferential contract of psychoanalysis because they themselves are nothing but what has been transferred. Thought transference is the imagined material mechanism of the invasion and symbolic annihilation of the psychotic.[64] As we have seen, Freud wants to set up a clear distinction between thought transference and psychoanalytic transference; the first, if it exists, is an entirely physiological phenomenon; the second happens psychically, in analysis and out of it, through unconscious representations and substitutions. But, as we have seen, this distinction is sometimes a difficult one to maintain because of the psychoanalytic merging of the physiological and the psychic. Freud finds himself drawn towards the thought transference of the psychotic in his most speculative moments, imagining it as a mechanism that reflects a primitive material form of communication.

The psychotic then is the subject at the outer limit of thought transference. He cannot be cured through psychoanalysis; he cannot engage in transference because he is himself the product of thought transference. His self consists entirely of the expropriated thoughts of the other.[65] In his theories Freud can admire psychosis – finding Schreber's delusions reassuringly supportive of his own theories – but in his practice he distances himself from both psychotics and the suggestive and annihilating forms of transmission they embody.[66] On the other hand Ferenczi – the 'deranged', seducing Ferenczi – collapses theory and practice, embraces annihilating forms of transmission, and redesigns psychoanalysis on the order of a psychosis. In the process he imagines a road not taken for psychoanalysis.

FERENCZI'S MATERIAL THEORIES: THOUGHT TRANSFERENCE, HOMOSEXUALITY, AND SEDUCTION

In contrast to Freud, Ferenczi's fascination with thought transference both influences and is influenced by his psychoanalytic theory and practice. He tells Freud:

My 'inclination toward occult matters' is not 'secret' but rather quite obvious – it is also not actually an inclination toward the occult, but rather an urge toward de-occultization, at the base of which there may be, in the final analysis, magic-religious strivings, which I am defending myself against by wanting to bring clarity to these matters. I am convinced of the actuality of thought transference. I believe, incidentally, that even an indication that *prophecies* are possible could or should not force one to abandon the scientific basis.[67]

Ferenczi not only engages his patients in telepathy experiments, but also begins to believe that unconscious thought transference is inevitably an integral part of psychoanalytic technique. Ferenczi's interest in telepathy merges with his psychoanalytic practice through his belief in what he calls the 'dialogue of the unconscious', which can develop between analyst and analysand, or between two people who are intimate: 'where the unconscious of two people completely understand themselves and each other, without the remotest conception of this on the part of the consciousness of either'.[68] As an outgrowth of this mutual communication already inherent in analysis, Ferenczi finds himself stretching the limits of transference by engaging in what he called mutual analysis with some of his most severely disturbed patients. Mutual analysis began with Ferenczi's sense that if he disliked or felt uncomfortable with a patient no analytic work would happen because the patient would pick up on these feelings. Therefore, the analyst might occasionally find it necessary to be absolutely open with the patient, to let the patient understand his own resistances. In mutual analysis, the analyst and patient actually change places in order to work through the resistances on both sides that are blocking the analysis.

Ferenczi stresses that mutual analysis is a final resort rather than a recommended method. There are obvious problems with it. For instance, if Ferenczi confesses his personal secrets to his patients, they in turn, as they conduct their own experiments in mutual analysis apart from the protected confidential space of the psychoanalyst's office, could tell his secrets to others[69]:

Thus I would be confronted with the possibility that people who are complete strangers to me will come into full possession of my most intimate, most personal emotions, sins, etc. Consequently I either have to learn to accept the impossibility, even madness, of this whole idea and technique, or I must go on with this daring enterprise and come around to the idea that it really does not matter if a small group of people is formed whose members know everything about one another.[70]

As we will see in his correspondence with Freud, this vision of mutual mind reading, a virtually psychotic society, becomes part of Ferenczi's ideal of a world changed by psychoanalysis through an open circuit of shared thought and shared honesty.

On 22 November 1910, Ferenczi writes to Freud, 'Interesting news in the transference story. Imagine, I am a great soothsayer, that is to say, a reader of thoughts! I am reading my patients' thoughts (in my free associations). The future methodology of [psychoanalysis] must make use of this.' Ferenczi goes on to describe his experiments with a homosexual patient in which the patient thinks of a person Ferenczi does not know and Ferenczi free associates his ideas about the person with some success although with generally mixed results. He concludes: 'this method will be suitable to catch the patient's most active complexes at work. – It can be refined even more! When I come to Vienna I will introduce myself as "court astrologer of the psychoanalysts".'[71] One may wonder what the patient felt about using up his psychoanalytic hour on Society for Psychical Research style experiments, but Ferenczi's tone, a mixture of triumph and self-deprecating humour, indicates that he at the very least felt that this was a worthwhile use of analytic space, even if he was not sure how Freud might react.

Freud's following letter, written the next day but clearly before he received Ferenczi's news, is not concerned with thought transference but rather with another difficult set of questions about the permeability and boundaries of the psyche. As previously discussed, Freud and Ferenczi had earlier attempted, unsuccessfully, to collaborate on the work on Schreber, which resulted in Ferenczi's accusations that Freud only wanted him as a secretary. In November of 1910 Freud foresees the publication of his (now solely authored) work on Schreber and suggests that Ferenczi should publish his own article on paranoia before Freud's comes out because 'after that you will lose the effect'.[72] When Freud writes to Ferenczi the day after Ferenczi's delighted, if somewhat tongue-in-cheek, claims for himself as a mind reader, Freud says, not at all tongue-in-cheek, '[a]s regards paranoia, it would be better for you to make yourself independent of me'.[73] It is a short bitter letter complaining of Adler and Stekel's defections and ending, 'I tell you, it was often nicer when I was alone.'[74] The simultaneity of Freud's and Ferenczi's crossing letters points towards the competing affective claims of thought transference and solitude. Ferenczi's exuberant attempts to bring thought transference to bear as a psychoanalytic tool suggest that he believes the analysts most telepathically attuned to their patients' unconsciouses will be the best ones. Thought transference for Ferenczi is a method which can and should be refined for analytic use, like free association and dream interpretation.

The contexts of these two letters differ; Freud's depression about theoretical disputes with colleagues is not precisely equivalent to Ferenczi's enthusiasm for telepathic contact with patients. Yet Freud's emphasis on shutting down the possibility of sharing thought contrasts strikingly with Ferenczi's tone. When Freud advises Ferenczi to make himself independent of Freud's thoughts he is giving him an impossible order, because the institution of psychoanalysis, as well as Freud's theory of psychosis, is based on the recognition of the impossibility of keeping one's thoughts to oneself, and the impossibility of keeping one's thoughts from Freud. The order Freud gives Ferenczi resembles the impossible imperative the father bequeaths the Oedipal son: be like me/do not be like me. The structure of shared knowledge in psychoanalysis suggests that none of its early adherents were allowed to make themselves independent from Freud and still consider themselves psychoanalysts. All knowledge had to be traced back to its source/father Freud. As Roustang has shown, if Freud cannot tolerate independence of thought in his disciples, neither can he tolerate them fully understanding him, taking his ideas on board too well. Making oneself independent is just what Ferenczi cannot do with respect to Freud, and it is also what the structure of paranoid psychosis both desires and claims is impossible. The paranoid psychotic such as Schreber believes he stands alone in his central importance to the world order, but therefore his mind is subject to invasion, his thoughts are expropriated, his psyche is not his own.

After their failed attempt to collaborate on Schreber, Ferenczi sends Freud a soul-searching letter about his own desire for unimpeded access to Freud: 'I did, perhaps, have an exaggerated idea of companionship between two men who tell each other the truth *unrelentingly*, sacrificing all consideration.'[75] Ferenczi's utopian ideal is one of thought transference as a two-way street, a shared emotional and intellectual storehouse; Freud's fears are of being invaded, having his own (proper to himself) ideas stolen. But as Ferenczi also points out, Freud's positioning of him as simply a medium or transcriber of Freud's ideas foregrounds one of the contradictory ways in which Ferenczi sees himself in relation to Freud – he sees his own thought as simply an extension of Freud's:

[D]on't forget that for years I have been occupied with nothing but the products of your intellect, and I have also always felt the man behind every sentence of your works and made him my confidant. Whether you want to be or not, you are one of the great master teachers of mankind, and you must allow your readers to approach you, at least intellectually, in a personal relationship as well. My ideal of truth that strikes down all consideration is certainly nothing less than the most self-evident consequence of your teachings.[76]

Ferenczi, occupied with nothing but the products of Freud's intellect, resembles both the secretary he balked at becoming, and the paranoid psychotic who finds himself entirely a product of the thoughts of the other. Ferenczi's being 'nothing but' an outgrowth of the master gives him a particular sort of psychic intimacy with him:

So I am and have been much, much more intimately acquainted and conversant with you than you could have imagined. Strangely – and that is the point of my case history that appears neurotic, even demented – I forgot to take into account the fact that you could not have known all that – and even if you did know it, it would on no account have obliged you to dispense completely with your justified distrust of people (even of friends – after the *Fliess* case) and give yourself over to someone, e.g., an enthusiastic, impertinent youngster.[77]

Ferenczi's intimacy with Freud's intellectual work is inseparable from his experience of intimacy with Freud the man: 'I am convinced that I am not the only one who in important decisions, in self criticism, etc., always asks and has asked himself the question: How would *Freud* relate to this? Under "Freud" I understood his teachings and his personality, fused together in a harmonic unity.'[78] Ferenczi insists upon the indissociability of Freud the man from Freud the movement: 'there has certainly never been any *intellectual* movement in which the personality of the discoverer has played such a great and indispensable role as yours has in psychoanalysis. – You see it is *literally* true: you are not only the discoverer of new psychological facts but also the *physician*, who treats us physicians.'[79]

   The paradox of psychoanalysis is that it dismantles myths of authority and origins (in its analysis of the Oedipal conflict, transference, etc.) while installing its originator Freud in the place of absolute authority. For Ferenczi, desire for knowledge of Freud's ideas inevitably shades into desire for Freud the man, for the deep theoretical knowledge of the psyche that psychoanalysis promises and for the autobiography from which the theory springs. If transference provides a method for understanding and enacting emotional ties to others, then the manoeuvrings of the early analysts around Freud expose the ways in which theoretical knowledge in psychoanalysis arises from what can appear at times to resemble psychotic desire – transference out of bounds. Given Ferenczi's desire for, and understanding of, the psychoanalytic breakdown of the barrier between the intellectual and the emotional, it is not surprising that he both engages with such enthusiasm in thought transference experiments and expresses his relentless transferential desire for Freud through fantasies of thought transference. Unlike psychoanalytic transference, thought transference is not expected to employ substitute objects. It aims for absolute openness – wanting (and knowing) the man and his theory.

For Ferenczi this breakdown of barriers, this giving over wholly to another the truth of the self, becomes the utopian possibility towards which psychoanalysis should strive:

> You once told me that [psychoanalysis] was only a science of facts, of indicatives that should not be translated into imperatives – that latter are paranoid. According to this conception there is no [psychoanalytic] worldview, no [psychoanalytic] ethics, no [psychoanalytic] rules of conduct. I also know of no ethics other than those of pure reason; but the extension of reason into hitherto unconscious areas has also had a very significant influence on the worldview and behaviour of nonparanoids. The final consequence of such insight – when it is present in two people – is that they *are not ashamed in front of each other, keep nothing secret, tell each other the truth without risk of insult or in the certain hope that within the truth there can be no lasting insult*. . . . according to my [psychoanalytic] ideal there are no halfway standards; all consideration for people and conditions disappears beside my ideal of truth. Please don't misunderstand me. I really don't want to 'reform' society. I am not a paranoiac. I would only like to see *thoughts* and *speech* liberated from the compulsion of unnecessary inhibitions in the relations of [psychoanalytically]-minded men. –
>
> Unfortunately – I can't begin, you have to! After all, you are [psycho-analysis] in person![80]

But what if Ferenczi's ideal of truth is psychotic? Paranoia may be an appropriate response in a world where people are occupied with nothing but the products of your thoughts. For Freud, paranoia, as he is about to publish in 'Schreber', is indissociable from homosexuality. He claims that 'what lies at the core of the conflict in cases of paranoia among males is a homosexual wishful phantasy of *loving a man*'.[81] Freud's conclusions have been attacked, and in my view, rightly so, for assuming that homosexuality is equivalent to narcissistic desire or desire for the same, but his formulation of paranoia as a disavowal of homosexual desire provides a compelling logical mechanism through which to understand homophobic disavowals.[82] According to Freud what the paranoid disavows in his delusions of persecution is the working out of the simple sentence 'I (a man) <u>love him</u> (a man)' which is turned around into 'I hate him':

> This contradiction, which must have run thus in the unconscious, cannot, however, become conscious to a paranoic in this form. The mechanism of symptom-formation in paranoia requires that internal perceptions – feelings – shall be replaced by external perceptions. Consequently the

proposition 'I hate him' becomes transformed by *projection* into another one: '*He hates* (persecutes) *me*, which will justify me in hating him.' And thus the impelling unconscious feeling makes its appearance as though it were the consequence of an external perception:

'I do not *love* him – I *hate* him, because HE PERSECUTES ME.'[83]

Paranoia results from repressed homosexuality for Freud because of a deep-rooted, definitionally uncanny, fear of the same that is never questioned. This fear is connected to a constitutive fear of losing one's individual boundaries – a simultaneously seductive and frightening lack of barriers between minds and bodies which is, as I have shown, at the turn of the century often figured through thought transference. In paranoid logic the desired other, whose similarity fascinates but also threatens the borders of the self, can only be seen as persecuting. Adam Phillips has suggested that this uncanny valence of homosexuality makes it the occult for psychoanalysis – its forbidden form of sexuality.[84]

Ferenczi, living with and through these theories, circumvents them by diving in – by inviting both homosexuality and psychosis. In his pleading letter to Freud after the Schreber incident Ferenczi begs him to, 'let a part of your homosexual libido be refloated and bring more sympathy to bear toward my "ideal of honesty".'[85] He asks Freud for unimpeded access to him: 'My dream in which I saw you standing naked before me (naturally without feeling the slightest conscious (indeed, also in my dream still unconscious) sexual arousal) was the transparent symbolization of 1.) the ucs. homosexual tendency and 2.) the longing for absolute mutual openness.'[86] Homosexuality, along with thought transference, is a figure for Ferenczi of this absolute openness. Yet, of course, both configurations of relationship to the other are also more than figures. They both represent, in terms of psychoanalytic logic, simultaneously a sexual (for Ferenczi, generalized to societal-utopian) fantasy and the threat of paranoid psychosis. These anxious figures of intimacy – standing naked in front of someone, scooping out the insides of their mind, finding someone else in your place, with your thoughts, writing your psychoanalytic article about paranoia – seem at different times pleasurable and dangerous, rhetorical and material. Thought transference like homosexuality is imagined as simultaneously physically invasive, and dematerialized or purified: the almost Edenic dream of standing naked without sexual desire.

Reading Ferenczi's letters and theoretical writings one is never led to believe either that his interest in thought transference cloaks his homosexual desire for Freud, or that his naked desire for Freud is simply a figure for his telepathic need for absolute mutual openness. His dream presents both options as coexisting. His interest in thought transference experiments indicates some of the ways in which Ferenczi's sometimes outrageous practices figure the literal, and literalize the figurative in the slide between bodily and psychic intimacy. One particularly rich example of this slide occurs with Ferenczi's paranormally sensitive homosexual patient. Ferenczi writes to Freud about an incident in which his patient jumped up from the couch claiming there were worms on it. Ferenczi then records his own free associations, connecting them to his patient's telepathic abilities:

I had sexual intercourse on the same day. The thought occurred to me that it is not right to use the same couch for one's occupation and for making love. The woman with whom I had intercourse calls spermatozoa 'little worms' . . . On the same day I thought of the possibility that a person with a fine sense of smell could sense that something took place there. (It is improbable that material traces had remained on the couch. That had been seen to. But such a thing cannot be dismissed.)[87]

What sort of intimacy is appropriate to the psychoanalytic office in which Ferenczi first has sex with a woman and then apparently has his thoughts read by a gay man? John Forrester has suggested that Freud's interest in theorizing incest can be seen to emerge from the embroiled sexual, familial, and psychoanalytic relations which pre-vailed among the early analysts – Ferenczi being one of the most 'incestuous'.[88] Ferenczi's ongoing affairs with Gizella Pálos, whom he eventually married, and her daughter Elma, whom he analysed, fell in love with, wanted to marry and sent to Freud for further analysis, make his correspondence with Freud sometimes seem like a theoretically charged enactment of Levi-Strauss's theory of the circulation of women. On Ferenczi's couch, this other scene of circulation – of thought transference transacted between two men over the physical or psychical remains of a heterosexual encounter – becomes an occult version of Eve Sedgwick's *Between Men*. Ferenczi's telepathic exchanges with his patient are explicitly formulated by him as sexual: 'My homosexual is a first-rate masochist (his cruelty, naturally, is lodged behind it). This masochism (possibly) enables him to apperceive impulses toward which others are unreceptive. I *project* the stimulus words ucs., he *introjects* them. (I act like a man, he like a woman; he is, of course, a homosexual).'[89] He is, of course, a homosexual, but I am not, the sentence might continue, propelling itself seamlessly towards the first step of Freud's paranoid logic.

Generally, Ferenczi's writings on homosexuality mirror Freud's, claiming that 'paranoia is perhaps nothing else at all than disguised homosexuality'.[90] But if Ferenczi still obliquely pathologizes homosexuality by seeing paranoia as a defence against it then a paranoid lack of boundaries is also Ferenczi's psychoanalytic ideal, his 'ideal of truth'. His urging of Freud to release some of his homosexual libidinal cathexes onto himself suggests that Ferenczi's theories and practice are at odds. His need to construct himself as nothing but the product of Freud's intellect leads him to follow Freud in identifying homosexuality with paranoia, by simultaneously participating in and diagnosing the fear of the same. Yet in Ferenczi's own practice, which includes his experiments with thought transference, sameness is usually seen as promising rather than threatening.

In his article, 'On the Nosology of Male Homosexuality', Ferenczi's ambivalence becomes clear. He speculates about the construction of what he sees as unnatural barriers between men:

It is in fact astounding to what an extent present-day men have lost the capacity for mutual affection and amiability. Instead there prevails among men decided asperity, resistance, and love of disputation. Since it is unthinkable that those tender affects which were so strongly pronounced in childhood could have disappeared without leaving a trace, one has to regard these signs of resistance as reaction-formations, as defence symptoms erected against affection for the same sex.[91]

He continues with his own reaction-formation: 'I do not wish to be misunderstood: I find it natural and founded on the psycho-physical organization of the sexes that a man loves a woman incomparably better than his like, but it is unnatural that a man should repel other men and have to adore women with an obsessive exaggeration.'[92] What does become threatening for Ferenczi, instead of homosexuality, is an invasive model of heterosexual seduction and its potential to be completely determining of the childhood, as yet unformed self.

In his final paper, 'Confusion of Tongues', Ferenczi returns to Freud's earliest ideas about the traumatic causes of neuroses. Anticipating recent debates about the frequency of child sexual abuse, Ferenczi claims that children fall victim to rape more often than suspected, and that this abuse can result in an overwhelming identification with the aggressor, who is usually a parent or parent figure:

The abused child turns into a mechanically obedient being or becomes defiant, but can no longer account for the reason for the defiance, even to himself . . . The scientific importance of the observation is the assumption that *the still not well-developed personality (of the child) responds to sudden unpleasure, not with defense, but with identification and introjection of the menacing person or aggressor, and identification based on fear* . . . Now we must revert to ideas long ago developed by Freud, who even then pointed out that the capacity for object-love is preceded by a stage of identification.[93]

The violence of the seduction scene leads to this formative identification for Ferenczi because he literalizes the appropriation of the body and mind. Like the psychotic, Ferenczi theorizes and experiences the permeability of the psyche substantially, both in his theory of trauma and through his patients. He imagines mutual analysis as an exchange of unconscious ideas, but also of substance: 'The two unconsciouses thereby receive mutual help; the "healer" himself would gain some tranquillity from the healed and vice-versa. Both emphasizing this mutual flux be taken in the substantial sense and not merely explained in terms of psychology. Both have completely identical notions that hate and enmity (especially in the earliest years of childhood) effectively expel the personality's vital energies and could altogether destroy them . . .'[94] He takes the question of substance in the psyche literally, and shares this literalization with his psychotic patients. When his patient R.N., with whom he has been engaging in mutual analysis, pleads for removal of her psychic pain, Ferenczi treats her through semi-hypnotic suggestion:

In the case of R.N. the attack would intensify until it reached an unbearable climax, and the patient would passionately plead for help, often shrieking, 'Take it away, take it away!' . . . Sometimes I concur with her wishes and assert, so to speak, suggestively: 'Yes, now I am taking the pain away.' . . . The painful part of the psyche is represented in this instance materially, as a substance, and I am required to surround this matter with a strong, impenetrable covering, or to prevent the rest of the psyche, which is located in the head, from collapsing, by erecting suitably placed, solid, supporting beams. Furthermore it is asked of me that even when I go away I leave a part of myself with, or in, the patient as a guardian spirit.[95]

Ferenczi finds himself initially 'embarrassed' by his use of suggestive techniques: 'Quite frankly I was embarrassed for a very long time to get involved with suggestive machinations of this kind, since I was so far from believing in the reality of these strange mental images. But frequently I could not bring these attacks to an end without reciting word for word, somewhat ashamed, whatever the patient insisted upon.'[96] Like Freud and Breuer before him, Ferenczi then admits that the efficacy of suggestion is short-lived; the patient returns in a similarly hysterical state the next day.

Yet Ferenczi by no means dismisses suggestion or the substantial invasions his patients experience. He is fascinated by 'the general question of the physical and the psychical'.[97] In his *Clinical Diary* he continues with his Lamarckian speculations, suggesting the possibility that under certain circumstances substance itself can become motivated; the physical can begin desiring:

But just as very powerful external forces are capable of exploding even very firmly consolidated substances, and can also cause atoms to explode, whereupon the need or desire for equilibrium naturally arises again, so it appears that in human beings, given certain conditions, it can happen that the (organic, perhaps also the inorganic) substance recovers its psychic quality, not utilized since primordial times. In other words the capacity to be impelled by motives (*Bewegtwerden durch Motive*), that is, the psyche, continues to exist potentially in substances as well.[98]

Once again the remnant of prehistoric biology grounds the possibility of an organic response to psychic processes. For Ferenczi, as for Freud at times, this response grounds psychoanalysis's most radical claims for the powers of the psychical over the physical.

If, in 'Dreams and Occultism', Freud seems theoretically drawn towards 'the physical equivalent of the psychical act', he eventually shies away from announcing its existence. Ferenczi, by contrast, consistently brings the material world and psychic reality together by insisting that the transferential processes are both psychic and substantial. He suggests that the analyst should open himself up to the potential reality contained in the delusions of psychotics:

I do not exclude the possibility that delusional productions contain more objective reality than we have assumed until now. From the very beginning I was inclined to think that the hallucinations of the insane, or at least a part of them, are not imaginings but real perceptions, stemming from the environment and from the psyche of other human beings, which are accessible to them – precisely because of their psychologically motivated hypersensitivity – whereas normal people, focusing only on immediate matters of direct concern to them, remain unaffected. What comes to mind in this connection is the so-called occult powers of certain people, and the close relationship and easy transition between the two states: paranoia and psychic super-performance.[99]

For Ferenczi, occult powers are aligned with psychosis; paranormal hypersensitivity and psychic illness issue from the same causes. Paranoia may still be at root a disavowal of homosexual desire, but it is also often an indication of a heightened ability to experience a super-substantive reality. If homosexuality breaks down the barriers between desire and identification, creating for Ferenczi a metaphorics of substantive and cognitive exchange, it follows that paranoids also experience this psychic and physical permeability:

To what extent do those who have 'gone mad' from pain, that is, those who have departed from the usual egocentric point of view, become able through their special situation to experience a part of that immaterial reality which remains inaccessible to us materialists? And here the direction of research must become involved with the so-called occult. Cases of thought transference during the analysis of suffering people are extraordinarily frequent.[100]

This belief in the super-material experiences of his patients returns Ferenczi at the end of his life to the seduction theory. The infant who experiences an annihilating traumatic sexual attack reacts to it by introjecting and totally identifying with her aggressor. Ferenczi's theory of trauma suggests that the psychosis caused by a childhood sexual attack results in a collapsing of the body and the mind which can initiate clairvoyant or telepathic hypersensitivity. This collapsing becomes crucial, both as the content of the illness: the patient's over-proximate identification with the attacker, and the potential technique of the cure: the analyst's over-proximate identification with the patient. Instead of psychoanalytically interpreting the patient's delusions to uncover their hidden meanings, Ferenczi practises psychoanalysis literally, until one might claim he does not practise psychoanalysis at all. He takes the patient's story as truth. In the final years of his life he embraces the possibility of sharing in his patients' delusions.

For Ferenczi, the best analysts and the most damaged psychotics share the ability to transgress normal sense boundaries, linking the most immaterial forms of transmission with the most material. To return to the initial charges against Ferenczi, many of the entries in his *Clinical Diary* do read like the product of a deranged mind, but they do so for a specific set of reasons:

It seems that the hypersensitivity of the sense organs, as I have found with some mediums, was to be traced back to the anxious listening for any wish-impulses of a cruel person. Presumably therefore, all mediums are such overanxious people, who are attuned to the slightest vibrations, those accompanying cognitive and affective processes too, even from a distance. Here link with the telegraphic, electro-radio-telegraphic and -telephonic hallucinations of the mentally ill. Perhaps there are no hallucinations, but only an illusionary working through of real events. The isochronism of dreams corresponding to reality of several patients could be explained . . . perhaps my person is only a relay station, through which the two of them [his two patients, S.I. and R.N.] can come into immediate contact with one another. In this dream that shock tried to reassert itself, but the greater independence acquired in analysis refuses to accept the exogenous substance or emotion into the ego. She rejects, with, as it were, deadly determination, the fare offered to it, saying, 'Please eat it yourself! Deal with it yourself! I will not let myself be tortured instead of you.' In order to make this explanation even more plausible, it must be said that the most abominable cruelty that the patient was subjected to was in fact this: she was forced to swallow the severed genitals of a repugnant black man, who had just been killed.[101]

Here is one psychotic endpoint to an unwavering belief in the seduction theory: the literalization of introjection in a gruesome, surprisingly racialized scene, which Ferenczi takes literally. Beginning with his theories about the developed hypersensitivity of the abused, Ferenczi speculates on the possibility that all hallucinations are really 'an illusionary working through of real events'. Invoking the always useful teletechnology analogy, he continues on to propose that dreams might be telepathically shared, that the analyst can become simply a relay station between the thoughts of his patients as they communicate to and through each other. All of Ferenczi's most wild and disturbing suppositions here rely on a psychotic literalization of psychical processes. The danger of endorsing the possibility of direct transmissibility from world to mind is that the doctor starts to sound like the psychotic.

Theories of transmission abound in this passage: from the vibrations picked up by the sensitive, to the analogy to teletechnology, to the analyst as relay-site, to the introjection of exogenous substance or emotion. If Ferenczi's relentless attempts to theorize psycho-analytic transmission lead him down bizarre paths, this is in part because his theories are enmeshed in his radical practices – particularly his overwhelming identifications with his patients: 'Pride: I am the *first* crazy person who had acquired critical insight, and had *yielded to everyone . . .*'[102] Ferenczi yields by imagining a world without barriers between bodies or minds. Sexuality holds out different promises and dangers for him than for Freud because he reconfigures intimacy in analysis and out of it. For Ferenczi, the unsuccessful disavowal of homosexuality theoretically leads to paranoid psychosis, as it does for Freud, but a release of homosexual libido can promise a utopian collapse of boundaries that may also appear through thought transference. Conversely, heterosexuality, by the time of the *Clinical Diary*, is returned to the seduction theory; a violent, invasive rape becomes formative for subjectivity. Both scenarios suggest that the occult does return as sexuality in psychoanalysis, specifically as a sexuality that knows no borders, that posits people as too close, as overlapping, as disturbingly intimate. Freud's fears and Ferenczi's hopes erupt in this sexualized, spatialized arena.

In 1958 in a lecture titled 'Ferenczi: False Problem or Real Misunderstanding', Wladimir Granoff claims that 'Ferenczi has always and will always be the main character in psychoanalysis'. Granoff continues: 'If Freud invented psychoanalysis, Ferenczi did psychoanalysis. And more . . . he did analysis insofar as it is a living pulsation.'[103] Surely the Hungarian ventriloquist would have appreciated this gratifying, if potentially paranoid, promotion to main character. Undoubtedly, Ferenczi did and lived psychoanalysis. By theorizing and acting out his own spectacular transmissions and blinding identifications, one might even say, he swallowed it whole.

CODA

In a footnote to his biography, *Freud: A Life for Our Time*, Peter Gay complains that James and Alix Strachey's English translations of Freud sometimes substitute unnecessarily obscure Latinate neologisms for Freud's straightforward German terms: 'A particularly egregious instance is "cathexis", now wholly domiciled in English and American psychoanalytic terminology. It renders Freud's *Besetzung*, a word from common German speech rich in suggestive meanings, among them "occupation" (by troops) and "charge" (of electricity).'[104] Freud himself apparently suggested the English word 'interest' as the closest equivalent to *Besetzung*. Occupied as if by troops, charged as if by electricity, interested – how does one describe an affective involvement with another person, idea, thing? The late nineteenth/early twentieth century structurings of this relation – a relation I have been referring to throughout this monograph as intimacy – helped determine the ways in which the discipline of psychoanalysis emerged from its precursor, psychical research, which shared its desires to theorize scientifically, mysterious forms of transmission.

The available cultural analogies for what it means to know another intimately supply the means for defining the ways in which knowledge can be transmitted from one mind, or one place, to another, and for how we imagine ourselves as participating in communities. As I have suggested, at the turn of the century these leaps of knowledge and affect are often imagined in terms of simultaneously supernatural, technological and spatial connections. James's telegraphist identifies and disidentifies through her position as transmitter and receiver of information. On the line, she is connected to the world of another class, literally, in other people's lives, imaginatively as both voyeur and participator. James's secretary, Theodora Bosanquet, similarly works through the invasive, communicative and ghostly potential of the secretarial relation. James finds himself identificatorily *in* the convulsion of the First World War, much as the hero of his ghostly novel *The Sense of the Past* finds himself *in* the past. The hypnosis novels of the 1890s that I discuss invoke mind-entering, powerful aesthete villains whose detached, aesthetic attitudes towards life often disguise vampiric desires to literally suck up other lives or control other minds. The Society for Psychical Research's investigations into occult phenomena such as mediumistic transmission of messages from the dead, and telepathic transmission of messages from the living explore the economics of transmission – how do messages get from one place to another? – while also trying to establish what it means to formulate intimate connections between people through pushing the limits of existing psycho-physical models of the mind. Thought transference, I argued, allowed for scientific knowledge to cathect love, and vice-versa.

Ferenczi's strange clinical practices also embraced these connections. He employed psychical research's psycho-physical and telepathic fantasies to elaborate his own version of scientific and desiring transmission. His theories relentlessly broke down the barriers between bodies and minds; for him thought transference was a bridge between the material and the psychic. By suggesting that identification and empathy were made possible by a permeable psyche, he formulated a psychotic scene for psychoanalysis. Freud participated in Ferenczi's speculations up to a point; as I have shown, Freud's own intense interest in the physical equivalent of the psychical act underlies much of his own strangest speculations. Clearly, Freud's relationship to the occult is by no means as dismissive as Ernest Jones would have liked it to be. But if Freud finally rejects Ferenczi's treasured late beliefs in the occult, suggestion and the real event, we can still see Ferenczi's oeuvre as comprising one of the most significant ghost stories of psychoanalysis – what it attempts to leave behind and what it cannot do without.

Notes

INTRODUCTION

1 Adam Phillips, *Terrors and Experts* (London: Faber & Faber, 1995), p. 20.
2 See D. M. Thomas, *The White Hotel* (New York: Pocket Books, 1982) for a fictional Freud who recognizes the powers of telepathy and clairvoyance in one of his hysterical female patients.
3 See Michel Foucault, *The History of Sexuality*, trans. Robert Hurley, vol. 1 (New York: Random House, Inc., 1978) and Eve Kosofsky Sedgwick, *Between Men: English Literature and Male Homosocial Desire* (New York: Columbia University Press, 1985).
4 See Tim Armstrong, *Modernism, Technology and the Body* (Cambridge: Cambridge University Press, 1998); Friedrich Kittler, *Discourse Networks 1800/1900*, trans. Michael Metteer with Chris Cullens (Stanford: Stanford University Press, 1990); Ivan Kreilkamp, 'A Voice Without a Body: The Phonographic Logic of *Heart of Darkness*', *Victorian Studies* 40: 2 (Winter 1997), 211–244; Lisa Steinman, *Made in America: Science, Technology and American Modernism* (New Haven: Yale University Press, 1987).
5 See for example, Ivan Kreilkamp's discussion of the phonographic logic of Conrad's novels (Kreilkamp, 'A Voice Without a Body').
6 According to Laplanche and Pontalis, psychical reality is a 'term often used by Freud to designate whatever in the subject's psyche presents a consistency and resistance comparable to those displayed by material reality: fundamentally, what is involved here is unconscious desire and its associated phantasies' (J. Laplanche and J.-B. Pontalis, *The Language of Psychoanalysis*, trans. Donald Nicholson-Smith (New York: W. W. Norton & Company, 1973), p. 363).
7 Jeffrey Masson, *The Assault on Truth: Freud's Suppression of the Seduction Theory* (New York: Farrar, Strauss and Giroux, 1984).
8 'In sum: the Oedipus complex, infantile sexuality, the wish-fantasies, all of Freud's self-proclaimed "discoveries" are arbitrary constructions designed to explain away his patients' stories of incest and perversion while simultaneously excusing the method that had provoked them . . . He covered up the hypnosis that allowed him to obtain the stories,

while leaving the astonished world with an Oedipal unconscious' (Mikkel Borch-Jacobsen, 'Neurotica: Freud and the Seduction Theory', *October* 76 (1996), 43).

9   Although in the context of the 'memory wars' no statement can safely be considered uncontroversial. The larger context for these arguments is recent popular discussion of false memory syndrome, childhood sexual abuse, and Satanic and/or alien invasions of the psyche. Both sides of these debates – those who make the case for the prevalence of childhood sexual abuse and the repression of memories, and those who believe in the possibility of false memory syndrome – employ and condemn psychoanalysis strategically to support their cases. For believers in repressed memory, Freud tragically betrayed his hysterical women patients when he disavowed their stories of sexual abuse, instead founding psychoanalysis on the idea that fantasy could have psychic effects which were as deep-rooted and far-reaching as reality. But, if for the supporters of repressed-memory theory Freud was one of the first in a long line of villains to disbelieve the horrifying stories he heard, he also forged the theory of psychic trauma, in which an event (such as a sexual asault) that took place in pre-comprehending childhood could remain dormant until triggered into experience by another event later in life. The traumatic Freud understood the possibility for repressed memory even if the post-seduction-theory Freud denied the reality of childhood sexual abuse. For those who support the existence of false-memory syndrome and point to a boom-industry in suggesting therapists milking suggestible patients through twelve-step treatments to uncover alien encounters, the two Freuds are reversed. The Freud who recognized that fantasy could be as formative as reality is applauded, while the Freud whose deceptive unconscious opened up the possibility of repressed memory is taken to task. Underlying all of these claims is a Freud who puts an inevitably invasive, formative sexuality at the foundation of identity. See Ian Hacking, *Rewriting the Soul: Multiple Personality and the Sciences of Memory* (Princeton: Princeton University Press, 1995) for a helpful history of the roots of the repressed memory debate. See Frederick Crews, *et al.*, *The Memory Wars: Freud's Legacy in Dispute* (New York: New York Review of Books, 1995) for Crews's blistering critique of Freud and the repression theory, and some responses.

10 'In his hypnotic efforts, moreover, he may have experienced a sense of personal failure because he was unable to hypnotize every patient as deeply as he wished' (Melvin A. Gravitz and Manuel I. Gerton, 'Freud and Hypnosis: Report of Post-Rejection Use', *Journal of the History of the Behavioral Sciences* 17 (1981), 68).

11 Originally Freud formulates this idea from observing his patient, the Rat Man. See Sigmund Freud, 'Notes upon a Case of Obsessional Neurosis (Rat Man)', *The Standard Edition of the Complete Psychological*

Works of Sigmund Freud (hereafter, *SE*) trans. James Strachey, (1953–1974).
(1909), *SE* x, pp. 151–249.
12 Sigmund Freud, 'Totem and Taboo', *SE* xiii (1913), p. 83.
13 *Ibid.*, p. 85.

1 THE SOCIETY FOR PSYCHICAL RESEARCH'S EXPERIMENTS IN INTIMACY

1 Terry Castle, *The Female Thermometer: Eighteenth Century Culture and the Invention of the Uncanny* (Oxford: Oxford University Press, 1995), p. 123.
2 *Ibid.*, p. 123.
3 David E. Wellbery, introduction, Kittler, *Discourse Networks 1800/1900*, (Stanford: Stanford University Press, 1990), p. xii.
4 This chapter is not designed to be a history of the Society. Alan Gauld, *The Founders of Psychical Research* (London: Routledge & Kegan Paul Ltd, 1968), Frank M. Turner, *Between Science and Religion: the Reaction to Scientific Naturalism in Late Victorian England* (New Haven: Yale University Press, 1974) and Janet Oppenheim, *The Other World: Spiritualism and Psychical Research in England, 1850–1914* (Cambridge: Cambridge University Press, 1985) have covered the subject extensively. John Peregrine Williams' unpublished dissertation 'The Making of Victorian Psychical Research: an Intellectual Elite's Approach to the Spiritual World' (Cambridge University, 1984) is an indispensable guide to situating psychical research amongst other medical and scientific discourses of the day.
5 Gauld, *Founders*, p. 141.
6 Oppenheim, *Other World*, p. 111.
7 Turner, *Between Science*, p. 54.
8 See Castle, 'Phantasmagoria and the Metaphors of Modern Reverie' in *The Female Thermometer* for an explanation of how the mind came to be described in the language of haunting. Castle suggests that by the nineteenth century science had banished ghosts to the inside of the mind and consequently thought itself began to be conceived of as haunted, 'as if there were, at the very heart of subjectivity itself, something foreign and fantastic, a spiritual presence from elsewhere, a spectre-show of unaccountable origin' (p. 167). Although fascinating in many respects, Castle's thesis leaves aside the whole question of the craze for spiritualism which began in the mid-nineteenth century. I would maintain that ghosts have a more complicated, and more continuously externalized, history than Castle allows.
9 'Objects of the Society', *Proceedings of the Society for Psychical Research* (*PSPR*) 1 (1881–1882), 3–4.
10 Henry Sidgwick, 'President's Address', *PSPR* v (1888–1889), 272.
11 *Ibid.*, 272.

12 Alex Owen, *The Darkened Room: Women, Power and Spiritualism in Late Victorian England* (Philadelphia: University of Pennsylvania Press, 1990), p. 26.

13 *Ibid.*

14 Logie Barrow, *Independent Spirits: Spiritualism and English Plebeians, 1850–1910* (London, Routledge & Kegan Paul, 1986) confines the intersection of spiritualism and radical reform movements to the working class spiritualists. In a footnote Alex Owen argues that Barrow underestimates the crossing of interests between middle class spiritualism and the working class movement. (Owen, *The Darkened Room*, p. 250, footnote 27).

15 Gauld, *Founders*, p. 138.

16 The fascination with the split and uncertain nature of the mind also surfaces in popular literature at the time in the many books about doubling written towards the end of the century, such as Robert Louis Stevenson's *Dr Jekyll and Mr Hyde* (1886) and Wilde's *The Picture of Dorian Gray* (1891).

17 F. W. H. Myers, 'General Characteristics of Subliminal Messages', *PSPR* VII (1891–1892), 301.

18 *Ibid.*, 306.

19 Oppenheim, *Other World*, p. 258.

20 See Carlo Ginzburg, 'Morelli, Freud and Sherlock Holmes: Clues and Scientific Method', in *The Sign of Three: Dupin, Holmes, Pierce*, eds. Umberto Eco and Thomas A. Sebeok (Bloomington: Indiana University Press, 1983) for an article which situates Freud in the context of other nineteenth-century interpretative sciences. By contrast the Lacanian return to Freud insists that psychoanalysis is not a hermeneutics and that the force of Freud's thought lies in its refusal of hermeneutics.

21 Ernest Jones, *The Life and Works of Sigmund Freud*, p. 27. Joan Riviere and James Strachey both initially encountered Freud's thought via Myers and the Society for Psychical Research (Pearl King, 'Early Divergences between the Psycho-Analytical Societies in London and Vienna', in *Freud in Exile: Psychoanalysis and its Vicissitudes*, eds. Edward Timms and Naomi Segal (New Haven: Yale University Press, 1988), p. 124).

22 F. W. H. Myers, *Human Personality and its Survival of Bodily Death* (Longmans, Green & Co., London, 1903), p. xxv.

23 Jacques Derrida's body of work would be one place to look for the deconstructive tracing out of this dynamic. See especially *The Postcard*, trans. Alan Bass (Chicago: University of Chicago Press, 1987).

24 Mark Twain, 'Mark Twain on Thought Transference,' *Journal of the Society for Psychical Research* (*JSPR*) 1 (1884), 167.

25 *Ibid.*

26 Mark Twain, letter to F. W. H. Myers, 12 January 1892, Myers Papers, Wren Library, Trinity College, Cambridge University.

27 Mark Twain, 'Mental Telegraphy', *The Complete Essays of Mark Twain*, ed.. Charles Neider (New York: Doubleday & Company, Inc. 1963), p. 71. In his introduction to the article Twain explains that he has collected material on mental telegraphy for years but was afraid to publish it 'for I feared that the public would treat the thing as a joke and throw it aside, whereas I was in earnest' (p. 71).

28 Mark Seltzer, *Bodies and Machines* (New York: Routledge, 1992), p. 9. Twain jokes about the difficulty of distinguishing between 'magical' telepathic communication and the effects of the telephone in *A Connecticut Yankee in King Arthur's Court*, ed. Allison R. Ensor (New York: Norton, 1982). Also see Twain's article 'The First Writing-Machines', *The Complete Essays of Mark Twain*, ed., Charles Neider (New York: Doubleday & Company, Inc. 1963), pp. 324–326.

29 Twain, *JSPR* I, 167.

30 Nicholas Royle, *Telepathy and Literature* (Oxford: Basil Blackwell Ltd, 1990).

31 Kittler, *Discourse Networks*; Avital Ronell, *The Telephone Book* (Lincoln: University of Nebraska Press, 1989); Royle, *Telepathy and Literature*.

32 Thomas A. Edison, *The Diary and Sundry Observations of Thomas Alva Edison* (New York: Philosophical Library, 1948), p. 234. Virginia Woolf invokes a similar fantasy in her story 'Kew Gardens' in an overheard conversation about spiritualism. An old man explains the practical side of communicating with the dead in terms similar to Edison's: 'You have a small electric battery and piece of rubber to insulate the wire – isolate? – insulate? – well, we'll skip the details, not good going into details that wouldn't be understood – and in short the little machine stands in any convenient position by the head of the bed, we will say, on a near mahogany stand. All arrangements being properly fixed by workmen under my direction, the widow applies her ear and summons the spirit by sign as agreed' (Virginia Woolf, *A Haunted House and Other Short Stories* (1944; London: HarperCollins, 1982), p. 36).

33 Friedrich Kittler, 'Gramophone, Film, Typewriter', *October* 41 (1987), 111.

34 Edmund Gurney, Frederic W. H. Myers and Frank Podmore, *Phantasms of the Living*, 2 vols. (1886; facsimile reprint edn Gainesville, Florida: Scholars' Facsimiles & Reprints, 1970).

35 Thought transference experiments usually involved readers' attempts to correctly guess cards, numbers and names which were concentrated on by another. The records of these experiments make for gloriously dull reading, usually in the form of tables of guesses or narrative along the lines of 'Expt. 2. – The same young lady, M.B., seated at the table with her eyes bandaged, pencil in hand. Her uncle, standing about twelve feet distance, asked "What word am I thinking of?" M.B. wrote "Homo." 'This was right.' ('First Report on Thought Reading', *PSPR* I (1882–1883), 55). The tedium of psychical research in general is a point of scientific pride for many writers in the pages of the Society's Journal and Proceedings. Psychical researchers constantly insist that they are

not engaged in frisson-producing activity: 'Further we must warn future readers that the details of the evidence are in many cases not only dull, but of a trivial and even ludicrous kind; and that they will be presented for the most part in the narrator's simplest phraseology, quite unspiced for the literary palate. Our tales will resemble neither *The Mysteries of Udolpho* nor the dignified reports of a learned society. The romanticist may easily grow indignant over them; still more easily may the journalist grow facetious . . . However caused, these phenomena are interwoven with the everyday tissue of human existence, and pay no more regard to what men call appalling than to what men call ridiculous' (William Barrett, C. C. Massey, Rev. W. Stainton Moses, Frank Podmore, Edmund Gurney and F. W. H. Myers, 'Report of the Literary Committee', *PSPR* I (1882–83), 118).

36 Oppenheim, *Other World*, p. 358.

37 See Trevor Hall's *The Strange Case of Edmund Gurney* (London: Gerald Duckworth & Co. Ltd, 1964) for a highly speculative account of Gurney's death from an overdose of chloroform, in a Brighton hotel, in June 1888. Hall surmises that Gurney must have discovered evidence of trickery, including that of his friend, experimentee and personal secretary, G. A. Smith, and therefore committed suicide. Hall provides no convincing evidence for Gurney's alleged discovery, but the verdict of accidental death was at least regarded by some at the time as a cover-up. The suicidally minded Alice James, invalid sister of Henry and William, writing in her diary in August 1889 says, 'They say there is little doubt that Mr Edmund Gurney committed suicide. What a pity to hide it, every educated person who kills himself does something towards lessening the superstition' (*The Diary of Alice James*, ed. Leon Edel, (Middlesex: Penguin Books, 1964), p. 52).

38 A. Sidgwick and E. M. Sidgwick, *Henry Sidgwick: A Memoir* (London: Macmillan & Co, Ltd., 1906), p. 494.

39 *Ibid.*, p. 473.

40 Ethel Sidgwick, *Mrs. Henry Sidgwick* (London: Sidgwick and Jackson, Ltd., 1938), p. 191.

41 William Barrett, *On the Threshold of the Unseen*, 2nd edn, revised (London: Kegan Paul, 1917), p. 294.

42 F. W. H. Myers, 'Science and a future life', *Science and a Future Life, with Other Essays* (London: Macmillan, 1893), p. 40.

43 Robert A. Nye, *The Origins of Crowd Psychology: Gustave LeBon and the Crisis of Mass Democracy in the Third Republic* (London: Sage Publications Ltd., 1975), p. 41.

44 A. H. Pierce and F. Podmore, 'Subliminal Self or Unconscious Cerebration?', *PSPR* XI (1895), 332.

45 Robert D. Stein, 'The Impact of the Psychical Research Movement on the Literary Theory and Literary Criticism of Frederic W. H. Myers', diss., Northwestern University, 1968, p. 32.

46 Henry Sidgwick, 'Presidential Address', *PSPR* I (1882–1883), 66.
47 Barrett, *Threshold of the Unseen*, pp. 293–94.
48 Sigmund Freud, 'Dreams and Occultism', *New Introductory Lectures, SE* XII (1911), p. 55. I discuss this passage further in my final chapter.
49 F. W. H. Myers, 'Automatic Writing', *PSPR* III (1885), 32.
50 Gabriel Tarde, *The Laws of Imitation*, trans. Elsie Clews Parsons (New York, 1903), p. 70, quoted in Mikkel Borch-Jacobsen, *The Freudian Subject*, trans. Catherine Porter (Stanford: Stanford University Press, 1988), p. 266.
51 Gustave LeBon, *The Crowd* (London, Penguin Books Ltd, 1976), pp. 24, 30.
52 *Ibid.*, p. 6.
53 'First Report on Thought-Reading', *PSPR* I (1882–1883), 15–16.
54 *Ibid.*, 33–34.
55 Philippe Auguste Mathias Villiers de l'Isle Adam, *Tomorrow's Eve*, trans. Robert Martin Evans (Urbana: University of Illinois Press, 1982), p. 213. Italics in original.
56 Rudyard Kipling, 'Wireless', *Traffics and Discoveries* (New York: Doubleday, Page & Company, 1920), p. 204.
57 Bruno Latour, *Science in Action*, (Cambridge: Harvard University Press, 1987). Electricity is often portrayed at the time as simultaneously mysterious and commonplace, useful as an explanation for anything otherwise incomprehensible, but not easily explainable itself. 'Perhaps the classic story in this vein was about the student who, asked to define electricity, said he used to know but had forgotten. "How sad", replied his weary professor, "the only man who knew what electricity was has forgotten"' (Carolyn Marvin, *When Old Technologies were New* (Oxford: Oxford University Press, 1988), p. 47 quoting 'Interesting Lecture by W. J. Hammer', *Electrical Review* (March 19 1887), 5).
58 Kipling, 'Wireless', p. 213.
59 Heinrich Hertz was the discoverer of elecromagnetic radiation (Oppenheim, *Other World*, p. 379).
60 Reneé Haynes, *The Society for Psychical Research* (London: Mcdonald & Co., 1982), p. 61.
61 D. D. Home was the one medium who was never discovered in fraud of any kind. See Gauld, *Founders* for a discussion of the SPR's change from investigating physical mediums to investigating mental mediums.
62 See Alex Owen, *Darkened Room*.
63 William James, 'Presidential Address', *PSPR* XII (1896), 6.
64 Gauld reveals the assumptions underlying this scenario in his discussion of the medium Eusapia Palladino and sittings carried out at Myers's estate in Cambridge, Leckhampton House: 'what points of contact could there possibly have been between the ignorant and earthy Eusapia, who was liable upon awakening from her trances to throw herself into the arms of the nearest male sitter with unmistakable intent,

and a group of earnest and highly educated enquirers into the inmost secrets of the Cosmos?' (p. 240). It is precisely these literal, physical points of contact which interest me.

65 As Alex Owen describes it: 'Mary Rosina Showers had a threaded needle passed through the pierced hole in her left ear and was thus attached via five yards of thread, to the outside of the cabinet where every movement of the cotton was visible. Florence Cook submitted to a test in which she completed an electric circuit so that any significant movement on her part would register on a galvanometer' (*The Darkened Room*, p. 69).

66 *Ibid.*, pp. 230–231. Also see Con Coroneos, 'The Cult of *Heart of Darkness*', *Essays on Criticism* 45 (1995), 1–23 for a fascinating analysis of Cesare Lombroso's investigations of Eusapia Palladino: 'Not only was she subject to rigorous control throughout the séance (special ropes, continuous contact, etc.) but after the séance had ended she would be weighed and measured, internally examined, her temperature would be taken, her excreta checked and her perspiration examined for changes in chemical composition. Bodily abnormality could thus be read symptomatically, providing an index for understanding what was unavailable by direct examination' (12–13).

67 'First Report on Thought-Reading', *PSPR* 1 (1882–1883), 30.

68 Quoted in Turner, *Between Science*, p. 113.

69 Quoted in Gauld, *Founders*, p. 182.

70 Bram Stoker, *Dracula* (1897; New York: Signet Classics, 1965), p. 229.

71 Oscar Wilde and others, *Teleny* (London: GMP Publishers Ltd., 1986), p. 38. Further references are included in text.

72 *Teleny*, p. 79. Wilde was familiar with the work of the SPR as he shows when he makes fun of *Phantasms of the Living* in 'The Decay of Lying,' first published January, 1889. He complains about the drab nature that even hallucinations have taken on today: 'why, even sleep has played us false, and has closed up the gates of ivory, and opened the gates of horn. The dreams of the great middle classes of this country, as recorded in Mr. Myers's two bulky volumes on the subject and in the Transactions of the Psychical Society, are the most depressing things that I have ever read. There is not even a fine nightmare among them. They are commonplace, sordid, and tedious' (Oscar Wilde, 'The Decay of Lying', *The Complete Works of Oscar Wilde* (Glasgow: HarperCollins, 1994)), p. 1089.

73 See Michael Warner, 'Homo-Narcissism; or, Heterosexuality', in *Engendering Men: the Question of Male Feminist Criticism*, eds. Joseph A. Boone and Michael Cadden (New York: Routledge, 1990) for a brilliant critique of psychoanalytic thinking on homosexuality and its inevitable collapse into a solipsistic economy of the same. Elizabeth Guzynski's 1993 unpublished paper '"Homo-Narcissism" and the 1890s' extends Warner's ideas in an analysis of *Teleny* to which I am greatly endebted.

74 Sigmund Freud, 'On Narcissism', *SE* xiv (1914), p. 88.
75 In an article called 'A Thought-Reader's Experiences', Stuart Cumberland argues that women make bad thought transference subjects: ' . . .
with the natural perversity of her sex, she will commence to think of
everything or everybody in the room, or perplex herself with the
thought what Mrs. A. thinks of her, or what Miss B. would do in her
place, or whether Mr. C. is of opinion she is making an exhibition of
herself. With such thoughts running like wild-fire through her mind
there is no room for that dominant idea which the operator is in search
of' (Stuart C. Cumberland, 'A Thought-Reader's Experiences', *Nineteenth Century* 20 (December, 1886), 883). Cumberland's methods were
disdained by the Society for Psychical Research as he relied on physical
contact with his subjects and thus opened himself up to the suspicion of
muscle-reading. But his supposition that women's minds are too full of
other subjects, primarily their own narcissism, to concentrate on one
subject for long enough to be effectively 'read' is a fascinating one in
the light of my somewhat schematic assignment of the séance as a
primarily feminine space and the telepathy experiment as a primarily
masculine one.

2 WILDE, HYPNOTIC AESTHETES AND THE 1890s

1 The best recent sources for the history of hypnosis are Alison Winter,
Mesmerized: Powers of Mind in Victorian Britain (Chicago: University of
Chicago Press, 1998); Alan Gauld, *A History of Hypnotism* (Cambridge:
Cambridge University Press, 1992); Adam Crabtree, *From Mesmer to
Freud: Magnetic Sleep and the Roots of Psychological Healing* (New Haven:
Yale University Press, 1993). Also see Daniel Pick's *Svengali's Web: the
Alien Enchanter in Modern Culture* (New Haven: Yale University Press,
2000).
2 George Du Maurier, *Trilby* (London: J. M. Dent & Sons Ltd, 1992).
Further references included in text. *Trilby* became the first modern best-
seller in America. It sold more than 200,000 copies in its first year of
publication (Elaine Showalter, introduction to *Trilby* (Oxford University
Press, 1995), p. ix).
3 Quoted in Jonathan H. Grossman, 'The Mythical Svengali: Anti-
Aestheticism in *Trilby*', *Studies in the Novel* 28:4 (Winter 1996), 539.
4 Of course the aesthete does not have exclusive control of hypnotic
power at the turn of the century. There are many other hypnotizing
types that populate fiction. Perhaps one of the most interesting contrasts
to the aesthetes I discuss here would be Selah Tarrant, the hypnotizing
humbug of Henry James's 1886 novel *The Bostonians*. Unlike more high-
culture-identified figures such as Wilde, Svengali and Lord Henry
(although as we shall see, the most influential aesthetes tend to move
ambivalently between high and mass culture), Selah Tarrant is a fraud

of the people – a democratic mesmerizer, absolutely identified with the newspapers and the public whose attention he craves. Selah (who appropriately sells his daughter along with anything else he can) has a nature which is 'pitched, altogether in the key of public life' (Henry James, *The Bostonians* (1886; Middlesex: Penguin Books, 1966), p. 65). The ways in which a novel such as *The Bostonians* connects the problem of the suggestible political subject to the crowd-identified, publicity-seeking mesmerizer are unfortunately outside of the scope of this chapter, but would make an interesting foil for the kind of connections I posit here. For more on *The Bostonians* and publicity see Lynn Wardley, 'Woman's Voice, Democracy's Body, and *The Bostonians*', *ELH* 56 (Fall 1989), 639–665 and Ian F. A. Bell, 'The Personal, the Private and the Public in *The Bostonians*', *Texas Studies in Language and Literature* 32: 2 (Summer 1990), 240–256.

5 Aestheticism, of course has multiple definitions and competing histories. My use of the term presumes the centrality of Wilde. For a recent discussion that usefully broadens the definition of aestheticism see Talia Schaffer, *The Forgotten Female Aesthetes: Literary Culture in Late-Victorian Britain* (Charlottesville: University of Virginia Press, 2000).

6 See Alan Sinfield, *The Wilde Century: Effeminacy, Oscar Wilde, and the Queer Moment* (London; Cassell, 1994); Joseph Bristow, *Effeminate England: Homoerotic Writing After 1885* (Buckingham: Open University Press, 1995); Ed Cohen, *Talk on the Wilde Side: Toward a Genealogy of a Discourse on Male Sexualities* (New York: Routledge, 1993) for astute analyses of the changing nature of Wilde's sexual and gender images before and after the trials.

7 Winter, *Mesmerized*, p. 2.

8 *Ibid.*, p. 185.

9 Sigmund Freud, 'Group Psychology and the Analysis of the Ego' (1921), *SE* XVIII, pp. 65–143. Winter in *Mesmerized* has brilliantly disentangled the histories of the meanings of hypnotism and mesmerism, asserting that mesmerism was the key term for the nineteenth century. In contemporary discussions and reviews of *Trilby* both terms are employed, and Braid's distinctions are by no means adhered to. For instance the 1895 send-up of *Trilby*, *Drilby*, cautions, 'Let this story be a warning / It's written on that plan / Don't introduce your sweetheart to / Von hypnotizing man' (quoted in Daniel Pick, *Svengali's Web*, p. 96). If we stick closely to Braid's terms Svengali mesmerizes, rather than hypnotizes Trilby; it is, in fact, the mysterious, transferential and eroticized relations of mesmerism which the novel describes. But during the nineteenth century, hypnosis, however it is defined, cannot rid itself of these connotations; Svengali is both a mesmerizing and hypnotizing man.

10 See Jean-Roche Lawrence and Campbell Perry, *Hypnosis, Will and Memory: A Psycho-Legal History* (New York: The Guilford Press, 1988).

11 *Ibid.*, p. 202.
12 'In the latter half of the 1880s, and for much of the 1890s, no aspect of hypnotism attracted greater interest, popular, medical, scientific and literary, than that of its possible adaptation to criminal ends' (Gauld, *History*, p. 494). See Robert G. Hilman, 'A Scientific Study of the Mystery: the Role of the Medical and Popular Press in the Nancy-Salpêtrière Controversy on Hypnotism', *Bulletin of the History of Medicine* 39 (1965), 163–182.
13 See Winter, *Mesmerized*, chapter 12, 'The Social Body and the Invention of Consensus'.
14 J. MacLaren Cobban, *Master of his Fate* (Edinburgh and London: William Blackwood and Sons, 1890), p. 5. Further references included in text. Tim Armstrong's discussion of the novel in *Modernism, Technology and the Body* (Cambridge: Cambridge University Press, 1998) first drew my attention to the book.
15 Oscar Wilde, 'The Portrait of Mr W. H.', *Complete Works*, p. 302
16 Many of Julius's arguments, such as this one, align him with anti-aesthetic discourse, as well as an aesthetic one. The aesthetes were seen as some of the prime examples of degeneration. See Max Nordau's chapter on 'Decadents and Aesthetes', in *Degeneration* (1895; Lincoln: University of Nebraska Press, 1993). Francis Galton coined the word eugenics in 1883 (Daniel Pick, *Faces of Degeneration: a European Disorder, c.1848–c.1918* (Cambridge: Cambridge University Press, 1989), p. 198).
17 Regenia Gagnier argues that during the course of Wilde's trials his life and his works both began to signify a refusal of middle class norms: 'As his works were given equal time with his sexual practices during the trial, aestheticism came to represent a distinct and private realm of art and sexuality. Wilde's trials confronted the public with an art that refused to say nothing but the truth, that refused to take its interrogation solemnly, and a sexuality outside of the rational demands of reproduction. Thus aestheticism came to mean the irrational in both productive (art) and reproductive (sexuality) realms: an indication of the art world's divorce from middle-class life' (Regenia Gagnier, *Idylls of the Marketplace: Oscar Wilde and the Victorian Public* (Stanford University Press, 1986), p. 139).
18 *Dracula*'s ending which juxtaposes the shaky material record of Dracula's eventual capture, 'nothing but a mass of typewriting', with the 'true' reproduction, Mina Harker's son, attempts to dispel fears about mechanical or vampiric reproduction (and fears about the modern women who provoke these odd reproductions with their secretarial skills or spectacular vamping abilities) through a return to a comforting maternal version of reproduction. As many critics have argued, the reproductive anxieties remain and suffuse the novel. See Jennifer Wicke, 'Vampiric Typewriting: *Dracula* and its Media', *ELH* 59: 1

(Summer 1992), 467–493, and Mark Seltzer, 'Serial Killers (I)', *differences* 5: 1 (1993), 92–128.

19 Sinfield, *The Wilde Century*, p. 9.

20 Edgar Allan Poe, 'The Man of the Crowd', *Selected Poetry and Prose of Poe*, ed. T. O. Mabbott (New York: Random House, 1951), pp. 154–162.

21 Eve Kosofsky Sedgwick, *The Epistemology of the Closet* (Berkeley: University of California Press, 1990), p. 186n.

22 Daniel Pick's *Svengali's Web* is an exhaustive study of the cultural meanings of, and continuing fascination with Svengali. Also see Adam Phillips's interesting review of Pick's book, 'Unfathomable Craziness', *The London Review of Books* 22: 10 (18 May 2000), 8–10.

23 Du Maurier, *Trilby*, p. 23. Further references included in text.

24 Grossman, 'The Mythical Svengali', 531.

25 Sedgwick, *Epistemology*, p. 193.

26 There is another story to be told about Trilby's feet and Freud's theories about the fetishistic disavowal of homosexual desire. In the economy of the novel Trilby becomes a commodity, literally a body in bits. Svengali may steal her voice but Little Billee and his friends also commodify her by painting her. And one of their favourite subjects for painting are her feet. *Trilby* along with Rider Haggard's novel *She* is a prime text for exploring the theme of foot fetishism in late nineteenth-century literature. Trilby's large but perfectly formed feet are described rapturously. They are repeatedly painted and drawn by Little Billee and his compatriots – drawings which later fetch huge sums. If Little Billee feels betrayed by the history written in Trilby's eyes, he initially falls in love with her because of her feet.

In his 1927 article, 'Fetishism', Freud interprets what it means to idolize a woman's feet. Freud claims that the foot is in reality a substitute for a missing body part – the penis the boy once believed his mother had. In later life the fetishist refuses to give up this treasured belief. Freud says, the fetishization of the foot 'saves the fetishist from becoming a homosexual, by endowing women with the characteristic which makes them tolerable as sexual objects' (*SE* xxi, p. 154). If what is desired by the child who is in the process of learning about sexual difference is the phallus (seen as a symbol of power and potency, as much as it is the real organ) then the man (it is usually a man) who turns to fetishism in Freud's explanation uses the fetishized object to ward off the frightening possibility of homosexuality. He uses the fetishized female foot to escape the possibility that what he really wants is another man. This interpretation dovetails neatly with Sedgwick's reading of the (homosexual) scandal in Bohemia. Fetishized Trilby and her fetishized foot make for wonderful objects of exchange between men.

27 In his article 'Powers of Suggestion: Svengali and the *Fin-de-Siècle*', in *Modernity, Culture and the Jew*, eds. Bryan Cheyette and Laura Marcus

(Cambridge: Polity Press, 1998), pp. 105–125, Daniel Pick emphasizes the imagined deadly and mesmeric power of the Jew: 'Svengali gave expression to fears of psychological invasion, showing the Jews' capacity to get inside – and even replace – the mental functioning of the gentile through mesmerism' (p. 107). Also see Pick, *Svengali's Web*.

28 Grossman, 'The Mythical Svengali', p. 536.
29 Daniel Pick, Introduction, *Trilby* (London: Penguin Classics, 1994), p. ix.
30 *Ibid.*, p. xii.
31 Edward Purcell, '*Trilby* and *Trilby*-Mania: the Beginning of the Best-seller System', *Journal of Popular Culture* 11 (Summer 1977), 69.
32 *Ibid.*, 71.
33 See Grossman, 'The Mythical Svengali'.
34 Oscar Wilde, *The Picture of Dorian Gray* (1891), in *Complete Works*, p. 159. Further references included in text.
35 Cohen, *Talk on the Wilde Side*, p. 113.
36 H. Montgomery Hyde ed. *The Trials of Oscar Wilde* (London: William Hodge and C. Ltd, 1948), p. 69.
37 See for instance Stephen Arata, *Fictions of Loss in the Victorian* Fin de Siècle (Cambridge: Cambridge University Press, 1996) as well as Cohen, *Talk on the Wilde Side*, Bristow *Effeminate England*, and Sinfield *The Wilde Century*.
38 Kerry Powell, 'The Mesmerizing of Dorian Gray', *The Victorian Newsletter* 65 (Spring 1984), 10–15.
39 Powell, 'Mesmerizing', p. 10 quoting *The First Collected Edition of the Works of Oscar Wilde*, ed. Robert Ross (London: Methuen, 1908), p. 413.
40 Max Nordau's influential *Degeneration* was published in English the same month that Queensberry left his calling card for Wilde. In *Degeneration*, Nordau too read Wilde's pose as a prime exemplar of his ideas – Wilde's eccentric dress, his vanity, his perverse tastes all signified his degeneracy.
41 Hyde, *The Trials of Oscar Wilde*, p. 169. In *De Profundis*, his famous letter to Bosie from prison, Wilde reversed the version of influence that had dominated the court-room, claiming, 'The basis of character is will-power, and my will-power became absolutely subject to yours' and 'My habit – due to indifference chiefly at first – of giving up to you in everything had become inevitably a real part of my nature' (*De Profundis*, in *Complete Works*, pp. 984, 985)
42 Richard Ellmann, *Oscar Wilde* (London: Penguin, 1988), p.391.
43 Hyde, *The Trials of Oscar Wilde*, p. 122.
44 Ellmann, *Wilde*, p. 404.
45 Robert Hichens, *The Green Carnation* (London: Robert Clark Ltd, 1992). Further references in text.
46 Ellmann, *Wilde*, p. 400.
47 Quoted in Arata, *Fictions of Loss*, p. 71.

48 Hyde, *The Trials of Oscar Wilde*, p. 316.
49 This compulsion or payment model I am hypothesizing is quite speculative. It might be further explored, and perhaps critiqued, via the mesmeric effect that the two lovers in *Teleny* exert on each other.
50 Gagnier, *Idylls*, p. 185.
51 *Ibid.*, p. 182.
52 See the definition of deferred action (*Nachträglichkeit*) in Laplanche and Pontalis, *Language of Psychoanalysis*, p. 111.
53 I explore the issue of Freud and the seduction theory at greater length in my final chapter.
54 Wilde, 'The Soul of Man under Socialism', *Complete Works*, p. 1195.

3 HENRY JAMES'S LIVES DURING WARTIME

1 Henry James, *The Portrait of a Lady* (1881; London: Everyman's Library, J. M. Dent, 1995), p. 99.
2 Leon Edel, *Henry James: The Master 1901–1916* (New York: Avon Books, 1972), p. 539.
3 Laplanche and Pontalis, *Language of Psychoanalysis*, p. 205.
4 See 'Group Psychology', section 7. Ferenczi also argues that identification precedes desire in 'The Confusion of Tongues Between Adults and the Child' trans. Jeffrey Masson and Marianne Loring, in *The Assault on Truth: Freud's Suppression of the Seduction Theory*, ed. Jeffrey Masson (New York: Farrar, Strauss and Giroux, 1952). See my final chapter.
5 Martha Banta, *Henry James and the Occult: The Great Extension* (Bloomington: Indiana University Press, 1972).
6 Rebecca West is one early reader of James who argues that metaphor in James's later fiction has 'as real and physical an existence as the facts' (Rebecca West, *Henry James* (London: Nisbet, 1916), p. 112). Ralf Norrman, among others, has connected James's 'verbal magic' to Freud's analysis of magical thinking or the 'omnipotence of thought' (Ralf Norrman, *The Insecure World of Henry James's Fiction* (New York: St Martin's Press, 1982), p. 131).
7 Christopher Nealon, 'Affect-Genealogy: Feeling and Affiliation in Willa Cather', *American Literature* 69: 1 (March, 1997), 10.
8 Henry James, *The Sense of the Past* (Glasgow: W. Collins Sons & Co. Ltd, 1917), p. 41. Further references included in text as *SP*.
9 James's enthusiasm for the British cause is usually seen as an anomaly in a remarkably passive, aesthetic career. The fact that James wrote propaganda at all is noted with some amazement by historians of the War. In his book *The Death of the German Cousin: Variations on a Literary Stereotype, 1890–1920* (Lewisburg: Bucknell University Press and London: Associated Presses, 1986) Peter Edgerly Firchow notes that 'Henry James, who had devoted nearly a lifetime to persuading his readers that the truth was invariably a relative quantity and that

omniscient narration of any event could only be untrustworthy, felt no hesitation whatsoever about informing his readers that the Germans had a peculiar relish for destroying anything marked with a Red Cross' (p. 170).

10 Henry James, 'To Henry James III,' 24 June 1915, in *Letters 1895–1916*, ed. Leon Edel, vol. IV (Cambridge: Harvard University Press, 1984), p. 760.

11 *Ibid.*, p. 761.

12 Violet Hunt, *The Flurried Years* (London: Hurst & Blackett, 1926), p. 264.

13 *Ibid.*, p. 269.

14 In *Henry James and the Art of Power* (Ithaca: Cornell University Press, 1984) Mark Seltzer argues that what I am calling the enforced 'we' of *The Golden Bowl* is a product of the inextricability of love from the policing functions of power in the novel. As I see it communication, and the potential for intimacy, in late James is always troubled by this double dynamic. James's three late novels, *The Golden Bowl*, *The Ambassadors* and *The Wings of the Dove*, all hinge on the misconstrual of alliance – relationships which are misperceived as intimate (and relationships which are misperceived as not intimate) by the consciousnesses of the main characters who come to new understandings of the limitations of their previous conceptions of alliance and intimacy. This problem of establishing intimacy, what I am calling the unsustainable 'we', is taken to its logical conclusion in late James, but is already operative and in fact explicit in earlier works such as *The Portrait of a Lady*: '[Gilbert Osmond] was more careful than ever to speak as if he and his wife had all things in sweet community, and it were as natural to each of them to say "we" as to say "I"' (p. 499). Or later when Gilbert is rebuking Isabel for wanting to go and visit the dying Ralph Touchett: 'Your cousin's nothing to you; he's nothing to us. You smile most expressively when I talk about *us*; but I assure you that *we, we*, Mrs Osmond, is all I know. I take our marriage seriously; you appear to have found a way of not doing so' (p. 529).

15 Eve Kosofsky Sedgwick, 'Queer Performativity: Henry James's *The Art of the Novel*', *GLQ* 1 (1993), 5.

16 As Lacan stresses about the mirror stage, it is a repeated *staging*, rather than a single moment or a developmental stage.

17 Joseph Litvak, *Caught in the Act: Theatricality in the Nineteenth-Century English Novel* (Berkeley: University of California Press, 1992), p. 203.

18 Henry James, *Autobiography* (London: W. H. Allen, 1956), p. 415. Further references included in text as *A*.

19 'The stable fire served and serves as James's metaphorical substitute early and late for his failure to serve in the war' (Paul John Eakin, 'Henry James's "Obscure Hurt": Can Autobiography Serve Biography?' *New Literary History* 19 (1987–1988), 689).

20 The annihilation of the Midmores by Ralph's 'very care for them' is an

explicit, if ghostly, example of what Mark Seltzer has identified as the 'vigilance of care' at work in *The Golden Bowl*, a dynamic in which love and the manipulations of power are inextricable and deployed simultaneously (*Art of Power*).

21 Henry James, *Within the Rim and Other Essays* (London: W. Collins Sons & Co. Ltd 1918), p. 32. Further references included in text as WR.

22 Hunt, *Flurried Years*, p. 265.

23 *Ibid.*, p. 266.

24 *Ibid.*, pp. 266–67.

25 In his autobiography *Return to Yesterday* (New York: H. Liveright, 1932), Hunt's lover Ford Madox Hueffer relates a similar anecdote about his final encounter with James in St James Park, in which James claims that 'he loved and had loved France as he had never loved a woman!' (*Return to Yesterday*, p. 220 as quoted in Peter Buitenhuis, *The Great War of Words* (Vancouver: University of British Columbia Press, 1987), pp. 119–120). This is yet another instance of the particular biographical conspiracy around James's sexuality – what is there, what can and cannot be exposed in early biographies and criticism, provoking all these nudge-nudge moments.

26 Benedict Anderson, *Imagined Communities: Reflections on the Origin and Spread of Nationalism* (London: Verso, 1983), p. 16.

27 See Andrew Parker, Mary Russo, Doris Sommer and Patricia Yaeger's introduction to *Nationalisms and Sexualities* (New York: Routledge, 1992).

28 Edel, *The Master*, p. 515. It is important to remember that James's assumption of British citizenship takes place in the context of the question of America's neutrality – how or if it will enter the war. His reactions to the war, especially in his propaganda, always seem pitched towards enlisting the enthusiasm of an American audience.

29 Henry James, 'To Clare Sheridan', 30 May 1915, in *Letters*, p. 755.

30 Henry James, 'To Edward Marsh', 28 March 1915, in *Letters*, p. 745.

31 Susan M. Griffin points out that, 'James's World War I essays . . . focus disproportionately on the wounded' (Susan M. Griffin, 'Tracing the Marks of Jamesian Masculinity', *Arizona Quarterly* 53: 4 (Winter 1997), 63).

32 Fred Kaplan discusses James's identification with Whitman in his biography of James (Fred Kaplan, *Henry James: the Imagination of Genius* (London: Hodder & Stoughton, 1992), p. 555).

33 Henry James, 'To Hugh Walpole', 21 Nov 1914, in *Letters*, p. 729.

34 There are many ways of charting this out in the popular imagination of the early 1900s. My favourite example is a cartoon by Max Beerbohm of James on the witness stand at a trial with the caption: 'A nightmare. Mr Henry James subpoenaed as a psychological expert in a cause celebre' – 'Cross-examining counsel: "Come, Sir, I ask you a plain question and I expect a plain answer!"' (Kaplan, *Henry James*, pp. 304–305).

35 Allon White, *The Uses of Obscurity: the Fiction of Early Modernism* (London: Routledge & Kegan Paul, 1981).

36 Litvak, *Caught in the Act*, p. 196.

37 See Eve Sedgwick's reading of 'The Beast in the Jungle', in *Epistemology* for the ways in which late nineteenth-century homosocial panic contributes to James's obscuring of his referents.

38 Preston Lockwood, 'Henry James's First Interview', *New York Times, Sunday Magazine*, 21 March 1915, 3–4.

39 *Ibid.*, 3.

40 *Ibid.*

41 *Ibid.* In her diary, James's secretary, Theodora Bosanquet, indicates that James's mania for control over the interview was extreme, and that he was at first dissatisfied with the results: 'H. J., finding that it wouldn't do at all from his point of view, has spent the last four days re-dictating the interview to the young man, who is fortunately a good typist. I should love to see the published result. I think the idea of H. J. interviewing himself for four whole days is quite delightful!' (Theodora Bosanquet, *Diary Notes*, Monday, 1 March 1915, bMS Eng 1213.2, Houghton Library, Harvard University, p. 144).

42 Lockwood, 'Henry James's First Interview', 4.

43 *Ibid.*

44 Edel, *The Master*, p. 531.

45 Kaplan, *Henry James*, p. 560, quoting editorial, *New York Times*, 29 July 1915.

46 H. Montgomery Hyde, *Henry James at Home* (London: Methuen & Co. Ltd, 1969), p. 258.

47 This scene is also interesting in terms of his relationship with Wharton during the war. Wharton was in France when the war broke out and sent James letters, from, as it were, the front lines. James's wartime letters to her are full of deference to her own more immediate experience of the horrors, as in this one of 23 March 1915: 'I won't attempt to explain or expatiate – about this abject failure of utterance: the idea of "explaining" anything to *you* in these days, or of any expatiation that isn't exclusively that of your own genius upon your own adventures and impressions!' (*Letters 1895–1918*, p. 740). In this light James's insistence upon excluding Wharton from the imperial stomach reads defensively, as if James is trying to make up phantasmatically for his own lack of actual experience of the convulsion – placing the boys with the boys and the girl outside.

48 Eakin, 'Henry James's "Obscure Hurt"', 675–692.

49 David McWhirter, 'Restaging the Hurt: Henry James and the Artist as Masochist', *Texas Studies in Literature and Language* 33: 4 (1991), 466.

50 Adrian Poole, 'Henry James, War and Witchcraft', *Essays in Criticism* 4 (1991), 292.

51 Sedgwick, 'Queer Performativity', 14.

4 ON THE TYPEWRITER, *IN THE CAGE*, AT THE OUIJA BOARD

1 Attributed to G. K. Chesterton, Wilfred A. Beeching, *The Century of the Typewriter* (Bournemouth: British Typewriter Museum Publishing, 1990), p. 34.
2 Edel, *The Master*, p. 363.
3 Kittler, *Discourse Networks*, p. 352.
4 Beeching, *Century of the Typewriter*, p. 35.
5 Morag Shiach, 'Modernity, Labour and the Typewriter', in *Modernist Sexualities*, eds. Hugh Stevens and Caroline Howlett (Manchester: Manchester University Press, 2000), p. 116.
6 Edel, *The Master*, p. 94.
7 See George Gissing, *The Odd Women* (1893; New York: W. W. Norton & Company, Inc., 1971) for a fictional representation of such a school.
8 Henry James, 'To William James,' 20 April 1898, in *Letters*, p. 75.
9 Cohen, *Talk on the Wilde Side*, p. 121.
10 *Ibid.*, p. 124. Eric Savoy has read *In the Cage* in the light of Cleveland Street events to suggest that, 'James, in dramatizing heterosexual vulnerability to blackmail or prosecution, deploys a construction of the working-class person's knowledge that was generated by *homosexual* scandal' (Eric Savoy, '*In the Cage* and the Queer Effects of Gay History', *Novel* 28: 3 (1995), 287). Insofar as the Cleveland Street scandal obviously did link the figure of the telegraph employee to casual prostitution and gay sex in the popular imagination, I agree with Savoy. However, I believe that a subtler reading of *In the Cage* and telegraphing would focus on the linkages between the erotics and anxieties of contamination, blackmail and the vulnerability of information storage – recognizing the potential differences that inhere in heterosexual and homosexual versions of these erotics while not simply claiming that the heterosexual version is always a displacement of the *real* fear which, in the 1880s and 1890s, is always finally of gay male sexuality. (This may be an exaggerated version of what Eve Sedgwick has wrought but it is basically what Savoy's article says – the reductive claim that, in the 1890s, every secret masks the real secret of homosexuality.)
11 Henry James, *What Maisie Knew* (1897; Middlesex: Penguin, 1966) p. 42.
12 Edel, *The Master*, p. 94.
13 *Ibid.*, p. 93.
14 *Ibid.*, p. 94.
15 Friedrich Kittler and others have suggested that the inadequacies of women's education actually made them appear to be excellent secretarial material. Ignorant women, one German textbook on *The Entrance of Women into Male Professions*, suggested, can easily 'sink to the level of mere writing machines' (Kittler, *Discourse Networks*, p. 352).
16 Edel, *The Master*, p. 370.
17 Hyde, *Henry James at Home*, p. 150.

18 Theodora Bosanquet, *Henry James at Work* (London: Hogarth Press, 1924), p. 5.
19 Henry James, *In the Cage*, in *Selected Tales* (London: J. M. Dent & Sons Ltd, 1982), p. 119. Further references included in text.
20 Jacques Lacan, 'The Circuit', *The Seminar of Jacques Lacan*, Book II: *The Ego in Freud's Theory and in the Technique of Psychoanalysis 1954–1955* (New York: W. W. Norton & Company, 1988), p. 82. Further references included in text as TC.
21 See Jacques Derrida, 'Le Facteur de la Verité', in *The Postcard*.
22 Kittler, *Discourse Networks*, p. 354.
23 *Ibid.*, p. 357.
24 Jennifer Wicke, 'Henry James' "Second Wave"', *The Henry James Review* 10: 2 (1989), 147. This quote portrays the ideal woman/secretary as a prescient telepath – anticipating every male need in the office or out of it. The ideal mechanized version of this fantasy relationship is portrayed in Villiers de l'Isle's novel *Tomorrow's Eve*, whose android heroine Hadaly's limited vocabulary (she is programmed to respond to her lover's words in ways which anticipate his desire so precisely that eventually he does not need to speak at all) also resembles Lacan's fantasy of the Symbolic in 'The Circuit'.
25 Sharon Cameron, *Thinking in Henry James* (Chicago: University of Chicago Press, 1989).
26 Alexander Welsh, *George Eliot and Blackmail* (Cambridge: Harvard University Press, 1985), p. 58.
27 Savoy, 'Queer Effects of Gay History', 287.
28 Wicke, 'Henry James' "Second Wave"', 149.
29 *Ibid.*, 151.
30 *The Sacred Fount* (1901; New York: Grove Press, 1979) is another 1890s James text which explores this nexus of concerns – the uncanny aspects of what it means to 'get into relation' with another for James. The novel, in which a voyeuristic, possibly insane, narrator speculates on a vampiric exchange of qualities between lovers and suspected lovers at a house party, provides a bizarre Jamesian twist on the economics of intimacy – what it means to be invaded and or drained by another. See my chapter two.
31 Theodora Bosanquet, *Original Diaries*, Tuesday 29th October 1907, bMS 1213.1, Houghton Library, Harvard University.
32 E. Duncan Aswell, 'James's *In the Cage* – the Telegraphist as Artist', *Texas Studies in Literature and Language* 8: 1 (1966–1967), 379.
33 Edel, *The Master*, p. 364.
34 Hyde, *Henry James at Home*, pp. 147, 149; Edel, *The Master*, p. 364.
35 Theodora Bosanquet, Bosanquet Files, Box 3, undated – beginning of book on Immortality of the Soul, The Society for Psychical Research Archive (SPR), University Library, Cambridge.
36 Edel, *The Master*, p. 365.

37 Under the name Hester Travers-Smith, Mrs Dowden published a book, *Psychic Messages from Oscar Wilde*, ed. Hester Travers-Smith (London: T. Werner Laurie Ltd, 1924), which is a treat. Wilde later dictated an entire play to her entitled 'Is it a Forgery?' which was sadly never produced. See Edmund Bentley, *Far Horizon: A Biography of Hester Dowden, Medium and Psychic Investigator* (London: Rider & Company, 1951) for more on Hester Dowden.

38 Of Johannes, Hester Dowden says: 'he purports to be a Jew who lived in Alexandria about the year 200 BC. He has a most amazing objection to the Egyptians' (Mrs Hester Dowden (Travers Smith), '"Is it a Forgery?" – How I Received Oscar Wilde's "Spirit Play",' *The Graphic* (10 March 1928), 401).

39 SPR, Bosanquet Files, Box 2, 'Notes on a Sitting with Mrs. Hester Dowden, Feb 15, 1933', p. 2.

40 *Ibid.*, p. 4.

41 *Ibid.*, p. 6.

42 SPR, Bosanquet Files, Box 2, 'Automatic Writing through Mrs. Dowden. Evening of March 13th, 1933'.

43 Wicke, 'Henry James' "Second Wave"', p. 147.

44 Seltzer, *Bodies and Machines*, p. 10.

45 '. . . if the typewriter . . . *dis*articulates the links between mind, eye, hand, and paper, these links are *re*articulated in the dictatorial orality that "automatically" translates speech into writing' (*Ibid.*, p. 195).

46 Bosanquet, *Henry James at Work*, pp. 6–7.

47 *Ibid.*, pp. 7–8.

48 Bosanquet may have 'caught' graphomania, the late nineteenth-century disease of the addiction to writing, from her employer. Her archive is tremendous. Perhaps her gleeful inhabiting of the role of writing instrument, both in James's lifetime and after his death, is related to this inability to stop writing: 'These maladies . . . were in effect understood as maladies of mimesis, representation and writing: the addiction to imitation and particularly imitative writing that marks the degenerate, and highly contagious, condition of *graphomaniacs*. They were understood, more generally, in terms of what the time-motion expert Etienne-Jules Marey called *une langue inconnue* of the body-machine complex writing itself. The unknown language of the body-machine complex becomes visible precisely through the new technologies of registration and inscription, the graphic methods and writing instruments, that proliferate around the workplace at the turn of the century. As Marey expressed it: "When the eye can no longer see, the ear cannot hear, or touch cannot feel, or even when the senses appear to deceive us, these instruments perform like a new sense with astonishing precision" (Etienne-Jules Marey, *La Méthode graphique dans les sciences et expérimentales en physiologie et en médecine* 2nd edn. Paris: Masson, 1978, 108). What these graphic technologies register and decipher then is something like

languages issuing from matter, automatized bodies writing themselves' (Mark Seltzer, 'Serial Killers (I)', *differences* 5: 1 (1993), 103–104). With Bosanquet, the graphomaniacal secretary to the dead, we seem to have an automatized body and a mind as a battlefield.

49 See Seltzer, *Bodies and Machines*, on the body–machine complex.

50 Her talents as a secretary make reading the archive much easier. Included in the archive are her nearly illegible automatic writings, done by hand, but also her typed transcriptions of them.

51 SPR, Bosanquet Files, Box 2, '12, 15 March, 1933.'

52 *Ibid.*

53 Bosanquet, *Diary Notes*, 1912–1916, 'Sunday Sept 5th, 1915'.

54 SPR, Bosanquet Files, Box 2, '12, 15 March, 1933.'

55 *Ibid.*, 'Note of writing at 3 pm.'

56 *Ibid.*, 'Note of Writing, March 16th. 11.30' (ellipses included in original).

57 *Ibid.*, 'March 17, 1933 11.45 am.'

58 Bosanquet's response to Johannes's call for chastity becomes explicitly identified with her lesbianism in a diary note she writes on 30 March 1933. She is afraid that her love for a woman only identified as Tess might affect her ability to communicate with the spirit world, and conversely that the spirit world might interrupt her ability to love: 'for at this stage of development I would almost give up any attempt to go on if I thought my little mediumistic power was going to create any sort of barrier between us, but I am told that it won't – rather the contrary soon. Johannes tells me that I feel neutralised because I love Tess too physically, but if I have to think of her not as a beautifully built young woman but as a lily of the valley (which he says is what her mind is like) I cannot do it' (SPR, Bosanquet Files, Box 3, 'A New Experience – Thursday, March 30, 1933'). Perhaps, Johannes's call to renunciation might also be read as a contest between who she will be intimate with – dead men of letters or living embodied women.

59 Owen, *Darkened Room*, p. 149. See also, Walkowitz, *City of Dreadful Delight* (Chicago: University of Chicago Press, 1992) for more on the nineteenth-century boom business in committing spiritually minded women to asylums for the insane, often to the financial benefit of their husbands and the alienists who ran the asylums at a profit.

60 See Ian Hacking on the invention of multiple personality: 'Double consciousness . . . became the diagnostic category, in English, for most of the nineteenth century' (Ian Hacking, *Rewriting the Soul*, p. 50).

61 Sonu Shamdasani, ed., intro, in *From India to the Planet Mars* (Théodore Flournoy, 1899; New Jersey: Princeton University Press, 1994), p. xxxi.

62 See Sonu Shamdasani, 'Automatic Writing and the Discovery of the Unconscious', *Spring* 54 (1993), 100–131. Myers of course also believed in, and hoped for, proof of both human personality and its survival of bodily death.

63 James answers no to the question 'Is there life after death?' but this is

because his idea of the power of consciousness is so vast that survival after death becomes beside the point. See Henry James, 'Is There a Life After Death?', in *The James Family*, ed. F. O. Matthiessen (New York: Alfred A. Knopf, 1947), pp. 602–614. Also see Sharon Cameron *Thinking*, on the expansive weirdness of the colonizing consciousness in James.

64 SPR, Bosanquet Files, Box 2, Folder 4, 'Impressions, Coming War – 1939, Fragment, February 18, 1939'.

65 Kittler, *Discourse Networks*, p. 347.

66 SPR, Bosanquet Files, Box 2, '16.3.33, 6 pm.'

67 *Ibid.*, 'Monday March 20th, 1933.'

68 William, describing his impression of Henry after his long residence in Europe, said: 'He's really . . . a native of the James family, and has no other country' (Matthiessen, *The James Family*, p. 69).

69 *Ibid.*, p. 338.

70 *Ibid.*, p. 339.

71 A particularly apropos incident of ventriloquism concerns which brother will talk about the possibility of speaking to the dead. In 1890, F. W. H. Myers asked William James to write up his observations of the Boston medium, Mrs Piper, for the *Proceedings of the Society for Psychical Research*. After Myers received William James's report he asked Henry to read it to the Society. Henry reluctantly agreed to do it:

> . . . Frederic Myers has written to ask *me* to read your letter on Mrs. Piper at a meeting of the Society for Psychical Research at the Westminster Town Hall on the 31st of this month, and I have said I would, though so alien to the whole business, in order not to seem to withhold from *you* any advantage – though what 'advantage' I shall confer remains to be seen. Therefore imagine me at 4 P.M. on that day, performing in your name . . . (Henry James 'To William James', 9 October 1890, *William James on Psychical Research*, eds. Gardner Murphy and Robert O. Ballou (London: Chatto and Windus, 1961), pp. 100–101).

> William replied 'I think your reading of my Piper letter . . . is the most comical thing I ever heard of' ('To Henry James', 20 Oct 1890, p. 101) and continued: 'Alice says I have not *melted* enough over your reading of my paper. I *do* melt to perfect liquefaction. 'Tis the most beautiful and devoted brotherly act I ever knew, and I hope it may be the beginning of a new career, on your part, of psychic apostolicism. Heaven bless you for it!' (p. 101)

72 See Bosanquet, *Henry James at Work*, for her comments on some of the changes James made in the New York Edition versions of his work.

73 Henry James, 'To Henry James III', 15–18 Nov 1913, in *Letters*, p. 800.

74 *Ibid.*, pp. 802–803. In a brief understated comment on this passage Cameron claims 'we are not dealing with an ordinary understanding of textual revision' (Cameron, *Thinking*, pp. 183–184).

75 Henry may have reluctantly participated in some séances aimed at

getting in touch with his brother initiated by William's wife Alice at William's pre-death request (Edel, *The Master*, p. 449).

76 Theodora Bosanquet, 'To Edith Wharton', 12 Dec 1915, in *Henry James and Edith Wharton Letters: 1900–1915*, ed. Lyall H. Powers (London: Weidenfeld and Nicolson, 1990), p. 376.

77 *Ibid.*, pp. 372–373.

5 FREUD, FERENCZI AND PSYCHOANALYSIS'S TELEPATHIC TRANSFERENCES

1 Freud to Jung, 31 December 1911, 290F *The Freud/Jung Letters,* ed. William McGuire, trans. Ralph Manheim and R. F. C. Hull (London: Penguin Books Ltd, 1991), pp. 252–253.

2 *Ibid.*, p. 123.

3 Sandor Ferenczi, 'Confusion of Tongues', pp. 291–303.

4 See Jean Laplanche and J.-B. Pontalis, 'Fantasy and the Origins of Sexuality', in *Formations of Fantasy*, eds. Victor Burgin, James Donald and Cora Kaplan (London: Routledge, 1989), pp. 5–34, for the best exegesis of Freud's early reworkings and refinings of the seduction theory.

5 Martin Stanton, *Sandor Ferenczi: Reconsidering Active Intervention* (New Jersey: Jason Aronson Inc., 1991), p. 1.

6 *Ibid.*, p. 1.

7 Ernest Jones, *The Life and Work of Sigmund Freud*, vol. III (New York: Basic Books Inc., 1955), p. 407.

8 He delivered a lecture on 'Experiments with thought transference' to the Vienna Society on 19 November 1913. It was not the first time the Society had discussed thought transference: 'On February 8, 1910, a debate was held on the phenomena of spiritualism and clairvoyance at the meeting of the Viennese Psychoanalytic Association, where Freud remarked that if one assumes the existence of such phenomena, then their nature would be rather physiological than psychological' (György Hidas, 'Flowing Over – Transference, Countertransference, Telepathy: Subjective Dimensions of the Psychoanalytic Relationship in Ferenczi's Thinking', in *The Legacy of Sandor Ferenczi*, eds. Lewis Aron and Adrienne Harris (Hillside: The Analytic Press, 1993), p. 209).

9 See particularly François Roustang, 'Suggestion over the Long Term', *Psychoanalysis Never Lets Go*, trans. Ned Lukacher (Baltimore: Johns Hopkins University Press, 1983).

10 Phillips, *Terrors and Experts*, p. 19.

11 See Roger Luckhurst, '"Something Tremendous, Something Elemental": on the Ghostly Origins of Psychoanalysis', in *Ghosts: Deconstruction, Psychoanalysis, History*, eds. Peter Buse and Andrew Stott (Basingstoke: Macmillan, 1999), pp. 50–71 for a fascinating argument about the ghostly (and psychical research influenced) origins of psychoanalysis.

12 'Psychoanalysis has always struggled to distance itself from supposedly discredited things like religion, glamour, mysticism, radical politics, the paranormal, and all the scapegoated "alternative" therapies. Psycho-analysis, that is to say, has used its discovery of the unconscious to legitimate itself' (Phillips, *Terrors and Experts*, pp. 18–19).

13 Jones, *Life and Work of Sigmund Freud*, vol. III, p. 38.

14 Peter Gay, *Freud: A Life for Our Time* (London: Papermac, 1989), p. 445.

15 See Geoffrey Gilbert, *Before Modernism Was* (Basingstoke: Palgrave, forthcoming) for more on the relationship between privacy, smoking, anti-semitism and psychoanalysis.

16 Freud to Ferenczi, 11 May 1911, letter 216, in *The Correspondence of Sigmund Freud and Sandor Ferenczi (Freud/Fer)*, eds. Eve Brabant, Ernst Falzeder and Patricia Giamperi-Deutsch, trans. Peter T. Hoffer, vol. I (Cambridge: Belknap Press of Harvard University Press, 1993), pp. 273–274.

17 *Ibid.*, p. 274.

18 Freud to Jung, 17 Feb 1911, 236F, *Freud/Jung*, p. 216.

19 Freud was first introduced to England via F. W. H. Myers. See my first chapter.

20 John Kerr, *A Most Dangerous Method: The Story of Jung, Freud, and Sabina Spielrein* (New York: Vintage Books, 1994), p. 317.

21 'If psychoanalysis were to renounce its effort to be a transmissible science, independent of its founder or of those who refound it through their theorizations, it would inevitably fall into occultism and magic – . . . This practice would fall back into the unsayable and the ineffable and thus into all the obscurantist manipulations without the aid of a theoretical apparatus. Any therapeutic effect would be reduced to personal power, to the qualities of the analyst, and one would never get beyond the level of faith healing and witchcraft: powers and gifts transmitted from one individual to another through the telling of a secret to be kept secret' (François Roustang, *Dire Mastery: Discipleship from Freud to Lacan*, trans. Ned Lukacher, (Baltimore: Johns Hopkins University Press, 1982), pp. 60–61).

22 Roustang, *Psychoanalysis Never Lets Go*, pp. 45–46.

23 *Ibid.*, p. 46.

24 This is, of course, the Freudian version of the story. For more sympathetic accounts of Jung see George Hogenson, *Jung's Struggle with Freud* (Notre Dame: University of Notre Dame Press, 1983); Peter Homans, *Jung in Context: Modernity and the Making of Psychology* (Chicago: University of Chicago Press, 1979); Linda Donn, *Freud and Jung: Years of Friendship, Years of Loss* (New York: Scribners, 1988).

25 John Forrester, *The Seductions of Psychoanalysis* (Cambridge: Cambridge University Press, 1990), pp. 4–5. Psychoanalysis's connections to fortune-telling are also made manifest in the phylogenetic fantasies that

Freud and Ferenczi explore; like teleological evolutionary models, they suggest development, progress and a goal. The Freud/Jung fissure also reveals an interesting moment when psychoanalysis might have turned more towards the claims of fortune-telling but did not. Jung actually wanted the theme of the Fourth International Psychoanalytic Congress of 1913 to be 'On the Teleological Function of Dreams', but this was vetoed by Freud and the title became the more modest 'The Function of Dreams' (Kerr, *A Most Dangerous Method*, pp. 460–461; Freud to Ferenczi, 19 May 1913, letter 396, *Freud/Fer*, vol. I, p. 487).

26 Sigmund Freud, *Beyond the Pleasure Principle, SE* XVIII, p. 22.
27 *Ibid.*
28 See Derrida, 'To Speculate – on "Freud"', in *The Postcard*.
29 Freud to Ferenczi, 6 Oct 1909, letter 74, *Freud/Fer*, vol. I, p. 79.
30 *Ibid.*, pp. 80–81.
31 Leon Chertok and Isabelle Stengers, *A Critique of Psychoanalytic Reason – Hypnosis as a Scientific Problem from Lavoisier to Lacan*, trans. Martha Noel Evans (Stanford: Stanford University Press, 1992), p. 71.
32 Henry James also wonders whether or not the best secretaries have empty minds. See my fourth chapter.
33 Freud to Ferenczi, 8 Nov 1909, letter 83, *Freud/Fer*, vol. I, p. 96.
34 Forrester, *Seductions*, p. 252.
35 Freud, 'Dreams and Occultism', p. 55.
36 Oppenheim, *Other World*, p. 147.
37 Stanton, *Sandor Ferenczi*, p. 77.
38 Sigmund Freud, *Introductory Lectures on Psychoanalysis SE* XV–XVI, p. 371. Freud's discussion of the transmission of primal phantasies in the *Introductory Lectures* was based primarily on his notes from the Wolfman case which he had completed two or three years earlier. Also see Freud's *A Phylogenetic Fantasy: Overview of the Transference Neurosis*, ed. Ilse Grubrich-Simitis (Cambridge: Cambridge University Press, 1987).
39 Jones, *Life and Work of Sigmund Freud*, vol. II, p. 219, quoting Freud letter to Karl Abraham, 11 November 1917.
40 Ludmilla Jordanova, *Lamarck* (Oxford: Oxford University Press, 1984), p. 81.
41 Lamarck's term *besoin* caused much controversy for his later interpreters. Because it could be translated as either 'desire' or 'need' Lamarck was accused of attributing a will and consciousness to animals' struggle for adaptation. According to Ludmilla Jordanova, Lamarck's intended meaning was closer to 'need'. *Besoin* was meant 'to suggest the biological imperative or drive which led animals to adapt to changing environmental conditions to ensure their survival' (*ibid.*, p. 102).
42 Laplanche and Pontalis, 'Fantasy', p. 17.
43 For Lacan telepathic transference springs from the same sources as thought transference: '. . . it is through being links, supports, rings in the same circle of discourse, agents integrated in the same circle of

discourse, that the subjects simultaneously experience such and such a symptomatic act, or discover such and such a memory'. But he also widens his idea of the Circuit claiming that the unconscious 'is the discourse of the circuit in which I am integrated. I am one of its links. It is the discourse of my father for instance, in so far as my father made mistakes which I am absolutely condemned to reproduce – that's what we call the *super-ego*. I am condemned to reproduce them because I am obliged to pick up again the discourse he bequeathed to me, not simply because I am his son, but because one can't stop the chain of discourse, and it is precisely my duty to transmit it in its aberrant form to someone else. I have to put to someone else the problem of a situation of life or death in which the chances are that it is just as likely that he will falter, in such a way that this discourse produces a small circuit in which an entire family, an entire coterie, an entire camp, an entire nation or half of the world will be caught' (Lacan, *The Seminar of Jacques Lacan*, pp. 89–90).

44 Helene Deutsch, 'Occult Processes Occurring during Psychoanalysis', in *Psychoanalysis and the Occult*, ed. George Devereux (1926; International Universities Press, Inc., 1953), p. 137.

45 Freud, 'On the History of the Psychoanalytic Movement', *SE* XIV (1914), p. 52.

46 Derrida, *The Postcard*; 'Telepathy', *Oxford Literary Review* 10, 3–40 and Royle, *Telepathy and Literature*.

47 Derrida, 'Telepathy', 13–14.

48 Jacques Derrida, 'Télépathie', *Psyché: Inventions de l'autre* (Paris: Galilée, 1987), p. 247.

49 Derrida, 'Telepathy', 16.

50 *Ibid.*, 36.

51 Marc Redfield, 'The Fictions of Telepathy', *Surfaces* 2: 27 (1992), 5.

52 'That Freud describes his disciples as a savage horde can be related to what he says in *Totem and Taboo*: the sons kill each other in order to take the place of the father. We propose the following hypothesis: when creating his own myth Freud simply looked around him' (Roustang, *Dire Mastery*, p. 16).

53 Sigmund Freud, 'An Autobiographical Study', *SE* XX (1925), p. 60.

54 Sam Weber, 'The Debts of Deconstruction and Other Related Assumptions', in *Taking Chances: Psychoanalysis and Literature*, eds. Joseph H. Smith and William Kerrigan (Baltimore: Johns Hopkins University Press, 1984), pp. 33–65.

55 Freud to Ferenczi, 8 Feb 1910, letter 110 *Freud/Fer*, vol. 1, p. 133.

56 Georg Groddeck, *The Meaning of Illness* (London: Hogarth Press, 1977), p. 37.

57 Helene Deutsch, *Confrontations with Myself* (New York: W. W. Norton & Co. Inc., 1973), p. 150.

58 See especially Roustang, *Dire Mastery*, on Victor Tausk. Freud refused to

analyse Victor Tausk because, like Nietzsche, he also seemed, uncannily, to prefigure and postfigure Freud's own thoughts. In *Dire Mastery*, François Roustang describes the transferential dynamics of this tragic relationship, which ended with Tausk's suicide in 1919. In her Freud journal, Lou-Andreas Salomé wrote of Tausk: 'I realize now that he will always tackle the same problems, the same attempts at solution that Freud is engaged in. This is no accident, but signifies his "making himself a son" as violently as he "hated the father for it". As if by a thought transference he will always be busy with the same things as Freud, never taking one step aside to make room for himself' (Roustang, *Dire Mastery*, p. 83, quoting Lou-Andreas Salomé, *The Freud Journal of Lou-Andreas Salomé*, trans. Stanley A. Leavey (London: Quartet Books Limited, 1987), pp. 166–167). Stepping aside to make room for oneself is an intriguing formulation of the problem.

59 Ferenczi to Freud, 28 Sep 1910, letter 168, *Freud/Fer*, vol. 1, footnote, pp. 214–215.

60 Daniel Paul Schreber, *Memoirs of my Nervous Illness*, trans. and eds. Ida Macalpine and Richard A. Hunter (Cambridge: Harvard University Press, 1988), p. 122.

61 Freud, 'Psychoanalytic Notes on an Autobiographical Account of a Case of Paranoia (Schreber)', *SE* XII (1911), pp. 78–79.

62 Eric Santner, *My Own Private Germany: Daniel Paul Schreber's Secret History of Modernity* (Princeton: Princeton University Press, 1996), p. 153, footnote 4. My discussion of originality and plagiarism in relation to the Schreber case and the early psychoanalysts intersects Santner's at many points.

63 Quoted in Hacking, *Rewriting the Soul*, p. 140.

64 In Victor Tausk's article 'On the Origin of the "Influencing Machine" in Schizophrenia', (*Sexuality, War and Schizophrenia*, ed. Paul Roazen, trans. Eric Mosbacher & others (New Brunswick: Transaction Publishers, 1991)) he discusses the typical schizophrenic hallucination of a machine which controls one's mind and body. He suggests that the patient usually initially explains sensations of physical or psychic invasion as coming from 'an external mental influence, suggestion or telepathic power, emanating from enemies . . . these complaints precede the symptom of the influencing apparatus, and . . . the latter is a subsequent pathological development' (pp. 187–188). This explanation posits thought transference as always preceding the more current explanations of machine culture. But the interchanges between technological and occult metaphors indicate to me that fantasies about technology and fantasies about mind invasion are mutually influential, and mutually formative of both doctors' and psychotics' views of the mind at the turn of the century.

65 'In psychosis, beliefs have an inner consistency; they speak of the nonsubject as a way of referring to the other. Thus one might say that

the psychotic is only belief and that he absolutizes what his other might say to him to such an extent that his psyche is *nothing but the set* of agglomeration of received ideas' (Roustang, *Dire Mastery*, p. 94).

66 In his biography of Freud, Peter Gay states that '[i]n April 1928 [Freud] told the Hungarian psychoanalyst István Hollós that he resisted dealing with psychotics: "Finally I confessed to myself that I do not like these sick people, that I am angry at them to feel them so far from me and all that is human"' (*Freud*, p. 537 quoting Freud to Hollós, 10 April 1928. Freud Museum, London). Ferenczi, in his *Clinical Diary* also faults Freud for despising his patients (*The Clinical Diary of Sandor Ferenczi*, ed. Judith Dupont, trans. Michael Balint and Nicola Zarday Jackson (Cambridge: Harvard University Press, 1988), pp. 92–93).

67 Ferenczi to Freud, 24 July 1915, letter 556, *Freud/Fer*, vol. II, pp. 70–71.

68 Sandor Ferenczi, 'Psychogenic Anomalies of Voice Production', *Further Contributions to the Theory and Technique of Psycho-Analysis*, ed. J. Richman, trans. J. Suttie, (London: Karnac Books, 1980), p. 109.

69 The whole question of the assumption and development of the confidentiality of the psychoanalytic office has been approached interestingly by John Forrester in his chapter on 'Telepathy and Gossip', in *Seductions*, and in 'Casualties of Truth', in *Dispatches from the Freud Wars: Psychoanalysis and its Passions* (Cambridge: Harvard University Press, 1997).

70 Ferenczi, *Clinical Diary*, p. 74.

71 Ferenczi to Freud, 22 Nov 1910, letter 182, in *Freud/Fer*, vol. I, pp. 235–236.

72 Freud to Ferenczi, 15 Nov 1910, letter 179, *ibid.*, p. 233.

73 Freud to Ferenczi, 23 Nov 1910, letter 183, *ibid.*, p. 236.

74 *Ibid.*

75 Ferenczi to Freud, 3 Oct 1910, letter 170, *ibid.*, pp. 217–218.

76 *Ibid.*, p. 219.

77 *Ibid.*, p. 219.

78 *Ibid.*, p. 219.

79 Ferenczi to Freud, 17 Mar 1911, letter 205, *ibid.*, pp. 261–262.

80 Ferenczi to Freud, 3 Oct 1910, letter 170, *ibid.*, pp. 219–220; italics in original.

81 Freud, '(Schreber)', p. 62; italics in original.

82 See Warner, 'Homo-Narcissism; or, Heterosexuality'. Christopher Craft also claims: 'Without doubt Freud must be credited with the radical insight into the mechanism of paranoia; the recognition that *in heterosexist culture* persecutory paranoia and "homosexuality" stand in a reciprocating, mutually identifying relation' (Christopher Craft, *Another Kind of Love: Male Homosexual Desire in English Discourse 1850–1920*, (Berkeley: University of California Press, 1994), p. 100).

83 Freud, '(Schreber)', p. 63.

84 Phillips, *Terrors and Experts*, p. 19.

85 Ferenczi to Freud, 12 Oct 1910, letter 173, *Freud/Fer*, vol. I, p. 226.

86 Ferenczi to Freud, 3 Oct 1910, letter 170, *ibid.*, p. 218.

87 Ferenczi to Freud, 17 Aug 1910, letter 160, *ibid.*, 206.

88 See 'Casualties of Truth', in *Dispatches from the Freud Wars*. Forrester goes on to suggest, in a formulation I would second, that the incestuous networks he traces may be another name for the cultural unconscious (p. 93).

89 Ferenczi to Freud, 17 Aug 1910, letter 160, *Freud/Fer*, vol. i, p. 209.

90 Sandor Ferenczi, 'On the Part Played by Homosexuality in the Pathogenesis of Paranoia', *Sex in Psychoanalysis*, trans. Ernest Jones (New York: Dover Publications, 1956), p. 133.

91 Sandor Ferenczi, 'The Nosology of Male Homosexuality (Homoerotism)', *Sex in Psychoanalysis*, trans. Ernest Jones (New York: Dover Publications, 1956), p. 266.

92 Ferenczi, 'Nosology', p. 267.

93 Ferenczi, 'Confusion of Tongues', p. 291; italics in original.

94 *Ibid.*, p. 12.

95 *Ibid.*, p. 107.

96 *Ibid.*

97 *Ibid.*, p. 5.

98 *Ibid.*

99 *Ibid.*, p. 58.

100 *Ibid.*, p. 33.

101 *Ibid.*, p. 140.

102 *Ibid.*, p. 161; italics in original.

103 Chertok and Stengers, *A Critique*, p. 103.

104 Gay, *Freud*, p. 465.

Bibliography

Anderson, Benedict, *Imagined Communities: Reflections on the Origin and Spread of Nationalism*, London: Verso, 1983.

Arata, Stephen, *Fictions of Loss in the Victorian Fin de Siècle*, Cambridge: Cambridge University Press, 1996.

Armstrong, Tim, *Modernism, Technology and the Body*, Cambridge: Cambridge University Press, 1998.

Aswell, E. Duncan, 'James's *In the Cage* – The Telegraphist as Artist', *Texas Studies in Literature and Language* 8: 1 (1966–1967), 375–384.

Auerbach, Nina, 'Magi and Maidens: The Romance of the Victorian Freud', in *Reading Fin de Siècle Fictions*, (ed.) Lyn Pykett, London: Longmans, 1996.

Banta, Martha, *Henry James and the Occult: the Great Extension*, Bloomington: Indiana University Press, 1972.

Barrett, William, *On the Threshold of the Unseen*, 2nd edn, revised, London: Kegan Paul, 1917.

Barrett, William., C. C. Massey, Rev. W. Stainton Moses, Frank Podmore, Edmund Gurney and F. W. H. Myers, 'Report of the Literary Committee', *Proceedings of the Society for Psychical Research* 1 (1882–83), 116–155.

Barrow, Logie, *Independent Spirits: Spiritualism and English Plebeians, 1850–1910*, London: Routledge & Kegan Paul, 1986.

Beeching, Wilfred A., *The Century of the Typewriter*, Bournemouth: British Typewriter Museum Publishing, 1990.

Beer, Gillian, *Darwin's Plots*, London: Routledge, 1983.
  "Wireless": Popular Physics, Radio and Modernism', in *Cultural Babbage: Technology, Time and Invention*, (eds.) Francis Spufford and Jenny Uglows London: Faber & Faber, 1996, pp. 149–66.

Bell, Ian F. A., 'The Personal, the Private and the Public in *The Bostonians*' *Texas Studies in Language and Literature* 32:2. (Summer 1990), 240–256.

Bentley, Edmund, *Far Horizon: a Biography of Hester Dowden, Medium and Psychic Investigator*, London: Rider & Company, 1951.

Borch-Jacobsen, Mikkel, *The Emotional Tie*, (trans.) Douglas Brick and others, Stanford: Stanford University Press, 1992.

The Freudian Subject, trans. Catherine Porter, Stanford: Stanford University Press, 1988.

'Neurotica: Freud and the Seduction Theory', *October* 76 (1996), 15–43.

Bosanquet, Theodora, *Henry James at Work*, London: Hogarth Press, 1924.

Bosanquet Files, Box 2, ms. and ts. The Society for Psychical Research Archive, University Library, Cambridge.

Bosanquet Files, Box 3, ts. The Society for Psychical Research Archive, University Library, Cambridge.

Original Diaries, bMS Eng 1213.1. Houghton Library, Harvard University.

Diary Notes, bMS Eng 1213.2. Houghton Library, Harvard University.

Jamesiana, bMS Am Eng 1213.4. Houghton Library, Harvard University.

Bristow, Joseph, 'Wilde, *Dorian Gray* and Gross Indecency', in *Sexual Sameness: Textual Differences in Lesbian and Gay Writing* (ed.) Joseph Bristow. London: Routledge, 1992, pp. 44–63.

Effeminate England: Homoerotic Writing after 1885, Buckingham: Open University Press, 1995.

Buitenhuis, Peter, *The Great War of Words*, Vancouver: University of British Columbia Press, 1987.

Buse, Peter and Andrew Stott (eds.), *Ghosts: Deconstruction, Psychoanalysis, History*, Houndmills: Macmillan Press Ltd., 1999.

Butler, Judith, *Gender Trouble: Feminism and the Subversion of Identity*, New York: Routledge, 1990.

Cameron, Sharon, *Thinking in Henry James*, Chicago: University of Chicago Press, 1989.

Castle, Terry, *The Female Thermometer: Eighteenth-Century Culture and the Invention of the Uncanny*, Oxford: Oxford University Press, 1995.

Chertok, Leon, and Isabelle Stengers, *A Critique of Psychoanalytic Reason – Hypnosis as a Scientific Problem from Lavoisier to Lacan* (trans.) Martha Noel Evans, Stanford: Stanford University Press, 1992.

Cobban, J. MacLaren, *Master of his Fate*, Edinburgh and London: William Blackwood and Sons, 1890.

Cohen, Ed, *Talk on the Wilde Side: Toward a Genealogy of a Discourse on Male Sexualities*, New York: Routledge, 1993.

Connor, Steven, 'The Machine in the Ghost: Spiritualism, Technology, and the "Direct Voice" in Buse, Peter and Andrew Stott (eds.), *Ghosts: Deconstruction, Psychoanalysis, History*. Houndmills: Macmillan Press Ltd, 1999, pp. 203–225.

Coroneos, Con, 'The Cult of *Heart of Darkness*', *Essays on Criticism* 45 (1995), 1–23.

Crabtree, Adam, *From Mesmer to Freud: Magnetic Sleep and the Roots of Psychological Healing*, New Haven: Yale University Press, 1993.

Craft, Christopher, *Another Kind of Love: Male Homosexual Desire in English Discourse 1850–1920*, Berkeley: University of California Press, 1994.

Crews, Frederick, *et al.*, *The Memory Wars: Freud's Legacy in Dispute*, New York: New York Review of Books, 1995.

Cumberland, Stuart C., 'A Thought-Reader's Experiences', *Nineteenth Century* 20 (1886), 867–885.

Derrida, Jacques, *The Postcard* (trans.) Alan Bass, Chicago: University of Chicago Press, 1987.

'Télépathie', *Psyché: Inventions de l'autre*, Paris: Galileé, 1987.

'Telepathy', *Oxford Literary Review* 10 (1988), 3–40.

Deutsch, Helene, *Confrontations with Myself*, New York: W. W. Norton & Co. Inc., 1973.

'Occult Processes Occurring During Psychoanalysis', in *Psychoanalysis and the Occult* (ed.) George Devereux, International Universities Press, Inc. [1926] 1953, pp. 133–146.

Donn, Linda, *Freud and Jung: Years of Friendship, Years of Loss*, New York: Scribners, 1988.

Dowden (Travers-Smith), Hester, *Psychic Messages from Oscar Wilde*, preface by Sir William F. Barrett, FRS, London: T. Werner Laurie Ltd, 1924.

'"Is it a Forgery?" – How I Received Oscar Wilde's "Spirit Play"', *The Graphic* 10 March 1928, 401.

Du Maurier, George, *Trilby*, London: J. M. Dent & Sons Ltd, 1992.

Eakin, Paul John, 'Henry James's "Obscure Hurt": Can Autobiography Serve Biography?' *New Literary History* 19 (1987–1988), 675–92.

Edel, Leon, *Henry James: the Master 1901–1916*, London: Avon Books, 1972.

Edison, Thomas A., *The Diary and Sundry Observations of Thomas Alva Edison*, New York: Philosophical Library, 1948.

Ellmann, Richard, *Oscar Wilde*, London: Penguin, 1988.

Ferenczi, Sandor, *The Clinical Diary of Sandor Ferenczi* (ed.) Judith Dupont (trans.) Michael Balint and Nicola Zarday Jackson, Cambridge: Harvard University Press, 1988.

'The Confusion of Tongues between Adults and the Child' (trans.) Jeffrey Masson and Marianne Loring, in *The Assault on Truth: Freud's Suppression of the Seduction Theory* (ed.) Jeffrey Masson. NY: Farrar, Strauss and Giroux, 1984, pp. 291–303.

First Contributions to Psycho-Analysis (trans.) Ernest Jones, London: Hogarth Press, 1952.

Further Contributions to the Theory and Technique of Psycho-Analysis (ed.) J. Richman (trans.) J. Suttie, London: Karnac Books, 1980.

'The Nosology of Male Homosexuality (Homoerotism)', *Sex in Psycho-analysis* (trans.) Ernest Jones, New York: Dover Publications, 1956, pp. 250–268.

'On the Part Played by Homosexuality in the Pathogenesis of Paranoia', *Sex in Psychoanalysis* (trans.) Ernest Jones, New York: Dover Publications, 1956, pp. 131–156.

Firchow, Peter Edgerly, *The Death of the German Cousin: Variations on a Literary Stereotype, 1890–1920*, Lewisburg: Bucknell University Press; London: Associated Presses, 1986.

'First Report on Thought Reading', *Proceedings of the Society for Psychical Research* 1 (1882–1883), 13–34.

Forrester, John, *Dispatches from the Freud Wars: Psychoanalysis and its Passions*, Cambridge: Harvard University Press, 1997.

The Seductions of Psychoanalysis, Cambridge: Cambridge University Press, 1990.

Foucault, Michel, *The History of Sexuality* (trans.) Robert Hurley, vol. 1. New York: Random House, Inc., 1978.

Freud, Sigmund, *Studies on Hysteria*, vol. 11. *The Standard Edition of the Complete Psychological Works of Sigmund Freud (SE)* (trans.) James Strachey, 1953–1974, (1893–1995).

'Notes upon a Case of Obsessional Neurosis (Rat Man)', *SE* x (1909), pp. 155–249.

'Psychoanalytic Notes on an Autobiographical Account of a Case of Paranoia (Schreber)', *SE* xII (1911), pp. 1–82.

'Totem and Taboo', *SE* xIII (1913), pp. 1–162.

'On Narcissism', *SE* xIV (1914), pp. 67–102.

'On the History of the Psychoanalytic Movement', *SE* xIV (1914), pp. 7–66.

Introductory Lectures on Psychoanalysis, *SE* xV–xVI (1916–1917).

'From the History of an Infantile Neurosis (Wolf Man)', *SE* xVII (1918), pp. 1–122.

Beyond the Pleasure Principle, *SE* xVIII (1920), pp. 7–64.

'Group Psychology and the Analysis of the Ego', *SE* xIV (1921), pp. 65–143.

'An Autobiographical Study', *SE* xx (1925), pp. 3–74.

'Fetishism', *SE* xxI (1927), pp. 147–157.

'Dreams and Occultism', *New Introductory Lectures*, *SE* xxII (1933), pp. 31–56.

A Phylogenetic Fantasy: Overview of the Transference Neuroses (ed.) Ilse Grubrich-Simitis, Cambridge: Cambridge University Press, 1987.

Freud, Sigmund and Sandor Ferenczi, *The Correspondence of Sigmund Freud and Sandor Ferenczi* (eds.) Eve Brabant, Ernst Falzeder and Patricia Giamperi-Deutsch (trans.) Peter T. Hoffer, 2 vols. to date, Cambridge: Belknap Press of Harvard University Press, 1993– .

Freud, Sigmund, and C. G. Jung, *The Freud/Jung Letters* (ed.) William McGuire (trans.) Ralph Manheim and R. F. C. Hull, London: Penguin Books Ltd, 1991.

Friedman, John A, 'Ferenczi's Clinical Diary: On Loving and Hating', *The International Journal of Psycho-Analysis* 76 (1995), 957–975.

Gagnier, Regenia, *Idylls of the Marketplace: Oscar Wilde and the Victorian Public*, Stanford University Press, 1986.

Gauld, Alan, *The Founders of Psychical Research*, London: Routledge & Kegan Paul Ltd, 1968.

A History of Hypnotism, Cambridge: Cambridge University Press, 1992.

Gay, Peter, *Freud: a Life for Our Time*, London: Papermac, 1989.

Gilbert, Geoffrey, *Before Modernism Was*, Basingstoke: Palgrave, forthcoming.

Ginzburg, Carlo, 'Morelli, Freud and Sherlock Holmes: Clues and Scientific Method', in *The Sign of Three: Dupin, Holmes, Pierce* (eds.) Umberto Eco and Thomas A. Sebeok. Bloomington: Indiana University Press, 1983, pp. 81–118.

Gissing, George, *New Grub Street* (1891). Middlesex: Penguin Books Ltd., 1976. *The Odd Women* (1893), New York: W. W. Norton & Company, Inc., 1971.

Gravitz, Melvin A., and Manuel I. Gerton, 'Freud and Hypnosis: Report of Post-Rejection Use', *Journal of the History of the Behavioral Sciences* 17 (1981), 68–74.

Griffin, Susan M., 'Tracing the Marks of Jamesian Masculinity', *Arizona Quarterly*, 53: 4 (Winter 1997), 61–82.

Groddeck, Georg, *The Meaning of Illness*, London: Hogarth Press, 1977.

Grossman, Jonathan H., 'The Mythical Svengali: Anti-Aestheticism in *Trilby*', *Studies in the Novel* 28: 4 (Winter 1996), 525–542.

Gurney, Edmund, F. W. H. Myers, and Frank Podmore, *Phantasms of the Living*, 2 vols. (1886); facsimile reprint ed. Gainesville, Florida: Scholars' Facsimiles & Reprints, 1970.

Guzynski, Elizabeth, '"Homo-Narcissism" and the 1890s', unpublished essay, 1993.

Hacking, Ian, *Rewriting the Soul: Multiple Personality and the Sciences of Memory*, Princeton: Princeton University Press, 1995.

Hall, Trevor, *The Strange Case of Edmund Gurney*, London: Gerald Duckworth & Co. Ltd, 1964.

Haynes, Reneé, *The Society for Psychical Research*, London: Mcdonald & Co., 1982.

Hichens, Robert, *The Green Carnation*, London: Robert Clark Ltd, 1992.

Hilman, Robert G., 'A Scientific Study of the Mystery: the Role of the Medical and Popular Press in the Nancy–Salpêtrière Controversy on Hypnotism', *Bulletin of the History of Medicine* 39 (1965), 163–182.

Hogenson, George, *Jung's Struggle with Freud*, Notre Dame: University of Notre Dame Press, 1983.

Homans, Peter, *Jung in Context: Modernity and the Making of a Psychology*, Chicago: University of Chicago Press, 1979.

Hueffer, Ford Madox, *Return to Yesterday*, New York: H. Liveright, 1932.

Hunt, Violet, *The Flurried Years*, London: Hurst & Blackett, 1926.

Huysmans, J.-K., *À Rebours* (trans.) Robert Baldick, 1884; London: Penguin Books, 1959.

Hyde, H. Montgomery, *Henry James at Home*, London: Methuen & Co. Ltd, 1969.
   ed. and Introduction, *The Trials of Oscar Wilde*, London: William Hodge and Co. Ltd, 1948.

James, Alice, *The Diary of Alice James* (ed.) Leon Edel, Middlesex: Penguin Books, 1964.

James, Henry, *The Sense of the Past*, Glasgow: W. Collins Sons & Co. Ltd, 1917.
Within the Rim and Other Essays, London: W. Collins Sons & Co. Ltd. 1918.
'Is There a Life After Death?', in *The James Family* (ed.) F. O. Matthiessen, New York: Alfred A. Knopf, 1947, pp. 602–614.
Autobiography, London: W. H. Allen, 1956.
The Golden Bowl (1904), New York: Dell Publishing Co. Inc., 1963.
The Bostonians (1886), Middlesex: Penguin Books, 1966.
What Maisie Knew (1897), Middlesex: Penguin, 1966.
The Sacred Fount (1901), New York: Grove Press, 1979.
Selected Tales, London: J. M. Dent & Sons Ltd, 1982.
Letters 1895–1916 (ed.) Leon Edel, vol. IV, Cambridge: Harvard University Press, 1984.
The Portrait of a Lady (1881), London: Everyman's Library, J. M. Dent, 1995.
James, Henry and Edith Wharton, *Henry James and Edith Wharton Letters: 1900–1915* (ed.) Lyall H. Powers, London: Weidenfeld and Nicolson, 1990.
James, William, 'Presidential Address', *Proceedings of the Society for Psychical Research* XII (1896), 4–7.
William James on Psychical Research (eds.) Gardner Murphy and Robert O. Ballou, London: Chatto and Windus, 1961.
Jones, Ernest. *The Life and Work of Sigmund Freud*, vols. II and III, New York: Basic Books Inc., 1955.
Jordanova, Ludmilla, *Lamarck*, Oxford: Oxford University Press, 1984.
Kaplan, Fred, *Henry James: the Imagination of Genius*, London: Hodder & Stoughton, 1992.
Kerr, John, *A Most Dangerous Method: the Story of Jung, Freud, and Sabina Spielrein*, New York: Vintage Books, 1994.
King, Pearl, 'Early Divergences between the Psycho-Analytical Societies in London and Vienna', in *Freud in Exile: Psychoanalysis and its Vicissitudes* (eds.) Edward Timms and Naomi Segal, New Haven: Yale University Press, 1988, pp. 124–133.
Kipling, Rudyard, 'Wireless', *Traffics and Discoveries*, New York: Doubleday, Page & Company, 1920.
Kittler, Friedrich, *Discourse Networks 1800/1900* (trans.) Michael Metteer with Chris Cullens, Stanford: Stanford University Press, 1990.
'Gramophone, Film, Typewriter', *October* 41 (1987), 101–118.
Kreilkamp, Ivan, 'A Voice Without a Body: the Phonographic Logic of *Heart of Darkness*', *Victorian Studies* 40: 2 (Winter 1997), 211–244.
Lacan, Jacques, 'The mirror stage as formative of the function of the I as revealed in psychoanalytic experience', *Ecrits*. (trans.) Alan Sheridan. New York: W. W. Norton & Company, 1977, pp. 1–7.
The Seminar of Jacques Lacan, Book II: The Ego in Freud's Theory and in the Technique of Psychoanalysis 1954–1955, New York: W. W. Norton & Company, 1988.
Laplanche, Jean, and J.-B. Pontalis, 'Fantasy and the Origins of Sexuality',

in *Formations of Fantasy* (eds.) Victor Burgin, James Donald and Cora Kaplan. London: Routledge, 1989, pp. 5–34.

The Language of Psychoanalysis (trans.) Donald Nicholson-Smith, New York: W. W. Norton & Company, 1973.

Latour, Bruno, *Science in Action*, Cambridge: Harvard University Press, 1987.

Lawrence, Jean-Roche and Campbell Perry, *Hypnosis, Will and Memory: a Psycho-Legal History*, New York: The Guilford Press, 1988.

LeBon, Gustave, *The Crowd*, London, Penguin Books Ltd, 1976.

Leys, Ruth, 'Death Masks: Kardiner and Ferenczi on Psychic Trauma', *Representations* 53 (1996), 44–73.

'Mead's Voices: Imitation as Foundation, or The Struggle against Mimesis', *Critical Inquiry* 19 (1993), 277–307.

Litvak, Joseph, *Caught in the Act: Theatricality in the Nineteenth-Century English Novel*, Berkeley: University of California Press, 1992.

Lockwood, Preston, 'Henry James's First Interview', *New York Times, Sunday Magazine*, 21 March 1915, 3–4.

Luckhurst, Roger, '"Something Tremendous, Something Elemental": on the Ghostly Origins of Psychoanalysis', in *Ghosts: Deconstruction, Psycho-analysis, History* (eds) Peter Buse and Andrew Stott. Baskingstoke: Macmillan, 1999, pp. 50–71.

Marvin, Carolyn, *When Old Technologies were New*, Oxford: Oxford University Press, 1988.

Masson, Jeffrey, *The Assault on Truth: Freud's Suppression of the Seduction Theory*, New York: Farrar, Strauss and Giroux, 1984.

Matthiessen, F. O., *The James Family*, New York: Alfred A. Knopf, 1947.

McWhirter, David. 'Restaging the Hurt: Henry James and the Artist as Masochist', *Texas Studies in Literature and Language* 33: 4 (1991), 464–491.

Myers, F. W. H., 'Automatic Writing', *Proceedings of the Society for Psychical Research* III (1885), 1–63.

Essays Classical and Modern, London: Macmillan Co., Limited, 1921.

'General Characteristics of Subliminal Messages', *Proceedings of the Society for Psychical Research* VII (1891–1892), 298–355.

Human Personality and its Survival of Bodily Death, London: Longmans, Green & Co., 1903.

Science and a Future Life, with Other Essays, London: Macmillan, 1893.

Nealon, Christopher, 'Affect-Genealogy: Feeling and Affiliation in Willa Cather', *American Literature* 69: 1 (1997), 5–37.

Nordau, Max, *Degeneration* (1895), Lincoln: University of Nebraska Press, 1993.

Norrman, Ralf, *The Insecure World of Henry James's Fiction*, New York: St Martin's Press, 1982.

Nye, Robert A, *The Origins of Crowd Psychology: Gustave LeBon and the Crisis of Mass Democracy in the Third Republic*, London: Sage Publications Ltd., 1975.

'Objects of the Society', *Proceedings of the Society for Psychical Research* 1 (1882–1883), 3–6.

Oppenheim, Janet, *The Other World: Spiritualism and Psychical Research in England, 1850–1914*, Cambridge: Cambridge University Press, 1985.

Owen, Alex, *The Darkened Room: Women, Power and Spiritualism in Late Victorian England*, Philadelphia: University of Pennsylvania Press, 1990.

Parker, Andrew, Mary Russo, Doris Sommer and Patricia Yaeger, Introduction, *Nationalisms and Sexualities*, New York: Routledge, 1992.

Pater, Walter, *The Renaissance: Studies in Art and Poetry*, (ed. with intro) Adam Phillips, 1873; Oxford: Oxford University Press, 1986.

Phillips, Adam, *Terrors and Experts*, London: Faber & Faber, 1995.

'Unfathomable Craziness', Review of Daniel Pick, *Svengali's Web*, *The London Review of Books* 22: 10, (18 May 2000), 8–10.

Pick, Daniel, *Faces of Degeneration: a European Disorder, c. 1848–c.1918*, Cambridge: Cambridge University Press, 1989.

'Powers of Suggestion: Svengali and the *Fin-de-Siècle*', in *Modernity, Culture and 'the Jew'* (eds.) Bryan Cheyette and Laura Marcus, Cambridge: Polity Press, 1998, 105–125.

Svengali's Web: the Alien Enchanter in Modern Culture, New Haven: Yale University Press, 2000.

Introduction *Trilby*, London: Penguin Classics, 1994.

Pierce, A. H., and F. Podmore, 'Subliminal Self or Unconscious Cerebration?', *Proceedings of the Society for Psychical Research* XI (1895), 317–332.

Poe, Edgar Allan, 'The Man of the Crowd', *Selected Poetry and Prose of Poe*, (ed.) T. O. Mabbott. New York: Random House, 1951, pp. 154–162.

Poole, Adrian, 'Henry James, War and Witchcraft', *Essays in Criticism* 4 (1991), 291–307.

Powell, Kerry, 'The Mesmerizing of Dorian Gray', *The Victorian Newsletter* 65, (Spring 1984), 10–15.

Purcell, Edward, '*Trilby* and *Trilby*-Mania: the Beginning of the Bestseller System', *Journal of Popular Culture* 11 (Summer 1977), 62–76.

Redfield, Marc, 'The Fictions of Telepathy', *Surfaces* 2: 27 (1992), 4–20.

Phantom Formations: Aesthetic Ideology and the Bildungsroman, Ithaca: Cornell University Press, 1996.

Roazen, Paul, *Freud and his Followers*, Middlesex: Penguin Books Ltd, 1971.

Ronell, Avital, *The Telephone Book*, Lincoln: University of Nebraska Press, 1989.

Roustang, François, *Dire Mastery: Discipleship from Freud to Lacan* (trans.) Ned Lukacher, Baltimore: Johns Hopkins University Press, 1982.

Psychoanalysis Never Lets Go, (trans.) Ned Lukacher, Baltimore: Johns Hopkins University Press, 1983.

Royle, Nicholas, *Telepathy and Literature*, Oxford: Basil Blackwell Ltd, 1990.

Salomé, Lou-Andreas, *The Freud Journal of Lou-Andreas Salomé* (trans.) Stanley A. Leavey, London: Quartet Books Limited, 1987.

Santner, Eric, *My Own Private Germany: Daniel Paul Schreber's Secret History of Modernity*, Princeton: Princeton University Press, 1996.

Savoy, Eric, '*In the Cage* and the Queer Effects of Gay History', *Novel* 28: 3 (1995), 284–307.

Schaffer, Talia, *The Forgotten Female Aesthetes: Literary Culture in Late-Victorian Britain*, Charlottesville: University of Virginia Press, 2000.

Schreber, Daniel Paul, *Memoirs of my Nervous Illness* (trans. and eds.) Ida Macalpine and Richard A. Hunter, Cambridge: Harvard University Press, 1988.

Sedgwick, Eve Kosofsky, *Between Men: English Literature and Male Homosocial Desire*, New York: Columbia University Press, 1985.

 The Epistemology of the Closet, Berkeley: University of California Press, 1990.

 'Queer Performativity: Henry James's *The Art of the Novel*', *GLQ* 1 (1993), 1–16.

Seltzer, Mark, *Bodies and Machines*, New York: Routledge, 1992.

 Henry James and the Art of Power, Ithaca: Cornell University Press, 1984.

 'Serial Killers (I)', *differences* 5: 1 (1993), 92–128.

Shamdasani, Sonu 'Automatic Writing and the Discovery of the Unconscious', *Spring* 54 (1993), 100–131.

Shamdasani, Sonu (ed.) Introduction, *From India to the Planet Mars* by Théodore Flournoy (1899) (trans.) Daniel B. Vermilye, New Jersey: Princeton University Press, 1994.

Shiach, Morag, 'Modernity, Labour and the Typewriter', in *Modernist Sexualities* (eds.) Hugh Stevens and Caroline Howlett, Manchester: Manchester University Press, 2000, pp. 114–129.

Showalter, Elaine, Introduction to *Trilby*, Oxford: Oxford University Press, 1995.

Sidgwick, A. and E. M. Sidgwick, *Henry Sidgwick: A Memoir*, London: Macmillan & Co, Ltd., 1906.

Sidgwick, Ethel, *Mrs. Henry Sidgwick*, London: Sidgwick and Jackson, Ltd, 1938.

Sidgwick, Henry, 'President's Address', *Proceedings of the Society for Psychical Research* 1 (1882–83), 65–69.

 'President's Address,' *Proceedings of the Society for Psychical Research* v (1888–1889), 271–278.

Sinfield, Alan, *The Wilde Century: Effeminacy, Oscar Wilde, and the Queer Moment*, London: Cassell, 1994.

Stanton, Martin, *Sandor Ferenczi: Reconsidering Active Intervention*, New Jersey: Jason Aronson Inc., 1991.

Stein, Robert D., 'The Impact of the Psychical Research Movement on the Literary Theory and Literary Criticism of Frederic W. H. Myers', diss. Northwestern University, 1968.

Steinman, Lisa, *Made in America: Science, Technology and American Modernism*, New Haven: Yale University Press, 1987.

Stevenson, Robert Louis, *Dr Jekyll and Mr Hyde* (1886). New York: Bantam Books, 1981.

Stoker, Bram, *Dracula* (1897), New York: Signet Classics, 1965.

Tarde, Gabriel, *The Laws of Imitation*, (trans.) Elsie Clews Parsons, New York, 1903.

Tausk, Victor, 'On the Origin of the "Influencing Machine" in Schizophrenia', in *Sexuality, War and Schizophrenia* (ed.) Paul Roazen, (trans.) Eric Mosbacher and others, New Brunswick: Transaction Publishers, 1991, pp. 185–219.

Thomas, D. M., *The White Hotel*, New York: Pocket Books, 1982.

Turner, Frank M., *Between Science and Religion: the Reaction to Scientific Naturalism in Late Victorian England*, New Haven: Yale University Press, 1974.

Twain, Mark, *A Connecticut Yankee in King Arthur's Court*, (ed.) Allison R. Ensor, New York: Norton, 1982.

'The First Writing-Machines', *The Complete Essays of Mark Twain*, (ed.) Charles Neider, New York: Doubleday & Company, Inc. 1963, pp. 324–326.

Letter to F. W. H. Myers, 12 January 1892, Myers Papers, Wren Library, Trinity College, Cambridge University.

'Mark Twain on Thought Transference', *Journal of the Society for Psychical Research (JSPR)* 1 (1884), 166–167.

'Mental Telegraphy', *The Complete Essays of Mark Twain*, (ed.) Charles Neider, New York: Doubleday & Company, Inc. 1963., pp. 70–87.

Villiers de l'Isle Adam, Philippe Auguste Mathias, *Tomorrow's Eve* (trans.) Robert Martin Evans, Urbana: University of Illinois Press, 1982.

Walkowitz, Judith, *City of Dreadful Delight*, Chicago: University of Chicago Press, 1992.

Wardley, Lynn, 'Woman's Voice, Democracy's Body, and *The Bostonians*', *ELH* 56 (Fall 1989), 639–665.

Warner, Michael, 'Homo-Narcissism; or, Heterosexuality', in *Engendering Men: the Question of Male Feminist Criticism* (eds.) Joseph A. Boone and Michael Cadden, New York: Routledge, 1990, pp. 190–206.

Weber, Sam, 'The Debts of Deconstruction and Other Related Assumptions', in *Taking Chances: Psychoanalysis and Literature* (eds.) Joseph H. Smith and William Kerrigan, Baltimore: Johns Hopkins University Press, 1984, pp. 33–65.

Wellbery, David E. Introduction, *Discourse Networks 1800/1900* by Friedrich Kittler, Stanford: Stanford University Press, 1990.

Welsh, Alexander, *George Eliot and Blackmail*, Cambridge: Harvard University Press, 1985.

West, Rebecca, *Henry James*, London: Nisbet, 1916.

White, Allon, *The Uses of Obscurity: the Fiction of Early Modernism*, London: Routledge & Kegan Paul, 1981.

Wicke, Jennifer, 'Henry James' "Second Wave" ', *The Henry James Review* 10: 2 (1989), 146–151.
  'Vampiric Typewriting: *Dracula* and its Media', *ELH* 59: 1 (Summer 1992), 467–493.
Wilde, Oscar, *The Complete Works of Oscar Wilde*, Glasgow: HarperCollins, 1994.
Wilde, Oscar, and others, *Teleny*, London: GMP Publishers Ltd., 1986.
Williams, John Peregrine, 'The Making of Victorian Psychical Research: An Intellectual Elite's Approach to the Spiritual World', diss. Cambridge University, 1984.
Winter, Alison, *Mesmerized: Powers of Mind in Victorian Britain*, Chicago: University of Chicago Press, 1998.
Woolf, Virginia, *A Haunted House and Other Short Stories* (1944), London: HarperCollins, 1982.

Index

CAMBRIDGE STUDIES IN NINETEENTH-CENTURY
LITERATURE AND CULTURE

General editor
Gillian Beer, *University of Cambridge*

Titles published

29. Physiognomy and the Meaning of Expression in
Nineteenth-Century Culture
by Lucy Hartley, *University of Southampton*

30. The Victorian Parlour: A Cultural Study
by Thad Logan, *Rice University,* Houston

31. Aestheticism and Sexual Parody: 1840–1940
by Dennis Denisoff, *Ryerson Polytechnic University*

32. Literature, Technology and Magical Thinking, 1880–1920
by Pamela Thurschwell, *University College London*